Television.

A History by Francis Wheen.
Editorial Consultant: Peter Fiddick.

GUILD PUBLISHING
LONDON

Acknowledgements

The publishers would like to thank the following organisations and individuals for permission to use the photographs featured in the book: P6 Universal Pictorial Press; P9 Topham; P10 BBC Hulton Picture Library; P12 Punch Magazine; P18/19 Topham; P26 E.M.I. Archives; P30 Topham; P36/37 Topham; P40 Topham; P44 Topham; P48/49 Topham; P52/53 Popperphoto; P60/61 David Steen; P64 Popperphoto; P69 Menerlyche/GAMMA; P70 Rex Features; P79 Radio Times; P82/83 Topham; P86/87 Gamma; P91 Rex Features; P94/95 Gamma; P100 Transworld; P104/105 Granada; P108/109 Topham; P112/113 Topham; P116/117 Universal Pictorial Press; P119 BBC; P120 Transworld; P124/125 Shooting Star/Transworld; P128 Granada; P129 BBC; P132 Universal Pictorial Press; P137 Popperphoto; P140 Transworld; P144/145 Granada; P148 Leslie Woodhead; P149 Transworld; P152/153 Shooting Star/Transworld; P156 Lee Lyon 'Survival'/Anglia; P160 BBC; P163 Granada; P164/165 BBC; P170 Camera Pix/Hutchinson; P174 ITC Denham; P176 Leslie Woodhead; P178/179 Camera Pix/Hutchinson; P180 Granada; P182 Topham; P202 Transworld; P207 BBC; P210 Transworld; P214 Rex Features; P215 Popperphoto; P219 London Features International; P222 Adrian Morrell/Allsport; P227 Allsport; P230 Allsport; P234 Adrian Morrell/Allsport; P251 L. Gubb/Gamma.
Space makes it impossible to give individual credits for the small screen photographs but special thanks are due to the television companies, particularly Granada, the BBC, ITN and LWT, and to Topham, Gamma and UPI for their help in providing source material.

Designed by Pearce Marchbank.

Picture Research by Sue Ready.
Artwork and layout by David Fudger,
Phil Levene and Pearce Marchbank.
Additional research and picture editing by
Heather Page.

This edition published 1985 by
Book Club Associates
By arrangement with Century Publishing Co. Ltd.

Typeset by Ace Filmsetting.
Printed and bound in Great Britain
by Purnell & Son (Book Production) Ltd.,
Paulton, Bristol.
A Member of BPCC plc.

Television is based on a major documentary
series made by Granada Television.

(Previous page)
One of the earliest television recordings ever made, Baird's 'Phonovision' of a Miss Pounceford made on March 28th, 1928. The system used a disc similar to old 78rpm records.

Introduction.

Strolling through central London one spring afternoon in 1984, I was stopped in my tracks by a placard for an evening newspaper: 'Weekend TV Chaos Warning'. If the word 'TV' had been replaced by 'rail' or 'bus' I should probably not have given the poster a second glance: such headlines are all too common. However, although I knew – who doesn't? – that television was an important part of many people's lives, it was not until I saw the placard that I realised just how much it had been transformed from an entertaining diversion into an essential public utility like gas or water. If the weekend's television programmes are to be disrupted, a 'warning' is issued to the public, lest the shock of sudden deprivation be too great.

It all seems a far cry from the first, flickering transmissions of the 1920s, the period when John Logie Baird advertised for assistance with his experiments for 'seeing by wireless'. But it is also an appropriate moment at which to consider the history of the medium. We are now entering what is often called the 'Third Age of Broadcasting': first there was the radio age, then the television age, and now we have the era of cable, video, direct broadcasts by satellite, teletext, viewdata and computers. Before we are swept into this new age, it is worth investigating how television has acquired its current status.

Reflections such as these led David Plowright, Managing Director of Granada Television, to suggest that the time was right to produce a televised history of the medium in all its different manifestations around the world. The fourteen-hour series, which has been three years in the making, is being shown in 1985. It is a massive project. Hundreds of interviews have been conducted in numerous locations in Asia, Africa, Europe, North America and South America. Archives have been scoured for historic footage – an exhausting task. Hardly any recordings were made of programmes until at least 1956, and even since then recordings of many memorable moments in television have often been 'wiped' by broadcasting companies, presumably in the belief that a programme's life ends once it has been transmitted. Indeed, television has always had a strangely casual attitude to its own history. Millions of words have been written in newspapers, books and academic theses about particular aspects of the medium, but the screen itself has usually remained blank on the subject. It is therefore greatly to the credit of Granada's staff that they have broken the taboo, and done so in such a spectacular way – with a series that deals with everything from current affairs to comedy, documentaries to drama, in countries as different as Britain and Japan, or India and the United States. This book, drawing on the research for the series, is an attempt to display the diverse and fascinating material which the Granada team has discovered. The project could not have been better timed: we may be starting the Third Age of Broadcasting, but many of the pioneers of the Second Age are still alive and able to give first-hand accounts of what it was like to work in television at a time when money was short, technical equipment was primitive and the air was loud with cries of derision from the sceptics.

Alone and palely loitering: Bruce McCandless II during his historic 'free walk' from Space Shuttle Challenger in 1984, using a Manned Manoeuvring Unit.

Granada's initial research was divided geographically, but the programmes themselves are arranged by themes, to give a clearer picture of how particular genres have developed over the years. As a glance at the contents page will show, this is an approach which I have also taken. However, I should add that although Granada has been generous in allowing me to study and use its material, the way in which I have presented that material and the conclusions I have drawn are entirely my own. Moreover, I have conducted other research for the book separately from Granada, so there may well be differences of emphasis between this book and the television series. One other point needs to be made. Many of the quotations in the pages that follow are from interviews conducted by Granada, but others are not. To distinguish between the two, I have employed the simple device of slipping into the present tense whenever I quote from someone who was interviewed for the series; thus if you find a comment prefaced by the words 'Carol Burnett says' or 'Michael Parkinson recalls', you will know that it is a Granada interview.

I should like to thank all those involved in the series; although they were busy with their own work, they always found time to see me and discuss their findings and ideas. They are Michael Beckham, Brian Blake, Philip Casson, Stephen Peet and Leslie Woodhead (Producer/Directors); Michael Murphy and Norman Swallow (Producers); Steve Hopkins, David Wason and Kate Woods (Researchers); Avril Warner and Jane Mercer (Film Researchers). My 'liaison man' at Granada, Andrew Robinson, has been helpful far beyond the call of duty. Peter Fiddick, the book's consultant editor, shared with me his large store of knowledge and experience of television. I am also grateful to my agent, Pat Kavanagh, and my publishers at Century, particularly Gail Rebuck, Sarah Wallace and Sophia Yorke. The book was designed by Pearce Marchbank with picture research by Susan Ready: as Sir Christopher Wren once said, *si monumentum requiris, circumspice*. Michael Jackson kindly lent me his collection of press cuttings and other documents, while David Kogan and Mike Coren both made valuable suggestions. Susan Roles and Graham Lock provided me with a place in which to work at a time when I needed it. Finally, Joan Smith made the heat and burden of the day seem immeasurably more bearable. As a classical scholar, she would probably appreciate a remark which is supposed to have been made by C. P. Scott, the famous editor of the *Manchester Guardian*: 'Television? The word is half Greek and half Latin. No good will come of it.' We shall see.

Francis Wheen

Soviet viewers: young trainees from a vocational school in the Vladimir region watching a broadcast from Moscow in the clubroom of their hostel.

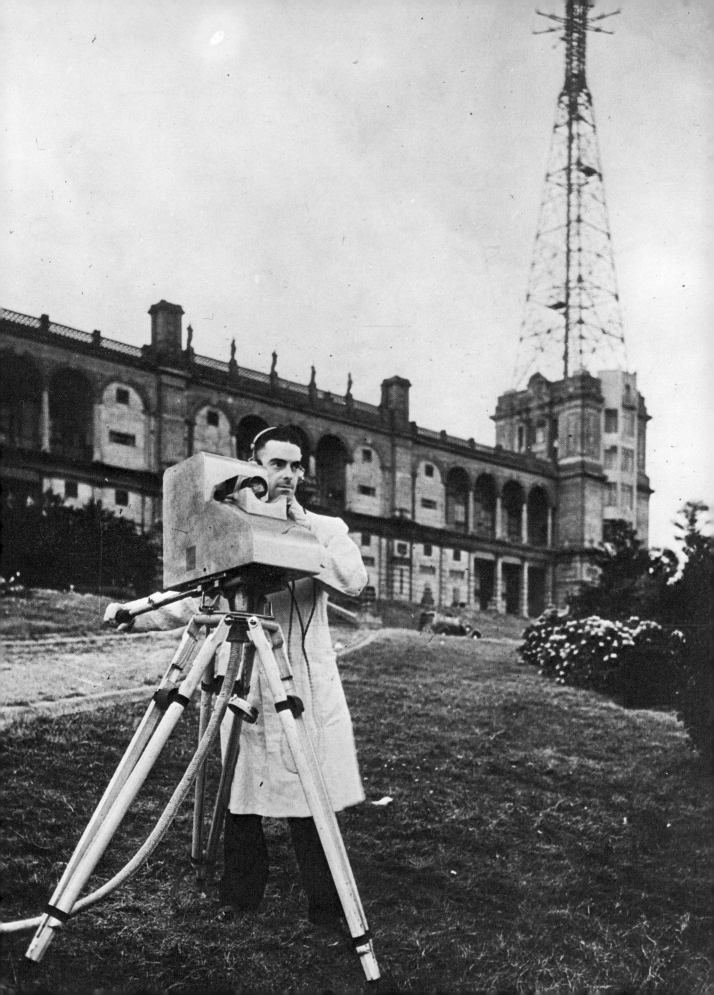

Who Invented Television?

On 27 June 1923 *The Times* of London carried the following advertisement: 'Seeing by wireless. Inventor of apparatus wishes to hear from someone who will assist (not financially) in making working model. Write Box S. 686.'

The man lurking behind this box number was John Logie Baird. Within two-and-a-half years he moved from the personal column to the news pages: on 28 January 1926 *The Times* reported that 'Members of the Royal Institution and other visitors to a laboratory in an upper room in Frith-street, Soho, on Tuesday saw a demonstration of an apparatus invented by J. L. Baird, who claims to have solved the problem of television.' Noting that the image as transmitted was 'faint and often blurred', the newspaper commented: 'It has yet to be seen to what extent further developments will carry Mr Baird's system towards practical use.' Ten years later, the British Broadcasting Corporation, in collaboration with Baird and EMI-Marconi, opened what was claimed to be the first regular 'high definition' television service in the world.

John Logie Baird looks through his Nipkow disc, the device which helped him realise his dream of 'seeing by wireless'.

Baird's story is an engaging one, and it is no wonder that several generations of British schoolchildren have been taught that he 'invented' television. But he was not alone.

He was certainly not the first person to have had the idea of 'seeing at a distance'. In 1879, George du Maurier drew a cartoon for *Punch* which showed a mother and father watching, on the wall of their English home, a tennis match in Ceylon in which their daughter was playing. They were also able to speak to her, over a long-distance telephone.

In 1882, six years before Baird was born, the French artist Robida produced an even more startling series of drawings, in which moving pictures were transmitted on to the walls of people's living rooms. One of the screens showed a teacher giving a mathematics lesson; another showed a dressmaker displaying his wares (a prediction of 'shopping by television' a century before it became reality); another had a ballet being performed; and yet another showed a full-scale desert war being fought, while the viewers gazed in horror from their comfortable chairs.

Progress towards television was not confined to the fancy of cartoonists and artists. In 1884 the German scientist Paul Nipkow had patented his invention of a metal 'disc', spirally perforated with small holes through which a strong light shone. When rotated, the disc could 'scan' an object by breaking its image into small pieces. The different strengths of light reflected by the object and its background were then turned into electric impulses of varying strengths by photosensitive selenium cells, which had been discovered in 1873. By using another scanning disc, these impulses could theoretically be converted back into an image of the original object.

Although he had devised the theory of scanning, Nipkow

Alexandra Palace, the first home of television, went on the air on 26 August, 1936.

EDISON'S TELEPHONOSCOPE (TRANSMITS LIGHT AS WELL AS SOUND).

(Every evening, before going to bed, Pater- and Materfamilias set up an electric camera-obscura over their bedroom mantel-piece, and gladden their eyes with the sight of their Children at the Antipodes, and converse gaily with them through the wire.)

Paterfamilias (in Wilton Place). "BEATRICE, COME CLOSER, I WANT TO WHISPER." *Beatrice (from Ceylon).* "YES, PAPA DEAR."
Paterfamilias. "WHO IS THAT CHARMING YOUNG LADY PLAYING ON CHARLIE'S SIDE?"
Beatrice. "SHE'S JUST COME OVER FROM ENGLAND, PAPA. I'LL INTRODUCE YOU TO HER AS SOON AS THE GAME'S OVER?"

failed to put it into practice. However, a number of other scientists began to interest themselves in the possibility of television. Not all of them approved of Nipkow's system. Its main drawback was that the scanning disc had to be rotated mechanically, limiting the speeds that could be achieved and, therefore, the clarity of the picture.

The two pioneers of an 'alternative' method were A. A. Campbell Swinton, a British scientist, and Boris Rosing, a Russian, working independently. Campbell Swinton concluded that the mechanical scanning disc should be replaced by an electronic 'cathode-ray tube' in which the image would be picked up on a thin plate coated with a photosensitive substance. The plate would be bombarded with electrons from a 'gun' at the other end of the tube. This fusillade, sweeping from side to side and up and down, would provide electrical impulses matching the image being received on the plate – impulses which could then be transmitted. At the other end of the apparatus, the image-receiver – that is, the television set – would convert the impulses back into a picture on a fluorescent screen.

The cathode-ray tube had been invented in 1897 by a German named Karl Braun, but it was Campbell Swinton and Rosing who showed how it could be used for television. Rosing's method was actually inferior to Campbell Swinton's, since the Russian envisaged the tube being used only for the receiver, not for the scanner.

Early televisors (from top): the 17 TN1 set made by Tovbin in Leningrad in 1939; the Baird Televisor front view; the first commercially produced television, 1930.

Rosing filed a patent for his system in 1907. In 1908, unaware of this (since the patent had not yet been published in England), Campbell Swinton wrote a remarkable letter to *Nature* magazine, revealing his proposals and concluding that 'distant electric vision will, I think, come within the region of possibility'. The system described in *Nature* is, with some refinements, still the basis of television today, so Campbell Swinton has a strong claim to be accepted as the true inventor of television. What he did not do, however, was to put his principles into practice.

This was John Logie Baird's great strength. Although rather shy, he was also, paradoxically, a showman, with an almost evangelical belief in television as a practical reality, not merely something to be written about in the pages of scientific journals. His tragedy was that when he began to experiment with television, in 1922, he used the Nipkow disc, even though it had been superseded by the work of Rosing and Campbell Swinton; and as the evidence accumulated that he ought to change to electronic scanning, he still obstinately refused to do so.

He had always been something of an oddball. Before turning his attention to television, he had had several other entrepreneurial adventures. These included making artificial diamonds from carbon, marketing 'Baird Undersocks' which kept the feet cool in summer and warm in winter, producing chutney in the West Indies and, finally, selling soap in London ('Baird's Speedy Cleaner'). Then, aged thirty-four, he retired to Hastings, in Sussex, to address himself to 'the problem of television'.

(Opposite) Du Maurier's cartoon for Punch in 1879 depicting a mother and father in England watching their daughter playing tennis in Ceylon on 'Edison's Telephonoscope'.
Contrary to what one might expect, Baird was not a practical man. 'He was no good with his hands,' according to Norman Loxdale, who was a schoolboy in Hastings at the time. 'He could describe what he wanted, but he couldn't make it himself, and that's where he got other people to make things for him.' The thirteen-year-old Loxdale was soon enlisted to make Nipkow scanning discs by breaking up old tea chests.

Another assistant was Victor Mills, a local wireless enthusiast. Early in 1923, he remembers, 'a ring came at the door and my mother came back and said to me, "There's a strange man at the door. He says he would like to speak to you, that you know something about wireless and you should know something about resonance."' Baird told Mills that he had fitted out an apparatus for transmitting pictures, 'and he says, "I can't get it to go, it's making a terrific noise."' When Mills went down to Baird's workshop, he was unimpressed: 'He had a collection of junk, that's what it boils down to; no, quite truly, I wouldn't have given two pounds to sell the lot.' He quickly discovered the cause of Baird's problem with 'noise' – his selenium cells were too big.

Stukey Bill, the long-suffering ventriloquist's dummy used for Baird's experiments, is now preserved in the Science Museum in London.

On his next visit to Baird's workshop, Mills took some of his own wireless equipment, 'because I couldn't trust anything that Baird had got'. Once Mills had switched on the system, he put his hand in front of the apparatus to check the illumination. 'I decided it was about right,' he recalls, 'but in the meantime Baird had yelled out "It's here, it's here!"' And that was the first picture he'd ever seen, it was a true picture of my hand.'

It was, of course, a rudimentary picture: the hand was shown only as a silhouette, without any gradations of light and shade. Nevertheless, it was enough to convince Baird that he was on the right course, and soon afterwards he placed his advertisement in *The Times*. The publisher W. J. Odhams saw the notice, but after investigating Baird's equipment he told the inventor that he could see no future for 'a device which only sends shadows'. Others were more excited. Baird gave demonstrations to journalists in 1923 and early 1924 which led to enthusiastic articles in *Kinematograph Weekly* and *Radio Times*. By May 1924 Baird had been granted a patent for his 'System of Transmitting Views, Portraits and Scenes by Telegraphy or Wireless Telegraphy'. Greatly encouraged, he moved to London.

Victor Mills declined to go with him, since he was already convinced that Baird ought to be experimenting with cathode-ray tubes instead of Nipkow discs. Baird worked on alone in his new room in Frith Street, London. He was very short of money by then: he seldom ate and never bought new clothes. Those who met him in this period remember him looking like a tramp. He had a brief respite from penury in 1925 when Gordon Selfridge, owner of the famous department store in Oxford Street, paid Baird to demonstrate his apparatus.

Elizabeth Wood, who was then a schoolgirl, missed a hockey game to attend the first demonstration. 'It was a little disappointing really, because of black lines wiggling across,' she remembers, 'and it jumped up and down and you could only see part of the thing.' Eventually, after fiddling with the equipment, Baird produced a picture of a man's face, 'but we couldn't see any face, only the outline'. At the end of the demonstration, Gordon Selfridge made a speech of thanks, saying that television was going to be 'very great' in the future. 'And then we all clapped rather politely,' Elizabeth Wood says, 'because we were all rather frightened of television. I think the trouble was that we believed that, if they could make this film, they could see into our houses. We could see them, they could see us.'

Rudimentary but recognisable: a picture of a man's face transmitted by Baird in 1925.

Baird used a ventriloquist's dummy called Stukey for his experiments in Frith Street, since no human was likely to tolerate, for hours on end, the extremely bright lighting that Baird needed in his efforts to obtain a decent picture. On

1 October 1925, Baird experienced 'the one great thrill that research work has brought me': for the first time, Stukey's head appeared on the screen not as 'a mere smudge' but as 'a real image with details'. Inspired by this achievement, Baird arranged his demonstration for members of the Royal Institution on 26 January 1926; it was reported in *The Times* two days later, though the reaction of the distinguished audience was not recorded.

While Baird was transmitting images in London, other people were working along the same lines elsewhere in the world. They included a Hungarian called D. Von Mihaly who, like Baird, was committed to mechanical scanning; but instead of the Nipkow disc, he preferred a revolving drum which contained mirrors tilted at different angles. Gerhardt Goebel, a German who saw Mihaly demonstrating at the Berlin Radio Exhibition in 1928, remembers 'dark red television pictures the size of a rail ticket. His programme consisted of a pair of scissors opening, or a pair of pliers.' Mihaly's mirror-drum was later adopted by Baird himself, but although its pictures were of better quality, it still suffered from the essential defects of all mechanical television systems. Mihaly, like Baird, was transmitting 30-line pictures. To give some idea of how rough these were, it is worth noting that the Selsdon Committee in Britain, which reported in 1935, recommended that television should have at least 240 lines for its pictures to be satisfactory. (Today, television in European countries is transmitted on 625 lines, while the United States uses 525 lines.)

In Japan, a young lecturer in engineering named Kenjiro Takayanagi managed to transmit the Japanese character 'I' in 1927. 'At that moment I was very happy,' he says today, 'and I thought that now for the first time we have the basis of television.' Meanwhile, in the Soviet Union, scientists at the Leningrad Polytechnic Institute were under the impression that *they* were inventing television. At least the Russians had the sense to pursue electronic television almost straight away, instead of going through a 'mechanical' phase. One Soviet inventor, Boris Grabovsky, claimed to have made the first electronic broadcast as early as July 1926. 'Ivan Philipovich went to Leningrad,' he said later, 'where, under Professor Rosing's guidance, electronic tubes were made, and he brought them to Tashkent, and we carried out the first experiments in my apartment. Pictures of a bright spot were transmitted, and the movement of a hand.'

Not to be outdone, the Americans were 'inventing' television, too. Charles Francis Jenkins had started experimenting in 1923, using Nipkow discs. In 1925, shortly after Baird's show at Selfridge's, Jenkins gave a similar demonstration in the United States. Corporations involved in radio and telephones were also sponsoring research into television. At General Electric, Ernst Alexanderson was working on mechanical scanning. At Westinghouse, Vladimir Zworykin, who had experimented with television in Russia before emigrating in 1919, was more interested in electronic scanning, though his employers were none too sympathetic. In an interview some years later, he described how his equipment was received by a manager at Westinghouse: 'He was very impressed. So finally he asks me a few questions, like "How long did I work with this system?" and so on, then departed saying a few words to the director of the laboratory. Later on, I found out what he said was, "Put this guy to work on something more useful." '

Unretouched photographs of faces taken from the screen of a Baird Televisor in 1928; the bottom one is actually the front cover of a magazine being held up to the television camera.

David Sarnoff of RCA had no such doubts. In 1923 he predicted that 'every broadcast receiver for home use in the future will also be equipped with a television adjunct by which the instrument will make it possible to see as well as hear what is going on in the broadcast station'. A year later, his vision was undimmed. 'Let us think,' he said, 'of every farmhouse equipped not only with a sound-receiving device but with a screen that would mirror the sights of life. Think of your family, sitting down of an evening in the comfort of your own home, not only listening to the dialogue but seeing the action of a play given on a stage hundreds of miles away; not only listening to a sermon but watching every play of emotion on the preacher's face as he exhorts the congregation to the path of religion.' Once the American press took up the new medium, television fever became contagious. On 7 April 1927, the American Telephone & Telegraph Company (AT&T) gave a public demonstration of the apparatus which had been developed in its Bell Laboratories. In the course of it the US Secretary of Commerce, Herbert Hoover, gave a speech which was broadcast from Washington and watched in New York by an invited audience of 'business executives, editors and bankers'. (He thereby, incidentally, became the first politician to appear on television.) On the following day the event was the lead story on the front page of the *New York Times*. The newspaper could scarcely contain itself: 'FAR-OFF SPEAKERS SEEN AS WELL AS HEARD HERE IN A TEST OF TELEVISION', announced its headline, followed by a string of sub-heads: 'Like a Photo Come To Life', 'Hoover's Face Plainly Imaged as He Speaks in Washington', 'The First Time in History', 'Pictures Are Flashed By Wire and Radio Synchronising With Speaker's Voice'.

The audience in New York saw two broadcasts. The first, in which Hoover spoke, was transmitted by wire from Washington. The second, and perhaps more significant, was sent by radio from AT&T's experimental station in Whippany, New Jersey. The Whippany broadcast featured a comedian called A. Dolan, who was thus the first entertainer to perform on television. He appeared before the viewers 'as a stage Irishman, with side whiskers and a broken pipe, and did a monologue in brogue. Then he did a quick change and came back in blackface with a new line of quips in negro dialect.' In view of the standard of most television comedy today, this seems appropriate. The *New York Times* did not miss Dolan's symbolic importance, 'for the commercial future of television, if it has one, is thought to be largely in public entertainment – super news-reels flashed before audiences at the moment of occurrence, together with dramatic and musical acts shot on the ether waves in sound and picture at the instant they are taking place in the studio'.

Five months later, in Los Angeles, there was an equally historic development: Philo T. Farnsworth produced an electronic television system that worked. What made it particularly extraordinary was that the inventor himself was only twenty-one years old.

If John Logie Baird, as the begetter of the Baird Undersock, was an unlikely figure to be involved in the creation of television, so was Farnsworth. He came from a poor farming family in Idaho, who could not afford to buy books for him. However, he once discovered an old stack of popular science journals, which he read voraciously. When he was fifteen, he drew on a school blackboard a complete plan for an electronic television system, cameras and all. His chemistry teacher did

The desire to watch television in the comfort of one's own home was found in the Soviet Union, too; here, a Russian family views through a screen magnifier, though the dog seems less impressed.

Philo T. Farnsworth, the American prodigy who designed a complete electronic television system by the time he was fifteen.

not understand it but was most impressed, and encouraged young Philo to persevere. After working his way through college, Farnsworth found a benefactor in George Everson, a fund-raiser from California, who persuaded financiers to sponsor the young scientist on condition that he produced a transmission within a year. Two weeks before the deadline, Farnsworth summoned his wife and brother-in-law to the first demonstration.

His widow remembers: 'My brother Cliff, who had made the tubes, was in the transmitting room which was over the partition, and Philo said, "Put in a slide, Cliff," and we saw a line. It was a curvy kind of thick line, and he adjusted it and it became sharper, and he asked Cliff to turn it on its side and the line turned, and he turned to us and he said, "Well, there you have electronic television." ' After that success, Farnsworth was ready to show the system to his backers – especially the Executive Vice-President of the Crocker Bank, who kept asking when he could expect to see some return on his investment. Farnsworth invited him round to the laboratory. As soon as the banker began his habitual refrain – 'When are we going to see some dollars in this thing?' – a dollar sign appeared on the screen.

Farnsworth felt confident enough to apply for a patent. This was vigorously contested by the Radio Corporation of America (RCA), whose President, David Sarnoff, had decided that television had a future and that RCA – through its subsidiary, the National Broadcasting Company (NBC) – ought to dominate it. But the mighty corporation was unsuccessful and in August 1930 the twenty-four-year-old Farnsworth won his patent for electronic television. Soon afterwards Vladimir Zworykin, then working on electronic television for RCA, visited Farnsworth in San Francisco. 'When he saw the first television picture in Philo's lab, which was quite a clear picture,' Mrs Farnsworth recalls, 'he said, "Beautiful, I wish I had invented it myself." ' RCA's lawyers then began the long and expensive process of trying to buy Farnsworth's patents.

Even though they were stuck with mechanical equipment, other American pioneers were making progress. In May 1928 General Electric began making regular, thrice-weekly broadcasts from radio station WGY in Schenectady, New York. Ray Kell, who was one of General Electric's engineers at the time, says that on Christmas Eve, 1928, he sent a greetings message which was picked up by his parents on a television receiver in Indiana. Most of the broadcasts from Schenectady were less adventurous ('only the faces of men talking, laughing or smoking,' as one magazine reported), but there were a couple of notable breakthroughs. On 22 August 1928, WGY transmitted Al Smith's speech accepting his nomination for the US Presidency. The event took place in Albany, New York, and 24-line pictures were then sent back to Schenectady over a telephone wire.

On 11 September 1928, WGY broadcast the world's first television drama – *The Queen's Messenger*, by J. Hartley Manners. The play had only two characters in it, which was just as well, since anything with a large cast would have defeated General Electric's primitive equipment. Each camera could only scan an area twelve inches square – enough for a human head and not much else. Three cameras were used: one for the actress, one for the actor, and one for the two 'doubles'. These doubles had an essential part to play, as the main actress and actor could not move their heads without

Vladimir Zworykin's interest in television was kindled in Russia, where he worked with Boris Rosing; after emigrating to the United States Zworykin became one of the most important pioneers in the history of American television.

Matinee idol Jack Buchanan in his dashing white flannels with Baird on the roof at Long Acre, 1929.

going out of focus. Whenever the script called for some other shot – a hand holding a glass of wine, for instance – there was a switch to the third camera, where one of the doubles' hands would be seen. Despite these limitations, the play was a success, in technical as well as dramatic terms: amateur television enthusiasts on the West Coast wrote in to say that they had received it. By the time WGY transmitted its second play, eight months later, life was rather easier for the cast: the cameras had been improved, and the twelve-inch frame was replaced by a stage eight feet wide, eight feet high and six feet deep.

WGY was not the only American television station operating in 1928. From June onwards, Charles Francis Jenkins was broadcasting 48-line 'silhouette' pictures from Washington on Monday, Wednesday and Friday evenings. By the end of the year, there were eighteen experimental television stations licensed in the United States. Progress was spurred by the Americans' knowledge that they were engaged in a race with the British. Research into new equipment took place in great secrecy. Arthur Hungerford of NBC says: 'The idea was that we were trying to beat the British to get a continuing service of television on the air, and we didn't want anyone to know how well we were doing.' NBC's owner, RCA, was indeed doing well: late in 1928 it began secret tests with Zworykin's 'Iconoscope'. This was a cathode-ray camera which differed from other cameras, both electronic and mechanical, by 'storing' an image before scanning it, thus reducing the amount of light that needed to be cast on the image.

John Logie Baird was aware of the competition from across the Atlantic, but he was not at this stage unduly troubled by it. Instead, he was inspired to perform feats of one-upmanship. In May 1927, one month after AT&T's transmission from Washington to New York, Baird transmitted pictures of himself from London to Glasgow – more than twice the distance covered by AT&T. Four months later Ben Clapp, who had been hired the previous year as Baird's first employee, was sent to New York to prepare for Baird's next stunt – transatlantic television. He had a long wait, for it was not until 8 February 1928 that Baird was able to give a public demonstration. The pictures went by landline from Baird's new studio in Long Acre, London, to Clapp's house in Coulsdon, Surrey, where there was a transmitter which sent them to Hartsdale, New York, where Clapp was operating a receiving set. The *New York Times* described the transmission as an event of 'epochal importance', which 'deserves to rank with Marconi's sending of the letter "S" across the Atlantic – the first intelligible signal ever transmitted from shore to shore in the development of transoceanic radio telegraphy'.

The British press was also excited. Bill Fox, a reporter from the Press Association who had been helping Baird in his spare time, was one of the three people whose faces were transmitted (the other two were Baird himself and a Miss Howe). He went home in the early hours of the morning believing that the signal had not been received in New York. 'I'd hardly got in before my wife was saying "Get up, get up, Mr Baird wants you,"' he remembers. He went to Baird's house. 'He said, as soon as I got there, "We did it last night, and the press know all about it and they are simply invading Long Acre to see me. What am I to do?" And I said, "Well, I'll have to let the office know because I was supposed to be keeping an eye on you."' Fox rang his news editor at the Press Association, who was, not surprisingly, furious that Fox had missed the biggest

Two of Baird's staff, Birch and Bartlett, making sound-and-vision recordings at the Long Acre studio in 1928.

scoop of his life. 'He just about exploded. Why hadn't I left a biography of myself in the office, why hadn't I done this, that and the other thing? He said, "Everybody wants to know who it is whose face was seen on the other side."'

Baird's appetite for publicity became gargantuan. He gave a series of demonstrations of his inventions, including 'daylight television', 'noctovision', 'stereoscopic television', 'phonovision' and, on 6 July 1928, colour television. The colour was achieved by using a Nipkow disc fitted with green, red and blue filters. 'Delphiniums and carnations appeared in their natural colours,' according to one report, 'and a basket of strawberries showed the red fruit very clearly.' Investors rushed to put money into Baird's company, whose shares rose from 1 shilling to 30 shillings, and at last Baird could afford to hire extra staff.

Noctovision: Sir Oliver Lodge with Baird and a 'Noctovisor' at the Leeds meeting of the British Association, 1927.

But there was still one large obstacle. Public demonstrations and press conferences were all very well, but Baird wanted to go further – to be able to broadcast, in the literal sense. Few people were likely to buy Baird television sets unless there were programmes for them to watch. The BBC enjoyed a monopoly of broadcasting in Britain, under licence from the Postmaster-General. As early as 1926 Baird had 'unofficially' broadcast a few times from the BBC's aerial on top of Selfridge's after radio programmes had ended for the night, until a senior executive of the BBC got to hear of it and had the broadcasts stopped. Baird had then been granted a licence by the Post Office for experimental transmissions – without sound – from London to Harrow, but the Post Office would not allow full-scale regular 'broadcasts' until its engineers could be satisfied by Baird's technical standards. Baird, in turn, professed himself unhappy with the wavelengths the Post Office had allocated him. What he wanted was to broadcast from a BBC station, but the BBC's engineers and executives were almost unanimously hostile. Baird's supporters complained constantly about the BBC's attitude, suggesting that the lumbering bureaucracy was trying to crush the lone genius. The journalist Sydney Moseley, who was Baird's most fanatical publicist, wrote that 'the struggle to put Baird over with the BBC is more or less a *guerre à mort*, no holds barred'.

In fact, the BBC had good reasons for its scepticism. As Peter Eckersley, the BBC's chief engineer, put it in a memo, 'the Baird apparatus not only does not deserve a public trial, but also has reached the limit of its development owing to the basic technical limitations of the method employed'. The limitations, of course, were to do with Baird's refusal to use electronic equipment instead of his mechanical system. Nor was it only the BBC who thought that Baird had no future. A. A. Campbell Swinton himself, the man who had proposed electronic television twenty years earlier, wrote an angry letter to *The Times* in July 1928, complaining that 'the public are being led to expect, in the near future, that, sitting at home in their armchairs, they will be able to witness moving images'. Such an achievement, Campbell Swinton wrote, would be beyond the capacity of any mechanical device and could only be accomplished 'by using the vastly superior agency of electrons'. (He also described Baird as an unscrupulous rogue who was fleecing the innocent public, but this part of the letter was edited out by *The Times* for fear of a libel suit.)

However well-founded the BBC's reservations were, pressure on the Corporation increased. In September 1928, after being given a demonstration by Baird, the Post Office's engineers recommended that the BBC should allow him to experiment on one of its own stations. The BBC demanded to see Baird's apparatus for itself, and did so the following month. It remained unimpressed. Gladstone Murray, the BBC's Assistant Controller in charge of public relations, wrote that 'yesterday's demonstration would be merely ludicrous if its financial implications didn't make it sinister'. It had been 'an insult to the intelligence of those invited', and the Baird method was 'either an intentional fraud or a hopeless mechanical failure'. For public consumption, the BBC said that Baird had 'failed to fulfil the conditions which would justify trial through a BBC station'.

Baird was outraged; and, as usual, he managed to orchestrate some favourable publicity for himself. *The People* declared that 'the attitude of the BBC in regard to this amazing British invention is absolutely incomprehensible'. More seriously, the Postmaster-General warned the BBC that if it continued to be uncooperative he would simply issue Baird with a licence not unlike that of the BBC itself.

Faced with threats of this kind, the BBC agreed to give Baird another chance. On 5 March 1929, experts from the BBC and the Post Office watched a Baird demonstration; it was much the same as the earlier ones, showing only heads and shoulders, but a touch of glamour was provided by the appearance of the matinee idol Jack Buchanan, a friend of Baird.

The Corporation bowed to the inevitable. At 11 a.m. on 30 September 1929, Baird transmitted his first broadcast via the BBC station 2LO. It included Lulu Stanley singing 'He's Tall, Dark and Handsome', and Baird's secretary, Miss King, performing 'Mighty Like a Rose'. The earliest broadcasts were bizarre to behold. Since the BBC had allowed Baird only one transmitter, he could broadcast either sound or vision but not both simultaneously; so there would be a couple of minutes of pictures followed by a couple of minutes of singing or speech. In March 1930 Baird got his second transmitter, which enabled him to produce synchronised sound and vision. He celebrated by inviting Gracie Fields to sing 'Nowt for Owt'. In July, with help from the BBC's drama department, Baird broadcast the first televised play in Britain – *The Man With The Flower in His Mouth* by Pirandello.

The Man With The Flower In His Mouth, *the cumbersomely named drama by Pirandello, which was the first televised play in Britain, 1930.*

In March 1930 Baird had installed a television set at 10 Downing Street. Ramsay MacDonald, the Prime Minister, told him that 'you have put something in my room which will never let me forget how strange is this world – and how unknown'. Two months later the 'Baird Televisor' went on general sale, at a price of 25 guineas, but there were few buyers. Most people watching these early broadcasts were those who had already assembled do-it-yourself television kits.

Baird was allowed to broadcast only when radio was not on the air – in the morning and late at night. On 3 June 1931, however, he received special dispensation to make a transmission in the afternoon – the Derby, 'live' from Epsom. It was televised on a single camera mounted in a van which was parked near the winning post. The camera was connected by landline to the Baird studio in Long Acre, and from there to the BBC. 'All that we ever expected or could see were the horses just flashing past the winning post,' says Tony Bridgewater, a Baird engineer who was supervising the receivers in Long Acre. 'You wouldn't be able to tell one horse from another or one jockey from another, but you could at least tell they were horses.'

Feeling that he had proved his point in England, Baird extended his horizons. In the autumn of 1931 he sailed for the USA on board the *Aquitania* at the invitation of Donald Flamm, who owned radio station WMCA in New York. Although there were plenty of Americans working on television, and a number of experimental stations in operation, Flamm thought that Baird was in a different league. 'On a standpoint of showmanship – and I must explain that I'd been involved with the theatre all my life,' he says, 'I liked what Baird was doing – the idea that in that year, 1931, he had actually televised the finish of the Derby at Epsom and he had already broadcast the scene from a play by Pirandello, and done many exciting things.' But even such an accomplished showman as Baird found Flamm's razzmatazz slightly overwhelming. When Baird stepped off the *Aquitania* he was greeted by a band of Highland pipers. 'He was very embarrassed about that, it bothered him no end,' Flamm recalls. 'And the same stunt was pulled when the Mayor invited him to come down to City Hall to receive an official welcome and pipers preceded him.'

Flamm's intention was to sign a contract with Baird under which the Scotsman would put his technical knowledge at WMCA's disposal so that it could start a television service. On 18 October Flamm introduced Baird to WMCA listeners as 'the father of television – a man who, like so many other great inventors, was confronted with difficulties which a lesser spirit would have deemed insurmountable'. He added that 'it remains only for certain legal formalities to be met – for a television wave to be assigned to us by the Federal Radio Commission – before WMCA starts to broadcast its television programmes'. Unfortunately for Baird, these little legal formalities were not met. In March 1932 the FRC rejected Flamm's application for a licence, agreeing with an objection by RCA that foreign companies such as Baird's should not be given a foothold in American television.

Isaac Shoenberg, another expatriate Russian, was the inspiration behind EMI's work in London, which eventually led to the development of the Emitron camera and the demise of the Baird system.

Ironically enough, less than a year later Baird himself was protesting about foreign firms' involvement in television. In February 1933 he wrote to no less a figure than the Prince of Wales to complain that the BBC was 'wasting a pioneer British industry' by giving 'secret encouragement to alien interests'. The alien interests were his old American foes, RCA, who owned a substantial stake in the new British company EMI, the offspring of a merger in 1931. Under the direction of Isaac Shoenberg, a brilliant Russian émigré (and therefore a compatriot of Vladimir Zworykin and David Sarnoff of RCA), EMI's research department was throwing itself into the struggle to produce an electronic television receiver suitable for the general market. In November 1932 Shoenberg invited the new Chief Engineer at the BBC, Noel Ashbridge, to inspect the equipment. Ashbridge reported that the pictures were 'by far the best wireless television I have ever seen and are probably as good as, or better than, anything that has been produced anywhere else in the world'. However, he added that 'the apparatus is developed only for the transmission of films and I am informed that the development of the system for studio transmission might not be very easy'.

In 1961, on the twenty-fifth anniversary of the opening of a television service in London, EMI staged an exhibition of early television camera tubes at their research building in Hayes, Middlesex, where Shoenberg and his team had worked.

When Baird heard of the BBC's sympathetic interest in EMI, he exploded. 'This company is virtually controlled by the Radio Corporation of America,' he wrote to Sir John Reith, Director-General of the BBC, 'which surely controls quite enough of the world's communications without the home of British broadcasting taking it under its wing.' Although he did not know quite what was going on in EMI's laboratories, he must have at least suspected that he was being overtaken.

His fears were justified. Every expert who saw the EMI apparatus agreed that it was immeasurably superior to anything achieved by Baird. Moreover, by 1933 EMI had decided to use an all-electronic design not merely for its receivers but also for cameras (to be known as Emitrons), which were similar to Zworykin's 'Iconoscopes' in the United States. The commitment to electronic scanning was particularly farsighted, since EMI had already achieved 180-line pictures with its mechanical scanner and might have been tempted to persevere with that instead.

Meanwhile Baird knew that his 30-line transmissions were no longer adequate; he hunted for ways of obtaining higher-definition pictures. The scanning system he was currently using was a 'flying spot': spots of light were beamed from the scanning disc itself on to the face of the performer. Apart from that illumination, the studio was in total darkness. This caused some difficulties, particularly for dancers, as Baird's engineer Tony Bridgewater remembers: 'What with the darkness outside the beam and the flickering effect in people's faces, as soon as they were out of the scanning area, if they had to leap out in some act or gymnastic thing, they were liable to crash against the wall or fall on the floor.'

The Paramount Astoria Girls, who appeared in transmissions in 1932.

Sally the Seal enters by the goods entrance of Broadcasting House for her screen debut, 1932.

Lack of light was not the only problem. Lillian Rowley, who appeared regularly in Baird transmissions, recalls being asked to stage a routine with two other dancers: 'When we got there, on the floor in chalk was a five-foot square. That was our space, and if you can imagine three fairly solid girls trying to dance in a five-foot square – we were black and blue by the end of it. Knees up hit the one in front and hands out hit you on the chin. It was chaos.'

For his salvation Baird looked to Germany, where experiments with television were proceeding apace in the early 1930s. Conditions were just as chaotic as in Britain. Ten Haaf, who worked as a production assistant in Berlin, says: 'When the actors had to be in close-up, they had to move forward. In the dark, they couldn't find where they were supposed to be. On each side there were two people, two production assistants. They had to guide the actors – we crawled right low down on the floor and had to make sure that the actors stayed in the middle.'

W. W. Jacomb, Baird's chief engineer, often visited Germany, and at the beginning of 1933 he brought back a design for a 120-line film scanner. Baird built one and thought it excellent, but the BBC's engineers were unimpressed. Although the device transmitted film reasonably well, it was hopeless for 'live' pictures from a studio. Following the logic of this, Baird came up with another solution: why not film all studio performances and *then* scan them with the German machine? He thus adopted an 'Intermediate Film Technique'. Negative film from a studio camera was transferred directly into a developing tank, whence it would be put on to rollers and scanned while still wet. The pictures were not live, of course, since there was a one-minute delay between performance and transmission; and the equipment was extremely cumbersome.

Baird was forced to recognise the limitations of his own inventions. In 1933 he borrowed an electronic camera called an 'image dissector' from Philo T. Farnsworth's laboratories

An early test (1931) at the BBC, in a rather unglamorous studio near Waterloo Bridge.

in Philadelphia. Baird claimed that this did not mean he was abandoning his belief in mechanical cameras, but in truth it has to be seen as an admission of defeat.

It was prompted by the fact that his licence for experimental broadcasts from the BBC was due to expire in April 1934; he might never be allowed to broadcast again unless he could show that he was moving with the times. In May, the government announced that he was to be put to the test. A committee was set up, chaired by Lord Selsdon, to 'consider the development of television and to advise the Postmaster-General on the relative merits of the several systems and on the conditions under which any public service of television might be provided'. At the same time a new company was formed, Marconi-EMI, which brought together the Marconi company's experience with high-power transmitters and EMI's developments in cathode-ray tubes – notably the Emitron camera.

The Television Advisory Committee, chaired by Lord Selsdon, was appointed in 1935 by the Postmaster-General, Sir Kingsley Wood, to discuss the planning and development of Britain's television service.

Selsdon's report, published early in 1935, recommended that the BBC should start regular broadcasts in the London area as soon as possible, leading to the 'ultimate establishment of a general television service'. The minimum standard was 240 lines, but Selsdon refrained from adjudicating between the rival claims of Baird and Marconi-EMI. Both systems should be tried, operating on alternate weeks; this Box-and-Cox arrangement would then be reviewed after three months. Marconi-EMI's Emitron was already scanning on 405 lines, but Baird's engineers had quite a struggle to push their various types of scanner up to the 240-line minimum.

The BBC was also busy. It began converting Alexandra Palace, a huge Victorian pile in North London, into the home of the fledgling service. There had to be a good deal of duplicated effort – a Baird studio and an EMI studio, a Baird control room and an EMI control room, and so on. The first Director of Television was to be Gerald Cock, a former radio executive, who then advertised for two female 'announcer hostesses' and one male announcer. The glamour of it all drove the press into a frenzy of hyperbole. Jasmine Bligh and Elizabeth Cowell, who were chosen from more than 1,000 applicants, were described as 'Twin Paragons', while the male announcer, Leslie Mitchell, was dubbed 'TV Adonis' by the *Daily Mail*.

The BBC's 'twin paragons', Jasmine Bligh and Elizabeth Cowell.

The regular service was due to start in November 1936, but Gerald Cock jumped the gun in August by transmitting at the Radiolympia exhibition in London. Cock told Cecil Madden, who had just been appointed senior television producer, that 'the radio industry have come to us, Radiolympia has been a failure, they can't sell the stands, they don't know what to do so they've appealed to the BBC – this new television which is coming later, if you can do it, it will save Radiolympia'. Madden had just nine days to put together a programme, which he called *Here's Looking at You*. It was opened by Leslie Mitchell on 26 August with the following words: 'Good afternoon, ladies and gentlemen. It is with great pleasure that I introduce you to the magic of television.'

The magic consisted of a couple of films – a Gaumont British Newsreel and a discussion about books with Rebecca West, T. S. Eliot and Somerset Maugham – as well as a 'live' variety show which featured a Chilean tap-dancing duo called Chilton and Thomas, the Three Admirals (a singing group – 'big one at the piano and two small people round him'), a comedy act by Miss Lutie and her pantomime horse, as well as Miss Helen McKay singing a specially-written song:

Here's looking at you
From out of the blue
Don't make a fuss
But settle down and look at us.

On the first day, when the Baird scanners were being used, there were several technical breakdowns; the second day's performance, with EMI's 405-line camera, passed off without a hitch.

After Radiolympia, the BBC's new team had two months to prepare for the official opening. Leslie Mitchell remembers one rehearsal with a group of bathing beauties: 'They were all in pastel colours and it looked as though they had nothing on at all, which was great for the boys. But it never went out.' Such problems were nothing new. In August 1933 the *News Chronicle* had reported: 'Scientific progress took an unfore-seen turn yesterday, to the embarrassment of two BBC men who were experimenting with infra-red ray television. The engineers were "looking in" at a row of dancing girls who were being televised when, to their astonishment, they noticed that only one of the girls appeared to be clothed.' The ex-planation was simple: the dark dyes in the cotton dresses did not reflect the infra-red rays, which penetrated the loose fabric so that the television 'saw' everything. The only dancer to escape this indignity was wearing silk.

While Marconi-EMI intended to use nothing but its Emi-tron cameras, Baird had to work with a makeshift combina-tion of his 'flying spot' scanner, his Intermediate Film Technique and his rather unreliable Farnsworth camera. His equipment caused constant difficulties for both performers and engineers. Whereas the Emitron was mobile, Baird's camera was fixed – unable even to tilt up and down, or pan from left to right. Announcers sat on 'a screw-up chair, a sort of typist's chair, but even that didn't accommodate all sizes of people', remembers Tony Bridgewater, who was by then working for the BBC. 'So if we got a very little person and still the head wasn't fully in the picture, we had a range of tele-phone directories in stock in the studio, and we would just shove one or more of these underneath them.'

The Super-Emitron camera, developed in the EMI-Marconi laboratories, revolutionised British television.

Baird's 'flying spot' was especially awkward. 'There was a flickering light in front of your face, which made it almost impossible to see, but there were no lights in the studio itself,' Leslie Mitchell says. 'And behind me were two people I thought were friends of mine, one of whom pinched me in the right kidney to make me smile; the other pinched me in the left kidney to start me talking. Otherwise I had no idea what cue I was getting.' With the Emitron, on the other hand, 'it was more or less straightforward except that it was very much hotter, they had stronger lights'.

Joan Miller, a Canadian actress who had been hired to help Leslie Mitchell present a magazine programme called *Picture Page*, points to another difference. With the EMI system, 'we used make-up rather like film make-up', she says, 'pretty much what is used today'. For the Baird, however, 'we had a white base on the face and blue lips and blue eye shadow, and in fact you looked like a clown when it was finished'.

'Normal' television make-up in the 1930s: Jane Carr with whitened face and blue-black on her eyebrows, lashes, lips and sides of nose.

Baird's apparatus did have one advantage from the pre-senters' point of view: his delayed-action Intermediate Film Technique enabled them to see themselves on television. Leslie Mitchell explains: 'You could stand in front of the camera, say what you had to say, and if you ran pretty fast you could get into the engineers' room and watch yourself

August 1936: the control room at Alexandra Palace for the Marconi-EMI system, complete with sound amplifiers and the obligatory white-coated attendant.

Joan Miller, the Picture Page *hostess, with baby animals from the Children's Zoo in 1938; in the background, obscured by a lamp, is a member of a party of Norwegian athletes.*

coming up on film – it had been developed, printed, put through the container and in front of television in one minute.'

Nevertheless, doubts about Baird's system were already strong among BBC staff by 2 November 1936, the historic date on which Britain inaugurated the first public high-definition television service in the world. At the opening ceremony there was another snub to the man who considered himself to be the inventor of television 'One rather expected that Baird would figure in the line-up,' Tony Bridgewater recalls. 'I think he thought so himself, so he came to Alexandra Palace that day, but apparently nobody thought he should be invited – it was thought only important executives and government people should take part, and the poor man was left wandering up and down the passage waiting to be invited, and never was. Wasn't that sad?'

The service went on the air at 3 p.m. with speeches from the Postmaster-General and other worthies. After a five-minute newsreel from British Movietone, Adele Dixon performed a special song:

> A mighty maze of mystic magic rays
> Is all about us in the blue,
> And in sight and sound they trace
> Moving pictures out of space
> To bring a new wonder to you.
> The busy world before you is unfurled,
> Its songs, its tears and laughter too,
> And when they play their parts
> In this latest of the arts
> They bring new enchantment to you.

To prove that television was indeed bringing 'the busy world before you', Adele Dixon was followed by some Chinese jugglers and a pair of black American comedy dancers, Buck and Bubbles.

After being transmitted on the Baird equipment, the whole performance was repeated on Marconi-EMI's system an hour later. When the service resumed at 9 p.m. Leslie Mitchell introduced the first edition of *Picture Page* ('a magazine of topical and general interest'), which included interviews with a tennis player and an aviator. (The second day's programmes, it is worth noting, seem to have been even less alluring. 'A display by champion Alsatians from the Metropolitan and Essex Canine Society's Show' was followed by 'The *Golden Hind*, a model of Drake's ship made by L. A. Stock, a bus-driver, who will describe its construction'.)

The contrast between Marconi-EMI and Baird was embarrassingly obvious over the next few weeks. 'In the Baird studio there were complications, the thing often broke down, bubbles appeared on the film,' Cecil Madden says. 'And quite frankly the artistes just didn't want to appear on it. Quite important people came and practically prayed at my desk, saying "Don't put us on in the Baird week". So I think the finger of doom was on it.'

Leslie Mitchell (right) with Cecil Madden, the man who organised the BBC's inaugural broadcasts in 1936. Also shown: Joan Gilbert.

Nothing was going right for Baird. On 30 November 1936 his workshops at Crystal Palace in South London were burnt down, and in February 1937 the *coup de grâce* was executed: it was announced that the Baird system was being dropped altogether by the BBC. From then on, broadcasts were all done with Marconi-EMI's electronic equipment. At what should have been his moment of triumph, Baird found his life's work in ruins.

It was not only his employees who regretted his fall. Marc

Chauvierre, a French experimenter who had visited Baird in London in 1929, says: 'It was the richest person who won. In other words EMI won, and it was from that moment on that Baird was on the sidelines and almost forgotten. And, for my part, I understand the pain and sorrow he must have felt, to have failed in this way. And in reality television owes much more to Baird than it does to EMI.' His opinions are shared by Donald Flamm, the American who had sponsored Baird's fruitless trip to New York: 'In view of all that I know of Baird, and having been associated briefly with him, I feel that he deserves recognition as the inventor of television in the same sense that Alexander Graham Bell, his countryman, is recognised as the inventor of the telephone, or the Wright brothers the inventors of the aeroplane. They were the first to successfully present the telephone and the aeroplane and Baird definitely was the very first to successfully demonstrate television.'

The first live cabaret on German television (1937), with actors sitting on boxes disguised to look like beds.

While the BBC was deciding that its future in television would have no place for Baird, other countries were making progress. Indeed, the Germans claim that they actually beat the British by starting regular high-definition broadcasts in March 1935, twenty months before the BBC. Whether one accepts this is largely a matter of semantic interpretation. The Germans, using mechanical cameras, were transmitting 180-line pictures; but Lord Selsdon's verdict, in January 1935, was that 'high-definition' television required at least 240 lines. Oddly enough, it was Selsdon himself who brought about the early start of the German service, albeit unwittingly. When he was preparing his report he visited Germany; his hosts were given the mistaken impression that Britain would begin regular broadcasts at the end of 1935. 'At this, the head of State Radio, Eugene Hadamovsky, said that what the British were intending to do at the end of 1935 we could do well beforehand,' says Gerhardt Goebel, who worked for the Reichspost (Post Office) at the time. 'And so on 22 March 1935, from one day to the next, the first television broadcasting service in the world was begun.'

The inauguration was a quiet affair, although a press conference was held. Kurt Wagenfuhr, a journalist who attended it, says: 'It was noticeable that out of about fifty or sixty people who were present at this conference there was no Minister there, and no Secretary of State. Nor was there a senior man from the Party. We suspected that this had been done because, if everything went wrong, it could all simply be ignored. If things went well, a few good words about television could still be said in front of the camera.' Lord Selsdon's report, two months earlier, had noted that Dr Goebbels, the German Minister for Propaganda, was said to be very interested in television as a means of promoting Nazism. According to Kurt Wagenfuhr, the speeches by Hadamovsky and others on the first day reflected this: 'The central theme was: we're now beginning television with the ultimate aim of carrying the picture of the Führer into the hearts of all viewers – which, incidentally, never happened during the whole period from 1935 to 1944, because the Führer never spoke live directly from a studio on television.'

The Führer did, however, take a close interest. Until March 1935 the technical side of television, such as experiments with different cameras and receivers, had been the responsibility of the Reichspost. After the inauguration, Hadamovsky demanded that his State Radio (Reichsrundfunk) should take charge of technology. 'We wouldn't stand for that,' says

Gerhardt Goebel of the Reichspost. 'We telephoned Hitler, and Hitler decided that television technology was, and was to remain, part of the Reichspost.' Control of the programmes themselves was to be shared by the State Radio and the Propaganda Ministry. Anything which might affect national security was to be dealt with by Hermann Goering, the Luftwaffe Minister.

Like all television pioneers, the Germans had plenty of teething troubles – especially with lighting. At first they tried the 'flying spot' technique, in which the only light in the studio came from the scanner itself. 'I can remember a lady harpist, played wonderfully,' says Ten Haaf, one of the first producers. 'Suddenly she looked down at her strings. She stopped, went stiff, didn't play and began to weep buckets, because the light shone on to the strings, and she suddenly saw four, five or six strings in place of one. She just didn't know any more where she was supposed to put her fingers.'

Things were no better when the Germans tried equipment which required intense illumination. Elena Gerhardt, who started in television by presenting gymnastics classes, played her accompaniment on a piano which was painted bright green to make it look white on the screen. When she became a reporter, the heat generated by the lights caused her many a headache. An item about frozen food was wrecked when it all thawed; when she introduced a report about candles, she was left with nothing but melted wax.

Ten Haaf describes another restriction. Because the cameras were fixed in the early days, people who stood further away from the camera had to be higher than the people in front, so that they could be seen. The studio floor was correspondingly sloped, as were the individual pieces of decor on it. Glasses and plates had to be nailed to the tables to stop them sliding off. 'When anyone wanted to propose a toast with the glasses someone would say *"Zum Wohl"* and reach out for the glasses; and at the very moment when you reached out for the glass the other person would say, "Just a minute, there's something I want to tell you." You couldn't move the glasses. They were nailed down. You were always feeling that they were about to drink but nobody did.'

Most of the programmes were on film – newsreels, half-hour extracts from feature films, short documentaries and a show called *Mirror of the Day* which was shot in the streets of Berlin using a mobile unit made by Mercedes Benz. As television sets could not be bought in the shops, anyone who wished to see these programmes had to go to one of Berlin's eleven public viewing rooms, which were run by the Reichspost. Berlin also had a 'telecinema' with a large screen, four feet by three feet.

In August 1935 the Berlin Radio Exhibition, opened by Dr Goebbels, was destroyed by fire, and with it went the two television transmitters. The service re-opened in January 1936, and producers prepared themselves for the most ambitious outside broadcast yet staged anywhere in the world – the Berlin Olympics. They acquired three of Farnsworth's electronic cameras to cover the event. The cameras at the stadium, the gymnasium and the swimming pool were linked to two mobile television vans, which were connected by cable to the studio itself. 'The place where the camera stood was exactly the finishing line of the 100 metres sprint,' says Walter Bruch, the cameraman in the stadium. 'We were therefore able to broadcast how Jesse Owens won the gold medal.' Bruch says that through his viewfinder he had a better

August 1936: Adolf Hitler opens the Olympic Games in Berlin; the crowd gives Nazi salutes as the American athletes march past.

The black athlete Jesse Owens set an Olympic record in the 200 metres race at the Berlin games in 1936, thus marring Hitler's dream of a festival of Aryan success.

vantage point than Hitler. But he also had continual fights with the commentator provided by the State Radio, who kept referring to the brilliant colours of the scene. Bruch interpreted this as a sneering comment on the fact that television could only broadcast it in black and white. Eventually the antipathy between the two men turned to violence. According to Bruch, 'The commentator was always saying "Well here comes the Zeppelin over the stadium" or "Hitler is up there", but it was so high that I couldn't do anything with my camera because it wouldn't tilt so high – so what was left to me was to kick him in the back and sometimes even to curse.' The Propaganda Ministry ordered that 'the camera-man who swears so terribly must be dismissed'; but, Bruch says, 'There was no one else who could operate the camera so I just went on doing it.' The audience for these broadcasts, watching in the public viewing rooms, was estimated to be as high as 150,000.

Several other European countries were experimenting with television in this period, though none was as advanced as Britain and Germany. In France, 30-line pictures had first been demonstrated by René Barthélémy in 1929. Experimental transmissions from the top of the Eiffel Tower began in 1935. In the following year, mechanical equipment was replaced by much more advanced electronic scanners, and by 1938 France was already achieving a standard of 455 lines. Marc Chauvierre, who had a friendly rivalry with Barthélémy in the development of French television, thinks that one of the most important moments came in June 1939, when the Tour de France was filmed and then broadcast on television. 'It wasn't a live broadcast as it is today,' he says, 'and what surprised me, and proved that television had suddenly become a force to be reckoned with, was that in the workshop where television sets were being produced the workers would stop working and watch the Tour de France being shown.'

One nation which was particularly eager to keep up with the race for television was the Soviet Union. It was, after all, the country where Boris Rosing had designed a cathode-ray receiver back in 1907; it was also the homeland of such distinguished émigrés as Isaac Shoenberg, who had masterminded the Emitron camera in London, and Vladimir Zworykin, who had invented the Iconoscope for RCA. Indeed the Russians claim that they designed an electronic camera very like Zworykin's as early as 1931. The man who invented it, Semyon Katayev, feels slightly piqued that it was the expatriate who got all the credit. 'The name of "Iconoscope" was given to this tube by Zworykin,' he says, 'and it took hold in our language, too; but my patent application was less successful in its name. I called it a "radio eye", which didn't even get into the written language; the name was not a success.'

The first 60-line picture of Academician Yoffe of the Leningrad Institute, taken in 1930 by Yakov Ryvtin.

Zworykin himself visited the USSR in 1934 for the second time since his emigration in 1919. On his first trip, he had merely talked about his own work; on this second visit, however, he was apparently impressed by what he saw in the television laboratories of the Leningrad Institute of Telemechanics. One Soviet newspaper quoted him as saying: 'The first time I came to tell you of my discoveries. The second time I am leaving as a colleague. The third time I'm afraid I shall have a lot to learn from you.' By the time of Zworykin's 1934 visit, the institute in Leningrad had already built an electronic camera to Katayev's specifications, which was producing 180-line pictures.

Experimental 240-line transmissions began in Leningrad in July 1938; three months later, a 343-line service started in Moscow. As usual, tests were carried out to discover which colours looked best under studio lights. The producers decreed that everyone should wear green make-up – on the eyes, the lips and even the cheeks. Olga Vysotskaya, one of the first announcers on Soviet television, remembers interviewing three Russian aviators who had flown over the North Pole to the United States. One of the three arrived a little late, and found himself shaking the hand of a woman who was plastered with green make-up. 'He was completely stupefied,' she says. 'I said to him, "Valery Pavlovich, calm down! You'll look the same yourself in a minute." He said, "Not under any circumstances!" '

Equally inevitably, there were tricks of the light which made performers look naked – a feature of almost all early television transmissions throughout the world. When Olga Vysotskaya gave a televised gymnastics class, viewers wrote in 'asking, doubtfully, why the woman who demonstrated the gymnastics was not wearing any costume at all'. But in spite of the presence of gremlins, Soviet television did produce some impressive broadcasts, such as a performance by Prokofiev of his 'Five Melodies'.

The star female announcer on Soviet television in the early days, N. V. Kondratova, at Moscow's central studios; only one camera and one microphone appear to be in use.

Very few receivers were available in the first year of transmissions, and anybody who owned one swiftly acquired a host of new friends. Professor Novokovsky, who was appointed chief engineer at the Moscow television station in 1938, describes the scene that used to greet him when he returned home from work in the evening: 'I go into my apartment, and in the hall there are a lot of overcoats hanging on the stand, lying on the chair, on the table and even on the floor. Darkness is total. I timidly open the door into the television room and some voices shout, "Comrade! Shut the door! You're stopping us watching the television." When the transmission ended, the light was switched on, my wife introduced me, and everyone shook my hand and told me how pleased they were with television. So who were these television viewers? It turned out they were friends of friends of friends, whom of course I didn't know at all . . . We had guests every evening, twenty or thirty of them, all keen television watchers.'

As in Germany, television sets in the USSR were installed in public places – clubs, Houses of Culture and Pioneer Palaces. The only sets being built were those designed for collective viewing, which were bulky, expensive and difficult to control. In 1939 Mikhail Tovbin and Sergei Orlov created the first 'table-top' set, for use in the home. These went into mass production in Leningrad in 1940, but only a few hundred were made before the Soviet Union entered the Second World War. Broadcasting then ceased and the television factory was closed.

In Britain, television had been stopped on 1 September 1939, as Neville Chamberlain prepared to declare war on Hitler. 'A message was simply given to the engineers at Alexandra Palace: "Switch off everything, it's over," ' Cecil Madden recalls. 'And it just so happened that it was in the middle of a film.' A Mickey Mouse film, in fact; the last words before the plugs were pulled were 'Ah tink ah kees you now', delivered in a heavy Greta Garbo accent. As Madden complains, 'They hadn't even the courtesy or the taste to let us finish the film.' The reason for the urgency was that BBC television was the only station broadcasting on 45 megahertz, and the aerial at Alexandra Palace would therefore have made an ideal beacon from which German pilots could take their bearings. There was another reason: the government needed engineers trained in television techniques to run its radar chain.

April 1939: a performance of Shall We Join The Ladies? *at the BBC.*

Although happy enough to help the war effort, staff at the BBC were bitterly disappointed by the closure. Dallas Bower, who had produced some of the earliest television plays, says: 'We felt totally overwhelmed, in as much as we felt that conceivably we'd spent three years to no purpose.' After the long years of struggle, television had just begun to win the public's confidence. In September 1939 about 20,000 people owned sets, two-thirds of which had been bought in the last year. Most were within a twenty-five-mile radius of Alexandra Palace, but some people further away were prepared to gamble on picking up the signals. In February 1939 the *Radio Times* interviewed a farm labourer in Suffolk who had spent his life savings of £126 on a television set. The *Radio Times* praised him for his 'courage', 'spirit of sacrifice' and 'desire for self-improvement'; the man himself opined that 'television's far more entertaining and much less trouble than a wife would be'.

September 1938: Neville Chamberlain arrives at Heston Airport after talks with Hitler.

Sales of television sets had been greatly helped by some of the BBC's trail-blazing outside broadcasts. In May 1937 the coronation of George VI had been televised (although cameras were not allowed into Westminster Abbey for the service itself); later the same year viewers were able to watch the Remembrance Day ceremony from Whitehall; and in 1938 the BBC televised Neville Chamberlain's arrival at Heston Airport from Munich – the famous occasion when he waved a piece of paper which Hitler had signed, supposedly a guarantee of peace. Sport, too, was attracting viewers: by the time war broke out the BBC had already broadcast the Football Association Cup Final, the Boat Race, the Wimbledon tennis championship and a cricket test match from Lord's. But anyone who had bought a set on 1 September 1939 would have had to wait until June 1946 to see anything on it.

While Britain was abandoning its television service for the duration of the war, the United States was only just beginning its transmissions. Although several American corporations had been experimenting with television for years, progress towards regular broadcasts had been slow – not least because of lengthy wrangles about the ownership of patents. But there was no doubt that television was on the way. In 1935 RCA announced that it would spend $1 million on television demonstrations, which took place in a studio at Radio City in New York; the studio was connected by cable to a transmitter on top of the Empire State Building. By 1937 RCA's subsidiary, NBC, was making regular 'experimental programmes'. Among those prepared to take part, and thereby submit themselves to the indignity of wearing purple lipstick and green face make-up, was the film star Betty Grable.

Televising the test match between England and Australia at the Oval, August 1938; the cameraman had to sit on an upturned orange box.

RCA's technical standards continued to improve. The corporation's great advantage was that it employed Vladimir Zworykin and was thus able to use his Iconoscope camera for scanning, and another of his electronic inventions, the Kinescope, for receiving the pictures. In 1937 they were already scanning on 441 lines. The following year, NBC-RCA's 'mobile units' were completed, and were put into action on 15 September when NBC conducted interviews with passers-by in Rockefeller Plaza. In the view of David Sarnoff, RCA's President, it was time to start proper broadcasting.

Sarnoff had as great a flair for publicity as John Logie Baird. The occasion he chose for the inauguration of NBC's service was the New York World's Fair, which was to be opened by President Roosevelt on 30 April 1939. NBC produced a three-and-a-half hour telecast of the event, and FDR became the first President to appear on television. At last, Sarnoff announced, NBC was making 'the art of television available to the public'. This was something of an exaggeration. There were only about 100 television receivers in the whole of the New York area at the time of the World's Fair, many of which belonged to executives and engineers from NBC. The sets which RCA put on sale at the World's Fair cost between $200 and $600. Although the screens were only five or nine inches wide, the sets in which they were housed were four or five feet high. Burke Crotty, the producer in charge of NBC's transmission from the World's Fair, says that not even he was prepared to have one: 'Well, at that price, and that size, nobody wanted them, they couldn't sell them. I can recall distinctly, I bought a brand new car in 1940 for $1,000, and they wanted $660 for this TV set when there was virtually nothing on the air.'

NBC would have objected to the suggestion that there was nothing to watch. In its first year of regularly scheduled programmes, it provided from ten to fifteen hours a week of 'entertainment, enjoyment and inspiration that has won unstinted praise from a hypercritical metropolitan audience', in the words of a 1940 publicity brochure. Many of those hours were filled with outside broadcasts, also known as 'remotes', picked up by NBC's mobile units. There was a simple reason for this. 'If you go into a prepared studio set-up and you want to do a dramatic show, you have to get your cast and rehearse them,' Crotty explains. 'For a half-hour show, you do that for possibly four or five days, then you move into the studio for one solid day, and you rehearse on camera for a solid day. Now that gets costly.' For a sports game, on the other hand, 'it may have taken us four or five hours to make the set-up but we had three hours of programme material, and so we did baseball, football, hockey, tennis, you name it'. Other outside broadcasts included a 'Parade of the US Mechanised Cavalry' from Fifth Avenue, a water ballet from Manhattan Beach, and the New York opening of *Gone With the Wind*. But the studios were not entirely idle. NBC presented two dramatic productions a week, among which were Noel Coward's *Hay Fever*, Chekov's *A Marriage Proposal*, and Michael Arlen's *When the Nightingale Sang in Berkeley Square*.

1939: the first televised baseball match, between Columbia and Princeton.

After only one year of broadcasts, the Federal Communications Commission (FCC) announced in May 1940 that NBC would have to return to the status of an 'experimental' station until agreement was reached on a common technical standard for the American television industry. The problem was that RCA was committed to 441-line broadcasts while the Philco company in Philadelphia argued that 605 lines ought to be the norm. The FCC set up a National Television System Committee (NTSC) to investigate the matter. 'I was called by Dr Baker, the Chairman of the NTSC, while I was on a skiing vacation in northern Massachusets,' says Donald Fink, who was then editing *Electronics* magazine. 'He said, "I want you to write a paper which will get RCA and Philco out of the impasse and find somewhere in the centre, where they can agree." Well, I had to reply, it's easy to do because results that have come out of the Bell Laboratories

RCA's experimental studio in the Empire State Building, in action in 1937.

Lady David Douglas-Hamilton (Miss Prunella Stack) displays herself for the television camera at Selfridges' television studio in London.

say that any number of lines between 441 and 605 will do, it's equally satisfactory so long as the channel is set. "Well," Doc said, "what have you got in the way of numbers?" I said it ought to be an odd number, it ought to be composed of a small number of odd factors, how do you like 525? He said, "Sounds all right to me." ' As a result of this random choice, the FCC decided that full-scale commercial television, to a 525-line standard, could begin on 1 July 1941.

It was at this point that another company chose to challenge NBC's monopoly. Columbia Broadcasting System (CBS) had already become a serious rival to NBC in radio, but its research with television lagged far behind. In 1939–40, while NBC provided a regular broadcasting service, CBS was still at the stage of making experimental transmissions. Nevertheless, CBS elected to take advantage of the FCC's announcement of a starting date. At 2.30 p.m. on 1 July 1941 it went on the air. There was no opening ceremony or fanfare of any kind, since CBS executives felt this would merely draw attention to the fact that they were two years behind NBC. In any case, CBS's facilities were so limited that it could not have staged anything as spectacular as NBC's broadcast from the World's Fair. It had a studio at Grand Central Station with just two cameras and a small film channel for transmitting slides and still pictures. There was no outside broadcasting equipment at all. Anyone watching CBS's early output would scarcely have guessed that this was to become the biggest and richest television network in America. Afternoon broadcasts began with a fifteen-minute news programme, followed by a children's story. There was then either a dance lesson or a panel discussion. Evening viewing consisted of fifteen minutes of news, fifteen minutes of singing and a programme in which the Metropolitan Museum of Art displayed their treasures in the CBS studio, under heavy guard.

NBC, of course, had also started a full commercial service on 1 July. But neither NBC nor CBS had long to improve their new medium. On 7 December 1941, Japanese aircraft attacked the American fleet at Pearl Harbor. America was at war. There was not, as in Britain, an official order to stop broadcasting, and NBC and CBS continued to produce a few programmes; but no sets were being manufactured, and without an audience there seemed little point in continuing. By 1942 American television had all but petered out.

Britain and the Soviet Union were already off the air. German television had been suspended for a month during the invasion of Poland in September 1939, but it was then resumed. 'We continued with our programmes and pretended nothing had happened,' says Kurt Hinzmann, who was the General Manager of Berlin Television. By that time there were about 3,000 viewers in Berlin, most of them watching in the special public rooms provided by the Reichspost, as well as a few hundred more in Hamburg, which was connected to Berlin by cable. There were also about 350 privately-owned television receivers. Hinzmann suggested that these sets should be collected and set up in military hospitals, so that entertainment could be offered to wounded troops. 'We went on with our programmes,' Hinzmann says, 'and in addition, up to twice weekly, we organised variety, bands, theatrical performances – everything on the basis of "forces' welfare". This had the advantage that we had become an organisation vital to the war effort.'

France surrendered in June 1940. Later the same year Hinzmann visited Paris, where he learned that a German

general had ordered that the television aerials and transmitters on the Eiffel Tower should be dismantled so that they could be used as raw material by German industry. 'We were horrified, because for those of us in television it was nothing short of vandalism,' says Hinzmann, who instantly set about having the order rescinded. 'Then the idea occurred to us – why not try what we had been able to do so successfully in Berlin, that is, to put television to work for forces' welfare?' Hinzmann's proposal was accepted by the top brass in Berlin, who were keen to keep television alive and develop it technically; the Eiffel Tower, at 985 feet the highest transmitter in Europe, offered an opportunity not to be missed.

Hinzmann was in charge of the service. He built a large studio to take six cameras, with an auditorium for 250 people – the first 'studio audience'. Television sets were installed in all the Parisian hospitals containing wounded German soldiers, but French people watched as well. There was also a more surprising audience – British intelligence officers, who monitored the picture across the English Channel at Beachy Head. Hinzmann knew about this possibility: 'The Eiffel Tower transmitter had a 30 KW output – enormous! – and we were, naturally, quite aware of how far away it could be received.' Nevertheless, he did not actually realise that British intelligence was watching his broadcasts. 'If we had known about it, we would have had a nice word of greeting for them. But we didn't know about it. There are stories that British intelligence was able to make observations because of our weekly news broadcasts about how their bombing was turning out, but, good heavens, I don't believe it. I hope that the facilities of that organisation for getting information were rather better than our already censored weekly news.' In any case, apart from the weekly news, the programmes were made 'not for propaganda but for entertainment'. Hinzmann's broadcasts continued until shortly before the liberation of Paris, when the Nazis smashed the transmitter and removed their cameras; even so, they left much valuable equipment which was to prove extremely useful when the French set up their own television service in 1944.

In Germany itself, Berlin Television had continued to broadcast for two or three hours in the afternoons and another two hours in the evenings, from 8 p.m. to 10 p.m. As the bombing of Berlin intensified, the time of the evening programme was brought further and further forward until it was going out between 6 p.m. and 8 p.m., because in the evenings people wanted to be at home in their cellars, sheltering from air raids. On 23 November 1943 the television service ceased altogether: Allied bombers had scored a direct hit on the Berlin transmitter.

Images of Power.

'Dear Abbie, What can be done about friends who drop in unexpectedly while we are watching our favourite TV programmes? We hate to be rude, but we would rather watch our programme than visit with them . . .'

'Dear Abbie, This may sound crazy but I need your advice. I am divorced and the mother of a sweet four-year-old boy named Ronnie. We were at home recently when an armed intruder confronted us. The man was gentle and he quickly put Ronnie at ease – he wanted only money and promised not to hurt us. We both explained to Ronnie that Mommie would have to be tied up for a while; he seemed to understand. After I was bound and gagged, Ronnie was told to turn on the TV and when the programme was over, about twenty minutes, he could help me or call for help. I was taken to another room and the robber left. Abbie, my son spent the next three hours watching TV while I was bound and utterly helpless . . .'

'Dear Abbie, The minute my husband comes home from work he turns on the TV and watches anything that happens to be on. He even has me serve his dinner while he is watching. He doesn't talk to me or the children. Abbie, he stays up until 2 o'clock in the morning, long after we have all gone to bed. Of course we don't have a sex life any more . . .'

Parents the world over complain about how much time their children spend watching television; those same parents are usually glued to the box themselves as soon as the kids are in bed.

These are just three of the hundreds of letters concerning television which have been received in the last few years by Abbie van Buren, whose agony column is syndicated in newspapers across the United States and beyond. As the letters suggest, television can be a powerfully addictive drug. This would be alarming enough even if there were only a few dozen television sets in existence; but the experiences of Abbie's correspondents are repeated – albeit in a more moderate form – in mansions and mud huts around the world. There were 4 million television receivers in the USA in 1949; by 1969 there were 81 million; ten years later there were 150 million. In 1949, only four countries – Britain, France, the USA and the USSR – had a television service; by 1981 there were regular transmissions in no fewer than 137 countries, ranging from the People's Republic of China to tiny islands such as the Maldives.

Whenever and wherever the introduction of television has been proposed, one of the first questions to be settled has been that of whether it should be allowed at all. Israel, Tanzania and South Africa, though far apart politically, were all determined for many years to resist the arrival of television because of their governments' fears of its influence on the people. (In the case of Tanzania, it should be added, President Nyerere also felt that television would use money which ought to be spent on 'social priorities'.) Another country which held out until the 1970s was Sri Lanka: the Minister in charge of broadcasting, Dudley Senanayake, returned from medical

Before he became a Tory politician, Christopher Chataway was ITN's first newscaster; he was also the favourite announcer of Prudence the kitten, who (according to her owner) 'mewed petulantly' if she couldn't watch her pin-up boy.

treatment in the USA in 1966 to announce that 'after what I saw from my hospital bed I will not let you have television, which is the deadliest instrument to create a non-thinking generation of people, gun-happy and brought up on mayhem and murder'.

Once a nation has decided to accept television, the next question is the most important of all: how should it be financed and who should control it? Broadly speaking, there are three different models for a television system. In some countries, although it is theoretically operating under licence from the government, television is run as a straightforward commercial enterprise by private firms; the American networks are the largest example. A second possible arrangement is to have a 'public service' broadcasting organisation which, although financed by public funds, is supposed to be independent of the government – as with the BBC in Great Britain. Finally, there are countries where the television system is unashamedly a branch of the government, under as much central control as any other ministry.

The most obvious example of this last category is the Soviet broadcasting authority, Gosteleradio – or, to give it its full title, the USSR State Committee for Television and Radio Broadcasting, whose Chairman is a member of the Soviet government. There is no licence fee: television is financed entirely out of state and regional budgets. Its duty, as laid down by the 23rd Party Congress, is to 'mould a Marxist-Leninist outlook and promote the political and cultural development of all the Soviet people'. To this end, Soviet television broadcasts programmes with such titles as *The Leninist University of Millions* (dealing with the history of the Communist Party), *Your Leninist Library* (a series 'to help the broad masses of the people to acquire a better knowledge of Lenin's works') and *I Serve the Soviet Union* (about the army). These programmes are transmitted on the First Channel, which reaches more than 240 million people – 89 per cent of the Soviet population.

The dish on top of the Orbita station in Yuzhno-Sakhalinsk, a city in the Far East, enabling it to receive broadcasts from Moscow via Sputnik. For countries such as the Soviet Union, satellites help to promote 'national unity'.

One of Gosteleradio's greatest challenges is the fact that the Soviet Union is a heterogeneous nation: it has fifteen republics, spread across eleven different time zones. The Soviet government, while wishing to encourage national unity, is also obliged to recognise the special demands of, say, Georgia or Siberia. There is thus a network of regional stations, carrying what Gosteleradio calls a 'sensible blend' of central programmes and local transmissions, which are made in forty-five languages.

On the fringes of the Soviet Union, there is another problem: people living near the border can pick up broadcasts from neighbouring countries. Two of the most avidly watched programmes in Estonia are *The Muppet Show* and *The Benny Hill Show* – not because Gosteleradio has had a rush of blood to the head and decided to transmit them, but because Estonians can receive Finnish television.

Given the huge geographical expanse of the Soviet Union, the idea of a few Estonians watching Benny Hill is no more than a trifling inconvenience to the controllers in Moscow. Elsewhere in Eastern Europe, the phenomenon of 'cross-viewing' has become an epidemic, and has forced the 'socialist countries' to re-think their programming. East Germany, for instance, has a structure like that in the Soviet Union: television is controlled by the government, and its function is 'the formation of socialist state consciousness'. However, the people who run broadcasting in East Germany are also well aware that the 6 million owners of television sets in the country can – and do – receive transmissions from West Germany. The East German broadcasters have tried to defuse this dangerous incursion by running a weekly programme called *Black Channel*, in which West German television is denounced for its capitalist wickedness. The East German population continues to watch broadcasts from the West just the same. East German television has also tried a more ingenious (and more successful) strategy: it has chosen to beat the West at its own game, originally by showing sports matches and then by importing Hollywood movies. In 1983 it bought a large number of Robert Redford films, which were then transmitted at the same time in the evening as West German TV's main news bulletin. The ploy worked. The East German audience, normally hungry for news from across the border, found *Butch Cassidy and the Sundance Kid* and *All the President's Men* irresistible. So did many West German viewers: 'cross-viewing', until then largely a one-way street, began to work in the opposite direction.

At the 1964 Nice Carnival in France, one float showed 'the monster television', complete with antennae.

Laplanders, after a hard day following reindeer, like nothing better than to settle down with the telly: these in the far north of Sweden acquired their first set in 1961.

Nevertheless, East German television is still an instrument of the Party; its main task is to act as a weapon of propaganda for the government. This is the case throughout the nations of the Warsaw Pact. It is also the pattern for most of the 'developing countries'. Although commercial companies are allowed to operate television stations in some parts of the Third World, they are never left in much doubt as to what they can or cannot show. In Thailand, for example, there are two commercial channels, one channel owned by the army and a fourth channel owned by the government itself; but all are politically limited. In 1965, the official regulations stated that 'the first objectives of broadcasting are (a) to promote national policy and common interests in the areas of politics, military affairs, economics and social welfare, (b) to promote the loyalty of the citizens to the country, the religion and the King, (c) to promote the unity and mutual cooperation of the army and its citizens, and (d) to invite citizens to retort to and oppose the enemy, including those doctrines which are dangerous to the security of the nation'. More recently, in 1982, the Thai Radio and TV Control Board issued a new set of binding rules which dictated what kinds of programmes could be shown at certain times of the day.

In Thailand's near neighbour, the Philippines, television is officially 'independent'; in reality, it has been rife with political skulduggery and manipulation from its very first transmission, on 23 October 1953. The man responsible for that broadcast, Judge Antonio Quirino, is disarmingly frank about his motives in starting the service: his brother, then President of the Philippines, was running for re-election. 'He was a very sick man, he was almost a walking skeleton, and he could not campaign around the country. So I figured out that if he could have a television in the palace and he could broadcast from there, he might be able to reach many of the people round the country without having to go around. That was the immediate reason.' Judge Quirino placed 120 television sets in restaurants and other public places in Manila for the benefit of the electorate, but it was to no avail: his brother lost the election. Soon afterwards, the new government removed the television transmitter from Judge Quirino's back garden and handed him a tax bill for 3 million pesos.

During the late 1950s and early 1960s television in the Philippines was controlled by a few powerful families, but that did not make it any less political than an officially-

(WX15)WASHINGTON, Oct. 7—DEBATING THE ISSUES—This was the scene tonight as Sen. John Kennedy of Massachusetts and Vice President Richard Nixon, rivals for the presidency, debated the issues of the political campaign during a nationally televised debate from Washington. Between the candidates is Frank McGee, moderator of the program. Four newsmen, who asked the questions of the candidates, are silhouetted in the foreground.

(CDA-17)CLEVELAND, October 28—DEBATE SCENE—President Jimmy Carter (left) and Republican presidential candidate Ronald Reagan (right) face their panelists Tuesday night during their televised debate. They are shown in the Cleveland Convention Center.

directed service. In particular, they used the medium to attack Ferdinand Marcos, who was elected President in 1965 despite their best endeavours. After his re-election in 1969, Marcos began to exercise a greater influence over broadcasting; in 1972, when he declared martial law, he closed down all the television channels except one, which was used for Presidential broadcasts from the palace.

Marcos did eventually allow other television stations to re-open, but on his terms. The three main channels were to be controlled by Roberto Benedicto, one of his closest friends. One 'independent' channel was permitted, but its owners knew that they were unlikely to stay in business for long if they displeased Marcos. More recently, Marcos has set up a commercial channel whose task is to 'explain government programmes and thinking'. Rod Rayes, who is in charge of the channel, freely admits that 'we give priority to news emanating from official government sources, and of course high on the list would be what the President is doing. And so we normally would lead off on stories on the Presidency – unless there is an earth-shaking event elsewhere in the world.'

If any of the Manila stations step out of line, they can expect a telephone call from the palace. A few years ago a Filipino actress presented a series in which she appealed for money to pay for the education of poor children, or for hospital treatment. She was promptly banished from the air: a senior government official announced that there were no poor people in the Philippines and there was, therefore, no need to produce a programme for the poor.

'Marcos has an idolatrous worship of media – he believes in media the way other people believe in God,' says Father James Reuter, a Jesuit priest who directed drama productions during the early days of Philippines television. 'He does not believe that reality counts at all. He thinks that the only important thing is the image. So if everybody knows that what he is saying is false, that doesn't trouble him one little bit, as long as the image is correct. I think he believes that the only ones who know the truth are those who are close enough to see it, and there are so few that it doesn't make any difference.' Reuter concludes that 'as soon as somebody goes for complete power, he has to get the media first'.

As Reuter points out, this is true not merely in the Philippines but throughout the world. Most politicians are firm believers in the importance and power of television. One of President de Gaulle's ministers in France described television as *'le gouvernement dans la salle-à-manger'* (government in the dining room). Shortly before Rhodesia's unilateral declaration of independence in 1965, Ian Smith said that control of television was necessary in order to win 'the war for the minds of men'.

The politicians' desire to dominate the air-waves is, then, not confined to dictatorships. India, which prides itself on its status as 'the world's largest democracy', has a free and vigorous press; its radio and television, on the other hand, are run by the Ministry of Information and are correspondingly unadventurous. As *India Today* magazine put it in 1982, 'the tedium is the message'. *India Today* described the television service, Doordarshan, as being like 'a slack, inexorably slow and malfunctioning government department, no different from the local passport office', and controlled by 'the same puny, gutless babus desperate to ingratiate themselves with their political bosses'. One Doordarshan producer was sacked by the news department 'because the crowd scenes in

Politicians have almost always been firm believers in the importance of television; this broadcast came from the United Nations General Assembly in 1949.

1964: live television programmes come to the Middle East for the first time, transmitted from a studio at the British Trade Fair in Baghdad. All the equipment was shipped to Iraq by a British firm. Receivers stationed in shops around the city had to be withdrawn after 48 hours because of traffic chaos caused by crowds queueing to watch.

By the time of the 1980 debates, both candidates – Carter and Reagan – were well aware of the need for dark suits against a light background; as were Kennedy and Nixon for their second debate, after the fiasco of the first.

'During extremely difficult phases of development,' according to Indira Gandhi, 'there has to be some medium which helps to hold the people together.'

a Mrs Gandhi meeting were not adequately shot'. An Additional Director-General of Doordarshan was fired after trying to cancel a programme in which Mrs Gandhi's guru appeared. In July 1983 the Director of Doordarshan's Srinagar station, Albel Singh Garewal, was 'transferred' because he had not transmitted full enough reports of speeches by leaders of Mrs Gandhi's party.

It was also in 1983 that Mrs Gandhi decided to build the image of her new political heir-apparent, her son Rajiv. Doordarshan was obediently compliant. It made a point of 'cutting in' photographs and film of Rajiv whenever he was mentioned in news bulletins – a privilege which was not always granted even to Mrs Gandhi herself. Every function attended by Rajiv – the inauguration of a wrestling contest, a seminar on the packaging of fruits, the opening of a sports museum – was reported at length by Doordarshan. At the same time, the government announced a huge programme of expansion which would increase the proportion of the country that could receive Doordarshan from 25 per cent to 70 per cent; it was to be completed by the end of 1984 – in time for the election.

Mrs Gandhi believed that it was quite justifiable for television to project the government's point of view 'because the government doesn't have any paper of its own'. She also thought, like many leaders of developing countries, that state control of broadcasting was essential for the promotion of national unity: 'While you are going through extremely difficult phases of development, and you have a long way to go, this is the time of the greatest expectations as well as the greatest disappointment. So there has to be some medium which helps to hold the people together and project the national point of view.' The distinguished Indian journalist Arun Shourie gives a very different – and blunter – opinion: 'The function of radio and television is to lie on behalf of the government.'

It is popularly supposed that pressures such as these exist only in developing countries or dictatorships. In an industrialised democracy, so the theory goes, no government would dare to interfere in television's autonomy. It is certainly a theory which Western governments themselves would like people to believe; but it is only partly true. In the West and Japan (which, these days, is classed as a 'Western industrialised nation'), television channels may have more freedom than in, say, the Soviet Union; but political pressure is still present, albeit in more subtle forms.

Japan is the TV society: here, one member of a family watches a set equipped with earphones while the others look at a different programme.

Take the case of Japan, which is often regarded as the epitome of a 'television society' – even more so than the United States. A recent opinion poll asked Americans and Japanese what single item they would take to a desert island; 36.6 per cent of the Japanese respondents chose television, compared with just 4 per cent of the Americans. In 1982 it was estimated by A. C. Nielsen, the American market research organisation, that a typical Tokyo family watched television for eight hours and twelve minutes every day, as against six-and-three-quarter hours in the United States and between three and four hours in Western Europe.

Japanese television consists of NHK (the Japanese Broadcasting Corporation), a non-commercial body financed by licence fees, and a number of commercial networks. Broadcasters in Japan are proud of their 'independence' – justifiably so, most of the time. Yet even in Japan there are limits to the risks that television is prepared to take.

In 1965 an eminent Japanese programme-maker, Junichi

A guest at the Capsule Inn, Osaka, Japan, watches television before going to sleep; although the accommodation is little bigger than a coffin, every 'capsule' has a TV set.

Ushiyama, produced a three-part documentary for one of the commercial channels, NTV, entitled *Actions of a Vietnamese Marine Battalion*, in which he predicted why the United States was bound to lose the Vietnam war. More importantly, he filmed some horrifying scenes from the war. In the first programme, he showed South Vietnamese government troops entering a village to interrogate people who were thought to be spies for the Vietcong. Among them was a seventeen-year-old boy. After shooting him, the troops cut open his belly to see if there were any 'secret documents' in his stomach. They then cut off his head, and held it up to the camera for a few seconds before throwing it on the ground. Ushiyama says that he 'agonised a lot' about whether the scene should be included, before deciding that viewers ought to be shown what was happening in Vietnam.

Pictures of napalm-burned children in Vietnam may have been visually arresting but some critics complained that they told viewers little of the origins and complexities of a far-off war

In the event, the first programme was the only one of the three to be transmitted. As soon as it appeared, the Cabinet Secretary rang the head of NTV to demand that no more of the 'brutal' series should be broadcast; NTV meekly acquiesced. 'The programmes were taken off on the grounds that that scene was a gross infringement of the television code,' Ushiyama recalls. 'That was on the surface, but, underneath, there was the criticism of the Vietnam policy.'

Two years later, in 1967, television coverage of the Vietnam war again caused the government to 'lean on' broadcasters. The trouble started when another commercial station, TBS, screened *The Testimony of Hideo Den from Hanoi*, the first Japanese report from inside North Vietnam. The presenter, Hideo Den, challenged the prevailing view that America, because of its overwhelming military power, was winning the war. 'When I went to Hanoi, I became aware for the first time that the Vietnamese people were withstanding this fierce American onslaught very calmly,' he says, 'so that was what I emphasised in my reporting.' He also described American bombing raids on Hanoi as 'atrocities'.

James Cameron's BBC report from North Vietnam claimed to be the first western film brought back from Hanoi 'untouched, uncensored and unseen'.

One week after the broadcast several leading members of the ruling Liberal Democratic Party – which supported American policy in the region – summoned the Managing Director of TBS to a meeting at which, according to Hideo Den, 'they raised the question of why I had been sent to Hanoi and why such a programme had been broadcast'. He survived, but not for long. Two months later, the ruling party took exception to another of his reports, on the visit of the aircraft carrier USS *Enterprise*. Two months after that, in March 1968, TBS was accused by the government of supporting the campaign against the construction of a new airport at Narita. 'The Liberal Democratic Party leaders of the time put pressure on TBS by saying that they wouldn't renew the company's licence.' Hideo Den was promptly 'purged', and TBS's current affairs department was disbanded. After his departure, Hideo Den believes, 'the atmosphere in the Japanese television world was such that as far as possible people avoided political subjects'. Censorship usually took the form of 'self-regulation' rather than direct intervention by the government; all that was required was the occasional reminder by Ministers that licences for the commercial channels had to be renewed every three years.

A tendency to avoid controversy has been discernible at the public-service station, NHK, as well as the commercial networks. One of the more glaring examples of 'self-regulation' was NHK's documentary *Text Books Are Made in Such a Way* in 1982. This followed the deliberations of a Japanese committee which was 'revising' history textbooks to present Japan's conduct during the war in the Pacific in a more favourable light. The 'revisions' had caused an international storm, with protests from countries as politically disparate as Taiwan and China, North and South Korea. Yet the documentary itself failed to examine the political implications of the committee's work, or the outcry that it caused: an NHK executive felt that 'this would stimulate foreign reaction against the government'.

During the 1960s, official control over television was exercised largely by persuading stations not to broadcast programmes which were 'inconvenient' to the government, such as *Actions of a Vietnamese Marine Battalion*. But by the end of the decade the government was also, simultaneously, taking more positive measures to put its message across. In 1967 it created a body called the Japan Information Centre whose aim was to 'infiltrate government policy among the people without its being obvious that these were government information programmes', according to Hiroshi Matsuda, media correspondent of the *Nippon Keiza Shimbun*, Japan's leading financial newspaper. 'The government and financial circles put up money jointly to sponsor television programmes, and through these programmes to spread the government's views among the people without their being aware of what was going on.' Matsuda says that broadcasters are 'very resistant' to working on these programmes: 'But if you look at it from the point of view of the television companies, they're caught in a very weak position – through the licence, the government has the power of life and death over them. Because of that, they make programmes of that sort at the government's behest.'

It is understandable that the government should be so eager to dictate what appears on the screen. The Japanese watch more television than anyone else in the world, and they are influenced by what they see; people who appear regularly on television thus acquire a stature much greater than that of most politicians. When Hideo Den was forced out of TBS, he stood for the National Diet (Parliament) and was easily elected. One of NHK's first 'anchor-men' on news programmes, Hisanori Isomura, was also offered the opportunity of starting a political career: 'I was nicknamed the Walter Cronkite of Japan, that kind of household figure, and when the election of the Upper House came, every political party – including the Communist Party – asked me to stand for their party,' he says. He chose to stay at NHK instead, where he became President of the News Division.

This phenomenon is common to all countries with a large television-viewing public. A number of British television performers have become Members of Parliament, including Geoffrey Johnson-Smith (a reporter on the BBC's *Tonight* show), Tim Brinton (a newsreader), Austin Mitchell (a presenter on Yorkshire Television), Clement Freud (a humorist and gourmet who was best known for appearing in commercials for dog food alongside a mournful-looking bloodhound called Henry), and Christopher Chataway (the first newscaster on Independent Television News). Robin Day and Ludovic Kennedy both stood as Liberal candidates for Parliament in the late 1950s, when they were interviewers for ITN. Such was the moribund state of the Liberal Party at the time that not even their television fame was enough to secure their election, but they both managed to cause an increase in the Liberal vote in their constituencies.

The fame conferred by the medium often helps television celebrities gain political office: among British stars who have become Members of Parliament are (from top) Geoffrey Johnson-Smith, Austin Mitchell and Clement Freud.

The occasion which Ludovic Kennedy chose for his attempt on Parliament – the Rochdale by-election of February 1958 – was peculiarly appropriate, since it was also the first British election to be televised. Incredible though it may seem now, until 1958 the only references to politics on television during an election campaign were the Party Political Broadcasts; news and current affairs programmes remained silent on the subject, in the belief that any mention of the election might infringe the Representation of the People Act.

In retrospect, it seems extraordinary that it took so long for this mistaken belief to be challenged. But there was a good reason: until 1955, television broadcasts in Britain had been a BBC monopoly, and the BBC often seemed reluctant to deal with anything 'contentious'. In the early 1950s almost the only televised discussions of political issues took place on a programme called *In the News*, and even this became too much for the BBC. The regular panellists on *In the News*, from its inception in 1950, were two left-wing socialists, A. J. P. Taylor and Michael Foot, an iconoclastic Conservative, Robert Boothby, and a right-winger named W. J. Brown, formerly an Independent MP. Both the Labour Party and the Conservative Party protested that the panellists were not from the 'mainstream' of the two parties. The original team was first diluted and then phased out completely. When the BBC's monopoly was broken, the four troublesome 'extremists' were signed up for an ATV show called *Free Speech*: nothing could have better symbolised the difference between the BBC's nervous conservatism and commercial television's early adventurousness.

The idiosyncratic political views of (from top) Michael Foot, A. J. P. Taylor and Robert Boothby were too much for the BBC; but with the arrival of ITV the three men found themselves back on screen again, in Free Speech.

The greatest restriction on political broadcasting during the first half of the 1950s was the BBC's preposterous 'fourteen-day rule'. This had been in force, *de facto*, since the war, but it was first laid down in writing in 1948: it meant '(a) that the BBC will not have discussions or *ex parte* statements on any issues for a period of a fortnight before they are debated in either House and (b) that while matters are subjects of legislation MPs will not be used in such discussions'.

By 1955 the rule seemed increasingly absurd: on an *In the News* programme, for example, panellists were not allowed to discuss the hydrogen bomb because it was to be debated in Parliament in the next fortnight. However, when the BBC announced that it was preparing to abandon the rule, the Postmaster-General issued a regulation ordering the practice to continue; this was not withdrawn until 1956, after a vigorous campaign of lobbying by the new commercial companies.

The people behind the new Independent Television network were already experienced in political hurly-burly, since they had had a long and difficult struggle to convince Parliament that broadcasting should not be the sole prerogative of the BBC. In 1951 an official committee of inquiry, chaired by Lord Beveridge, had concluded that the BBC should keep its monopoly. Soon afterwards, however, the Labour government which had commissioned the report was replaced by a Tory administration markedly more sympathetic to the idea of competition. The Tories' support for commercial television was partly inspired by their suspicion that the BBC had a left-wing bias – even though the only evidence to support this belief was the fact that the BBC had once cancelled the repeat of a satirical play called *Party Manners* which had offended the Labour Party. After much heated argument, in 1954 Parliament passed the Television Act, which allowed the creation of a commercial television service under the control of an Independent Television Authority (ITA). Franchises were awarded, and on 22 September 1955 'independent' television went on the air for the first time, with Sir John Barbirolli conducting the Hallé Orchestra at a lavish ceremony in the Guildhall, London.

The ITA (which later became the Independent Broadcasting Authority, or IBA) was soon to prove itself as stern an invigilator of controversy as the BBC. It cancelled a programme in which Malcolm Muggeridge was to have criticised the monarchy; in the 1960s it banned several editions of Granada Television's innovatory current affairs programme, *World in Action*. As we shall see in the next chapter, in the thirty years since 1955 both the BBC and the IBA have often intervened to prevent 'contentious' material being included in current affairs coverage; and, as the chapter on drama will demonstrate, plays have not been free from censorship either. Even in the mid-1960s the 'liberal' Director-General of the BBC, Hugh Carleton Greene, forbade the screening of *The War Game*, a fictionalised account of life during nuclear war. He claims that he did so for 'humanitarian reasons'.

Nevertheless, some barriers had been destroyed, notably the fourteen-day rule and the moratorium on election reports. Politicians could no longer rely on television to maintain a discreet silence on political matters; instead they would have to learn to use the new medium to their own advantage.

Granada TV's transmissions from the Rochdale by-election in 1958 had been judged a success; they had, moreover, passed off without any legal challenge under the Representation of the People Act or the Television Act. The path had been cleared for something more ambitious. In 1959, Granada announced that during the general election it intended to run a series of programmes called *Marathon*, in which candidates from the area covered by Granada – the north of England – would be permitted to make a televised address. As a headline in the *News Chronicle* put it, 'Granada Offers TV Election'.

Granada's coverage of the Rochdale by-election in 1958 broke the taboo on political television.

Two weeks later the BBC said that it would televise statements by 'selected' candidates – although, in order to by-pass the complex laws governing elections, they would have to be introduced as 'regional spokesmen' for their parties. 'When is a candidate not a candidate?' the *Manchester Guardian* asked. 'The answer we are now asked to believe is: when he appears in a BBC election broadcast. This prize bit of humbug is the latest attempt to find a way out of the stranglehold of our archaic election laws.' It was only after the Cabinet had discussed the issue and several eminent lawyers had been consulted that election broadcasting was allowed to proceed.

For most of the candidates it was to be their first encounter with a television camera. Granada sent them some suggestions: 'What you wear is not of critical importance, but it would help your appearance on television if you wear a blue or light green shirt, which transmit best. Plain ties look better than striped. If you wish, wear your rosettes, but avoid things that shine. Badges and metal pen tops reflect light and do not help your picture . . . if you are used to talking to large audiences remember that television is a very intimate medium. Big oratorical speeches and gestures are not successful. They often seem pompous.'

The 1959 election broadcasts were modest compared with the extravaganzas that were to come in later years. But while some politicians sought to adjust to television, others continued to prefer the older method of outright suppression. In

November 1962 the BBC threw down the gauntlet to this latter group by starting a late-night satirical show called *That Was The Week That Was* (swiftly abbreviated to *TW3*). The idea for it came partly from the Director-General himself, Hugh Greene, who wanted to 'prick the pomposity of public figures', but it was developed by Ned Sherrin, Alasdair Milne and Donald Baverstock. Some public figures were none too enamoured of their approach, but others were surprisingly tolerant. 'After the first night, which was really rather a sensation,' Greene recalls, 'newspaper reporters got on to the Postmaster-General, Reg Bevins, and said: can any government stand for this sort of thing, will you be doing something about it? And Reg Bevins was foolish enough to say "Yes I will." Next morning, when he got to his office, as I know from a senior Post Office civil servant, he found on his desk a four-word memo from Harold Macmillan, just saying "Oh no you won't."' This support from the Prime Minister was especially magnanimous in view of the fact that one of *TW3*'s most successful and régular items was an unflattering impersonation of Macmillan, performed by Willie Rushton.

Some of the sketches on *TW3* were more savagely satirical than anything the BBC had ever broadcast; there was a particularly vicious attack on the Home Secretary, Henry Brooke, which was presented in a parody of the *This Is Your Life* format. Yet Hugh Greene thinks that in general the parties took it very well. 'Harold Wilson always claims that he enjoyed the programme very much,' he says. 'And when Dick Crossman was being nasty about it and saying that no Labour government could put up with that sort of thing, Harold said to me, "Don't you pay any attention to Dick." And there was a case when the programme dealt with a dozen MPs on both sides who had been in the House for donkey's years without opening their mouths. And one of them then got up in the House to speak for the first time in a decade – to claim that it was a breach of parliamentary privilege. Both sides of the House collapsed in helpless laughter, and he just sat down again.'

Harold Wilson's fondness for *TW3* may have been connected with the fact that most of the programme's satire was directed against the government rather than his party. The Conservatives had been in office since 1951 and presented an easy target for ridicule – especially when, in 1963, the party's leadership passed from one ageing aristocrat, Harold Macmillan, to another, Lord Home (who had to disclaim his peerage and become plain Sir Alec Douglas-Home to take on the job). Nothing could have been more pronounced than the contrast between Harold Wilson, who made visionary speeches about the white-hot technological revolution, and Sir Alec, who seemed to have spent much of his life on grouse moors. In the 1964 election, with both party leaders appearing regularly on television, viewers had the chance to notice the difference for themselves. Wilson had already mastered the art of performing for the cameras, but to Douglas-Home it was all unfamiliar territory. When Wilson was heckled at televised public meetings he made relaxed and witty replies, knowing that the microphones would pick up only his repartee and not the original heckle; when Douglas-Home spoke to a rowdy audience in Birmingham he began to shout at the top of his voice, unaware that the viewers at home would hear only his bellowing without the sound of hecklers. Douglas-Home believes that the election 'began to turn at that point'. He adds that 'I blame myself for not studying the techniques

Harold Macmillan was the butt of much of TW3*'s satire but seemed remarkably tolerant of it all.*

Henry Brooke, Home Secretary in the Tory government of the early 1960s, was one of the most reviled politicians of his day and a natural target for the satire of That Was The Week That Was.

Sir Hugh Greene (right) wanted That Was The Week That Was *to prick the pomposity of politicians, and he spoke from experience: here he meets Vice-President Nixon in 1958.*

(Opposite) The TW3 team tied up in videotape (right to left): Willie Rushton, Millicent Martin, Kenneth Cope, Roy Kinnear, David Kernan, Lance Percival, David Frost is (inappropriately) kneeling.

Alec Douglas-Home, who was once told by a make-up woman that he had 'a head like a skull', talking to Dean Rusk in a three-nation transatlantic discussion carried by Early Bird satellite, May 1965.

of television more than I did'; if he had known about the way in which directional microphones work, 'one would have looked more confident to the audience'.

Douglas-Home had another problem with his television image, for which there was no remedy. During the 1964 election he pleaded with a make-up woman in a television studio: 'I said, "Can you make me look better than I do on TV? I look rather scraggy, like a ghost." And she said "No" and I said "Why not?" and she said, "Because you've got a head like a skull." So I said, "Well, hasn't everybody got a head like a skull?" and she said "No" and that was the finish of the conversation.' As he touchingly concedes: 'Somehow I haven't got the looks of a natural.'

Harold Wilson had one final piece of assistance from television in that election. At 7.30 p.m. on election day, one-and-a-half hours before the polls closed, the BBC was due to transmit an episode of the popular comedy series *Steptoe and Son*. The BBC's intention was to grab a large audience early in the evening and hold it, thereby outdoing its rivals at ITV. However, in the first week of the campaign Harold Wilson went to see Hugh Greene and expressed his 'very real worry about *Steptoe and Son*': he feared that it might keep Labour voters away from the polling booths. Greene decided to postpone the transmission until 9 o'clock. 'When I told Harold Wilson about that on the telephone the next day, he said, "Well, Hugh, thank you very much. That might be worth a dozen seats to me." ' Greene adds that since Labour eventually won by just four seats, 'I've often wondered whether I should have a bad conscience.'

Steptoe and Son was postponed until after the polls closed, following a personal request made by Harold Wilson.

Relations are bound to be delicate between politicians and broadcasters – particularly with the BBC, because of its status as a publicly-financed body whose licence fee is determined by the government. If the BBC treats a politician's comments with some scepticism, it will be accused of 'hostility'; if it is deferential, it will then be lambasted for 'bias' by members of the other party. It is not surprising, then, that the tension between broadcasters and politicians has sometimes erupted in public. In the 1966 election the BBC built a special studio on the train which was to carry Harold Wilson back from his constituency in Liverpool to London on election night. Just before Wilson was to be interviewed in the studio he told his interviewer, John Morgan, words to the effect of 'I hope you won't forget your loyalty to your membership of the Labour Party'. Morgan replied that he would remember his duty as a journalist. Wilson then stormed out of the carriage, saying that he would talk only to ITV. (The BBC managed to salvage something from this débâcle. It arranged for Wilson's train to be met at Euston by Desmond Wilcox, who had only recently moved to the BBC. Thinking that Wilcox was still with ITV, Wilson happily gave him a televised interview.)

The most famous political interviewer in Britain, Robin Day, has often been at the centre of such incidents. During the 1979 general election the Labour Prime Minister, James Callaghan, walked out of a television studio in Cardiff halfway through an interview because Day insisted on questioning him about the strikes by public service workers which had helped to bring down his government. At the Conservative Party Conference in 1982 the Secretary of State for Defence, John Nott, abruptly terminated a live interview when Day referred to him as a 'here today, gone tomorrow' politician. So much attention is paid to politicians' attitudes towards

Politicians may walk out on Robin Day, but Brian Walden of Weekend World *– himself a former politician – is much less abrasive; he is said to be Margaret Thatcher's favourite interviewer.*

broadcasters that even the most unintentional slight can be transformed into a serious dispute. When the recently-knighted Sir Robin Day interviewed Margaret Thatcher at Downing Street during the 1983 general election, she called him 'Mr Day' instead of 'Sir Robin'; the press immediately interpreted this as being her way of showing displeasure with the BBC, despite denials from both Mrs Thatcher and Sir Robin. In her next interview with him, she made a point of referring to him as 'Sir Robin' throughout.

Probably the most celebrated example of a mountainous argument being created out of a molehill concerned Harold Wilson himself, the man who was normally such a relaxed television performer but who – as his tantrum on the train in 1966 had shown – was sensitive to any possibility that the BBC might be against him. The programme which caused the trouble was called *Yesterday's Men*; Marcia Williams, Wilson's personal secretary, wrote later that it was 'the only occasion when Harold was extremely angry'.

The project had begun harmlessly enough. After Labour's electoral defeat in 1970, David Dimbleby had the idea of making a programme which would show how Ministers adjusted to the loss of office. Everything proceeded smoothly until May 1971, when Dimbleby filmed an interview with Wilson for inclusion in the programme. Having dealt with various political topics, Dimbleby asked Wilson how much he had earned from his memoirs. 'What's it got to do with you then?' Wilson snapped. 'Why do you ask this question? I mean, why can people afford to buy £25,000 yachts, do the BBC not regard that as a matter for public interest?' This was a reference to the purchase of a boat named *Morning Cloud* by Wilson's Tory opponent, Ted Heath. Wilson then told Dimbleby that he wanted the interview stopped and the film destroyed: 'I'm really not having this if the BBC put this question to me without putting it to Heath.' He added, menacingly, that 'if this film is used or if this is leaked, then there's going to be a hell of a row'.

And there was. Although it agreed to cut most of the altercation, the BBC still intended to use a brief clip showing Wilson's refusal to say how much he had been paid for his book. Wilson's lawyer, Lord Goodman, protested vehemently and threatened legal action. Only hours before transmission, the BBC's Governors agreed to delete the offending passage.

Wilson and his colleagues were still not mollified. They took exception to the title *Yesterday's Men* and to the use of photographs showing Wilson's farm in Buckinghamshire; they also felt that the programme as a whole was 'gossipy' and 'sneering'. For weeks afterwards, senior Labour politicians attacked the BBC for its bias against their party – especially as the Corporation had, on the very day after *Yesterday's Men*, broadcast a favourable report on Heath's government. It confirmed Wilson in his long-standing preference for commercial television. As he had said during his censored exchange with Dimbleby, 'We never get this on the other channel, may I say; it's very interesting.'

Nevertheless, the Labour Party could not simply boycott the BBC. Television may need the support of politicians for its survival, but politicians are dependent on the exposure which television can give them, especially when they are to face the voters. As the British academic Ivor Crewe says: 'Today an election is what is seen on television. The election campaign *is* television and nothing else.' Although Wilson

David Dimbleby has continued his father's dynasty at the BBC, presenting Panorama *and other current affairs programmes; David's brother, Jonathan, makes current affairs documentaries for ITV.*

Harold Wilson's mastery of the medium included a canny understanding that it would help his image to be seen with other well-known television figures such as the cast of Coronation Street or (as in this picture) the English football manager, Sir Alf Ramsey.

Just before the 1974 general election, Labour Party advisers became seriously worried by Edward Heath's 'very smart image . . . with sixty-four tombstone teeth and a big laugh'; Labour hired a film director to make Wilson equally attractive.

had been able to outshine Sir Alec Douglas-Home without difficulty in 1964, by the time of the election in February 1974 his television image was becoming rather tattered. David Wickes, an English film director, was called in to help Wilson. 'Edward Heath at that time was presented as a rather jovial, overweight and always tanned grocer, with sixty-four tombstone teeth and a big laugh,' Wickes recalls. 'And although he might be suspect for wearing rope-soled shoes at weekends, and perhaps even suspected of blue-rinsing his hair to make it whiter, it was nevertheless a very smart image. Whereas Harold Wilson at that time was depicted by cartoonists, rather cruelly, as a sly garden gnome with a Yorkshire accent, with tobacco-stained teeth and a pipe, perhaps even bicycle clips.'

Wickes was a political agnostic, but he relished the challenge of 'packaging something'. His first action was to buy Wilson six new suits, three in blue and three in dark grey. The suits in each colour were identical, Wickes explains, 'so that it didn't look as if he had had a change between nine o'clock and quarter past nine in the morning, even though he obviously had to because he probably spent about fifteen minutes in the back of a car, hunched up with his papers. And so when he got out of the car, we made absolutely certain that he got out in a pristine crisp jacket and a clean shirt and a clean tie. The ties were identical and the shirts were identical so that he always looked as if he'd just travelled perfectly and uncreased.' Throughout the election campaign Wilson travelled with a valet, who spent most of his time at the ironing board, and a make-up man whose task was to keep Wilson's eyes 'de-bagged' and to ensure that the candidate did not look 'shining and sweaty'.

In previous elections, when the Labour leader arrived at a televised public meeting while someone else was speaking, there would be a brief interruption for applause before the speaker continued as though nothing had happened. Only when the speech finished would Wilson be introduced. Wickes changed all that. He stationed people with walkie-talkies outside the meeting-hall so that as soon as Wilson's car appeared they could alert Wickes, who was inside the hall. 'I would arrange for him to arrive up the centre of the hall with two spotlights on him,' Wickes says. 'And I would have a microphone which I would be able to use to cut off whoever was speaking at the platform, right in mid-sentence. Rude though that may have seemed, the television media were not actually recording that speech so it never came over as being cut off; nobody ever saw that. I would flick the switch on my microphone and bellow down through the huge loudspeakers that travelled with us everywhere: "Ladies and Gentlemen, the Prime Minister – the Right Honourable Harold Wilson!" And the gramophone operator would press his button and the theme tune "I'm Just Wild About Harry" would blast out of the speakers and everybody would rise and the spotlights would flash.' Wickes also made sure that the television cameras had the best vantage points in the hall so that they could have a clear shot of Wilson walking down the central aisle, waving regally. The only part of the procedure about which Wilson complained was the choice of theme tune. 'I'm Harold, not Harry,' he used to grumble. Apart from that, however, Wilson cooperated enthusiastically with any gimmick that Wickes proposed. 'I saw Harold one night come up the steps from the front of the hall on to the platform and he ran up the last two steps,' Wickes recalls. 'It looked very

In 1974 Harold Wilson's general election campaign was designed almost entirely for television; and it worked.

President Kennedy's use of television extended far beyond the shores of America; customers at this pub in south London, along with millions of other people in Europe, watched this live press conference from Washington transmitted by Telstar on 23 July 1962.

Adlai Stevenson at the Democrats' convention in 1952 – the last presidential candidate to make no concessions to the power of the small screen.

attractive, as if he was a very capable and physically robust man; instead of slogging up them he just skipped up them.' Wickes asked him to do it at every meeting thereafter; Wilson agreed, as long as precautions were taken to prevent him tripping over television cables on the steps.

If this all seems reminiscent of American televised politics, that is hardly surprising. Wickes had attended political conventions in the United States and had learnt from them the importance of transmitting the 'correct image'. Wilson, too, had always been influenced by his American counterparts' use of the media. He was well aware of the popular belief that television had enabled John F. Kennedy to win the Presidency in 1960 and although he denies that he tried to 'copy' Kennedy, he admits that he was impressed by him.

Kennedy was not, however, the first American politician to discover the manipulative power of television. As early as 1948 both the Republican Party and the Democratic Party had chosen to hold their conventions in Philadelphia because the city had just established a networking system whereby its broadcasts would also be shown by fourteen other stations along the East Coast.

Four years later the political impact of television was indisputably demonstrated. Both the Presidential candidates – Dwight Eisenhower for the Republicans, Adlai Stevenson for the Democrats – were suspicious of the new medium. 'Has an old soldier come to this?' Eisenhower groaned when his aides suggested ways in which he could 'project' himself to the viewers; Stevenson considered that television was 'selling the Presidency like cereal'. But while Stevenson refused to alter his style one jot for the benefit of the cameras, Eisenhower realised that, like it or loathe it, television had to be accommodated.

President Eisenhower, Stevenson's successful rival, adapted quickly to the demands of television image-makers.

Eisenhower proved to be a fast learner. The actor Robert Montgomery was brought in to teach Eisenhower how to relax in front of the cameras. One problem which worried Eisenhower's media advisers was his bald head, so he was instructed to keep it tilted back, thus reducing the amount of his pate which would be visible. Even so, it still shone under the television lights, and Eisenhower refused to have any make-up put on it. Carroll Newton, an advertising agent who helped in the campaign, says that this difficulty was surmounted by having a make-up man sneak up behind the candidate just before the cameras rolled and 'pop him on the head with the powder puff'. Once the make-up had been dealt with, his aides could rely on Eisenhower's personality for the rest. He had charm, he was well known as a war hero and – most importantly – he was a simple man, conveying simple ideas. Television has never had any problem in transmitting simplicity; where it does often stumble is in trying to cope with intellectual complexity, and this, unfortunately, was what Adlai Stevenson wanted it to do.

During the 1952 campaign, Eisenhower's team produced a number of slick and effective one-minute commercials in which their man was shown joking with his wife and giving one-sentence answers to a few easy questions. When the Democrats suggested that their candidate should do something similar, Stevenson waxed indignant: 'This is the worst thing I've ever heard of,' he told an adviser. 'How can you talk seriously about issues with one-minute spots!'

He was no more helpful when he had to deal with reporters from the networks. Stevenson's idea of a good campaign was a series of long, thoughtful but dense speeches. Camera crews begged him for some visual excitement. Couldn't they film him off-duty at home, or driving his car, or eating a meal, or playing with his children? The answer was always no. Stevenson's children were in fact of some importance, since he was a divorcee and his aides wanted to show that he remained a family man despite it all. One adviser, Lou Cowan, decided to use the children anyway, without warning Stevenson. At a rally in Chicago the day before the election, Stevenson's three sons would stand beside the podium; as their father walked past them, one son would pat him on the back and say 'Good luck, Dad'. It would be a heart-warming scene, and television reporters would be tipped off to ensure that they recorded it. At the last minute, however, Cowan had an attack of guilt at deceiving the candidate in this way. He told Stevenson of his plan and, as he had feared, it was instantly vetoed. 'Lou, old boy,' Stevenson said, 'we don't do things like that in our family.' He went on to lose the election, but Eisenhower would probably have won even without television.

Richard Nixon's Checkers speech, 1952: arguably the most influential broadcast ever made.

Nevertheless, television did affect the course of the 1952 election in a spectacular way; for it was also the campaign in which Richard Nixon, Eisenhower's running mate, delivered his legendary 'Checkers' speech and saved his political career. It had been revealed that a group of Californians had set up a secret 'special fund' for Nixon amounting to about $18,000. Some senior Republicans urged Nixon to stand down as the Vice-Presidential candidate, since Eisenhower's integrity had been continually stressed during the campaign. Instead, Nixon decided to fight. He persuaded the Republican National Committee to buy a half-hour slot on sixty-four television stations across the nation. 'We booked the studio time, but never really knew what he was going to say until he went on the air,' says Herb Klein, who was Nixon's press aide. 'He wrote the speech himself on a yellow pad.'

It was an extraordinary performance. Nixon began his speech by claiming, rather unconvincingly, that 'not one cent of the $18,000 or any other money of that type ever went to me for my personal use'. But he then turned to the real business of his broadcast – emotional manipulation of the audience. He did not think he ought to quit; he was not a quitter. 'Incidentally,' he added, 'Pat is not a quitter.' The camera then panned to show Nixon's wife sitting beside him. 'After all,' he continued, 'her name was Patricia Ryan and she was born on St Patrick's Day, and you know the Irish never quit.' Having neatly captured the Irish vote, Nixon proceeded to his sentimental climax. There was 'one other thing' he ought to mention: 'We did get something – a gift.' But it was nothing to do with slush funds. 'A man down in Texas heard Pat on the radio mention the fact that our two daughters would like to have a dog. And, believe it or not, the day before we left on this campaign trip we got a message from the Union Station in Baltimore saying they had a package for us. We went down to get it. You know what it was? It was a little cocker spaniel dog in a crate that he sent all the way from Texas. Black and white spotted. And our little girl – Tricia, the six-year-old – named it Checkers. And you know, the kids love that dog, and I just want to say this right now, that regardless of what they say about it, we're going to keep it.' With tears in his eyes, Nixon asked the viewers to 'wire and write to the Republican National Committee on whether you think I should stay or get off, and whatever their decision is, I will abide'.

Nixon returned to his suite at the Ambassador Hotel in Los Angeles, nervously wondering how the broadcast would be received. 'The first word we got that it had had a tremendous reaction,' Herb Klein says, 'was when somebody called from Miami and talked to me. And he said: "I couldn't get through on the Western Union because everybody's sending telegrams, so I thought I'd call and tell Mr Nixon I thought it was a great speech and I'm for him." ' Over the next few days the Republican headquarters was deluged with hundreds of thousands of telegrams supporting Nixon. There was no longer any question of removing Nixon from the ticket. 'You're my boy!' Eisenhower said, as he posed for photographs with his arm round Nixon. Herb Klein believes that 'if you look back, probably that speech had more impact and responses per viewing set than anything in television history. I think that's unquestionably true'.

Eisenhower and Nixon were elected by an overwhelming majority in November 1952. Four years later they repeated the triumph, assisted by the fact that the Democrats had again chosen as their candidate Adlai Stevenson, who still declined to make any concessions to the requirements of television. In 1960, however, when Nixon himself was the Republican candidate for President, he was confronted by a Democrat as unlike Stevenson as it was possible to be – John F. Kennedy. 'Kennedy was a natural for television,' says J. Leonard Reinsch, who worked with him in the 1960 campaign. 'It wasn't necessary to tell him to raise his head or turn and follow the camera. He just intuitively did the right thing.' Television had been Nixon's saviour eight years earlier; in 1960 it was his downfall.

The event which changed the course of the election was the first of four televised debates between the two candidates, transmitted on 26 September. It was an unmitigated disaster for Nixon. He had only recently come out of hospital. He had lost a good deal of weight, which made his shirt look loose. He refused to wear make-up. This was partly because Kennedy was not wearing make-up, but the difference was that Kennedy was strikingly sun-tanned, having spent a week campaigning in an open-topped car in California, whereas Nixon looked pale and tired. Another reason for Nixon's objection to make-up was that 'he had a great macho feeling and he didn't want to be seen with all that powder on', according to Herb Klein, who was assisting him. He was eventually persuaded to dab on a little Lazy Shave, a cosmetic which hid five o'clock shadow, but this only made matters worse since it ran under the television lights.

Nixon arrived for the first debate with Kennedy in a light suit, only to find that it merged into the background.

Nixon had spent hardly any time preparing himself for the encounter. Kennedy, by contrast, left nothing to chance. For hours beforehand he lay on his hotel bed while his 'strategy group' fired questions at him on every subject that might conceivably come up. But political issues turned out to be of secondary importance; what really counted was the practical preparation which Kennedy's staff had made for the staging of the debate. The director of the transmission, Don Hewitt of CBS, had already agreed to a suggestion from J. Leonard Reinsch that both candidates should stand at lecterns rather than sit in studio chairs. 'Nixon had had the misfortune of being in hospital with a bad leg,' Reinsch explains. 'Appearances on television are very important, and standing on his bad leg forced him to shift his weight during the debate. I just felt that that would go down to the favour of Kennedy.'

Some of the Republican team accused Don Hewitt and CBS of deliberately helping Kennedy. One of Nixon's

(Following pages) Weekend World, *the Sunday lunchtime current affairs programme from London Weekend Television. Brian Walden, the presenter, and editor Robin Paxton discuss the interview with the week's guest, the telegenic Labour leader, Neil Kinnock, seen with his press secretary, Patricia Hewitt, and during rehearsals and live transmission.*

WEEKEND WORLD

advisers, Carroll Newton, claims that CBS had told Nixon that the studio would have a dark background and he would therefore stand out better if he wore a light suit. When Nixon's aides arrived at the studio in the early afternoon they found that it had been painted a light colour, in front of which – since the broadcast was in black and white – Nixon's suit would all but disappear. 'They insisted that it be repainted,' Newton says. 'It was. It came out the same colour. They insisted it be repainted again and it was. It was still wet when the show went on, but it was still the light colour. In the meantime, Kennedy showed up in a dark suit, leaving a very strong suspicion that he was told this was the way it would be done.'

The Kennedy team were certainly meticulous. After checking the lighting in the studio, Reinsch suggested to Kennedy that he should change into a shirt that would show up better on the 'grey scale'. He also brought with him a pair of long socks, in case any of the camera angles should show part of Kennedy's ankle.

There was yet more controversy over the use of 'reaction shots' – moments when the camera would show the face of one candidate while the other was speaking. Reinsch had been very much in favour of these, because 'I knew that candidate Nixon had a tendency to perspire and that it was possible that somewhere along the line he might wipe his brow'. His hopes were realised. As Newton complains, 'They didn't turn the reaction shots on him until he was sweating profusely, because he had a fever; and when he started to sweat and bite his lip or wipe his forehead, then they put the reaction shots on him.'

By such tricks are Presidents made. The first debate was seen by a television audience of 75 million. It was also broadcast on the radio, which gives one a good opportunity to judge the difference made by the visual effects. A poll after the debate found that a majority of radio listeners thought that Nixon had won; television viewers, on the other hand, were in no doubt that Kennedy had come off best. After his election, Kennedy pointed at a television set and said: 'We wouldn't have had a prayer without that gadget.' Since he had won the Presidency by the narrowest of margins (34,221,463 votes to 34,108,582), he was probably right.

During his brief tenure of the White House, Kennedy made continual and brilliant use of television. He was the first President to allow his press conferences to be televised 'live' – a risky venture, but one which he handled superbly. Whenever he had difficulty answering a question, he would turn next to a female reporter from Texas with an eccentric taste in hats who invariably asked exceedingly parochial questions. Their double-act always raised a laugh, making viewers forget that he had not actually replied to the previous question.

Jackie Kennedy, young and glamorous, contributed greatly to her husband's brilliant use of television.

Kennedy also knew the value of addressing the nation directly. The CIA's bungled attempt to invade Cuba in April 1961, which swiftly became known as the 'Bay of Pigs fiasco', was an indefensible act of deception which alienated many of Kennedy's supporters; yet he managed to salvage something from the wreckage by giving the American people a televised Fireside Chat in which he admitted that 'the job is harder than I thought'. This unprecedented admission of human vulnerability by a politician brought some of his straying sheep back into the fold. In October 1962, during the Cuban missile crisis, he used television again to speak to the country as a whole – and, on this occasion, to the wider world. He delivered an apocalyptic ultimatum to the Soviet Union's leader, Nikita Khrushchev, urging him to 'move the world

Khrushchev, like Kennedy, knew the value of television; on his tour of the USA in October 1960 he was interviewed by David Susskind for the Open End *programme.*

back from the abyss of destruction' by removing Soviet missiles from Cuba. If the warning was not heeded, Kennedy said that he would not 'shrink from the risk' of fighting a 'worldwide nuclear war'. Few Americans can have slept well that night: it was more blood-curdling than a late-night horror movie. Fortunately for Kennedy and the world, he did not have to prove whether or not he would have carried out this threat. The Russians agreed to withdraw their missiles and the Third World War was postponed. Kennedy himself did not last much longer. On 22 November 1963 he was killed by an assassin's bullet. The Television President was dead.

Kennedy's successor, Lyndon Johnson, was also a Television President, though in a rather different sense: he had made his fortune from his wife's ownership of a television station in Austin, Texas. He was obsessed by the medium, yet he was also surprisingly ill-at-ease with it – aware, perhaps, that he could never live up to the standards set by Kennedy. For one thing, he did not have Kennedy's physical advantages: he was short-sighted and he had a bulbous nose. He tried numerous different types of spectacles, he tried contact lenses, he railed at make-up people who failed to make his nose look smaller. However often he appeared on television, he was never satisfied with his image. In his office at the White House he installed three television sets next to one another so that he could watch all three networks' evening news programmes simultaneously. If he disapproved of the way in which they presented him he would ring up to complain. CBS's White House correspondent, Dan Rather, was a regular recipient of abusive telephone calls from the President. Johnson felt that Rather, as a Texan, ought to show a greater loyalty to his fellow-Texan in the White House. On one occasion Johnson interfered with a news programme more dramatically: having just settled a railway strike, he decided to break the news himself. His car raced down to the CBS building, arriving just as Walter Cronkite was going on the air with the evening news. Johnson marched into the studio and made his announcement; the hapless Cronkite could only gape at this uninvited guest. Later that evening, when Johnson was asked by his wife why he had behaved so outrageously, he replied: 'Because I wanted to see the look on Walter Cronkite's face when I walked in the studio.'

Walter Cronkite, the most trusted man in America, had an uneasy relationship with President Johnson and contributed to his downfall.

Cronkite was to have his revenge. Although LBJ may have had a love-hate attitude to television, there was one point on which he had no doubts: people believed what they saw on television, and the person they believed more than any other was Walter Cronkite. He had been the first anchor-man on American television, and he was often described as the most honest man in America. Over the years, he had been approached by official delegations from both the major parties, and from both wings of those parties, asking him to stand for Congress, the Senate and even the Presidency itself. 'I don't think I could be elected,' Cronkite says, 'because I've got very strong feelings, positions that people don't know I have until I get out on the campaign trail. And then it's a little late: you are going to lose an awful large segment of the population. But besides that, what really bothers me is that not one of the delegations that has called on me has ever asked me first what I stand for.' Early in 1968 they found out, when Cronkite decided that he would go to Vietnam and, for once, would not attempt to hide his opinions. 'I would step out of my role as an impartial newscaster,' he says, 'and try to cut through all the confusion of the moment.'

As he travelled around the war zone Cronkite discovered that the Vietcong were far stronger than he had been led to believe. On his return, he broadcast a half-hour 'news special' in which he reported that, although America could win in Vietnam, the effort it would take would be much greater than it was worth; it would keep the US involved in South-East Asia for many years. 'I concluded that we ought to say that we had done the very best we could, we tried, it didn't work – and get out.'

Lyndon Johnson was profoundly influenced by Cronkite's broadcast. He told his press secretary that if he had lost Walter Cronkite, he had lost Middle America. A few weeks later, on 31 March, he went on television to address the nation. His aides all assumed that he would give a defence of American involvement in Vietnam, but he added two unscripted sentences at the end: 'I have concluded that I should not permit the Presidency to become involved in the partisan divisions that are developing in this political year. Accordingly I shall not seek, and I will not accept, the nomination of my party for another term as your President.'

Dean Rusk, who was Secretary of State at the time, denies that Cronkite's 'defection' persuaded LBJ to stand down. 'President Johnson had talked to me about a year before that,' he claims, 'and he'd told me that he would not run again. At that time he put almost the total emphasis on his health.' This is not a view which many others share. CBS's President, Frank Stanton, was one of Johnson's closest friends; he is convinced that Cronkite was the decisive influence: 'Johnson felt that Walter's broadcast had really cut the ground from under his position.'

Further evidence for this interpretation was provided by Johnson himself. On the day after announcing that he would not seek re-election he made a speech in Chicago which effectively blamed television for turning the country against him: 'Historians must only guess at the effect that television would have had during earlier conflicts on the future of this nation, during the Korean War, for example, at the time our forces were pushed back to Pusan, or World War II, the Battle of the Bulge . . .'

Similar criticisms were to be heard from many politicians in the late 1960s. Television was not only bringing the horror and futility of the Vietnam war into people's living rooms, it was also giving wide coverage to the anti-war protests in America itself. 'The whole world is watching' was the chant of demonstrators who were clubbed by police outside the Democratic convention in Chicago in 1968. Student radicals knew that television would seldom be able to resist a dramatic image, and that was what they provided. 'We were a generation brought up on television,' says Abbie Hoffman, the former Yippie leader. The Black Power symbol of a clenched fist was a potent 'media image', according to Stokely Carmichael, one of the most prominent figures in the movement. But Carmichael knew that the free publicity might be stopped at any moment. 'In a struggle,' he says, 'the communications system is necessary. But if you do not have a communications system and it belongs to the enemy, to the oppressor or the one with whom you are in conflict, you cannot assume that you can trick the oppressor and use that medium at all times and under all conditions.' The conditions of 1968 allowed Stokely Carmichael, Abbie Hoffman and other revolutionaries to become television celebrities. There was, however, an inevitable backlash from the 'oppressor'.

Black Panthers, like other protest groups of the 1960s, provided potent 'media images' which the networks gratefully transmitted.

After Richard Nixon's inauguration as President in 1969, Lyndon Johnson urged him to 'get a grip on television'. Nixon was happy to oblige. The medium had been kind to him in 1952, but since then he had come to see it as part of a conspiracy against him. In 1962 he had sulkily told television correspondents that 'you won't have Richard Nixon to kick around any more'. During his 1968 campaign he was so suspicious of 'unfriendly' newscasters that he appeared instead on a series of artificial 'shows' which were actually commercials paid for by his fund-raisers. In these shows Nixon was seen chatting to a cross-section of American people – housewives, blacks, farmers – who had all been carefully selected to ensure that they were 'sympathetic' to candidate Nixon.

As President, Nixon continued to try to by-pass intermediaries – anchor-men, interviewers and so on – when he appeared on television. His favourite device was the televised Presidential address, through which he could appeal directly to 'the great silent majority of my fellow Americans'. The only problem with these broadcasts was that network pundits subjected them to 'instant analysis' on the air immediately afterwards. Their comments were often unfavourable.

The Nixon Administration decided to intimidate the networks into silence. The man chosen for the task was Vice-President Spiro Agnew; the occasion was a speech in Des Moines on 13 November 1969. 'The purpose of my remarks tonight,' Agnew declared, 'is to focus your attention on this little group of men who not only enjoy a right of instant rebuttal to every Presidential address, but, more importantly, wield a free hand in selecting, presenting and interpreting the great issues of our nation.' He attacked the concentration of power 'in the hands of a tiny, enclosed fraternity of privileged men elected by no one and enjoying a monopoly sanctioned and licensed by government'.

Spiro Agnew, Nixon's Vice-President, denounced television commentators as 'nattering nabobs of negativism' who were 'elected by no one'.

Ironically, this denunciation was transmitted live by all three networks, who had been warned of what Agnew intended to say. But his reminder that networks were licensed by government had an effect, at least temporarily. 'Instant analysis' of Presidential addresses was halted. To exculpate themselves from Agnew's charge that they were 'nattering nabobs of negativism', broadcasting executives encouraged their newscasters to give less publicity to anti-war protests and other unhelpful phenomena. They often allowed themselves to be used by Nixon for his propaganda stunts, of which the most spectacular example was his trip to China in 1972. He arranged his arrival in Peking to coincide with prime-time viewing on American television. On his return, his plane waited in Alaska for a few hours so that his touch-down in Washington would also take place in prime-time. After his visit to Moscow, three months later, he flew immediately by helicopter to the Capitol, where he delivered a televised speech to Congress.

Nixon came to believe, as he had after the Checkers speech, that the magic of television would always bring the American people rushing to his side. But in 1973 and 1974, as the Watergate scandal unfolded, the magic no longer worked. Nixon continually went on the air to announce that 'I am not a crook' and 'there will be no whitewash at the White House', but this was contradicted by each day's new reports of deception in high places and by Nixon's own haggard and shifty appearance. Nixon's credibility was also damaged by the many hours of Congressional Watergate hearings which were televised in

Nixon resigns on television, 8 August 1974: a video made ten minutes before the speech, smuggled out by CBS technicians, showed him alternately smiling, threatening and giggling.

1973. It was singularly appropriate that when Nixon finally resigned, in August 1974, he did so in a prime-time televised address. On the day after this speech he allowed television cameras into the White House to record his departure, though it is hard to know why: he was a shambling, broken figure. With a last, feeble wave of the hand, he climbed into his helicopter and flew off into exile.

As Nixon discovered, television is a two-edged sword which can destroy politicians just as easily as it can help them by destroying their opponents. Those who denounce the medium's insidious power are often the very same people who go to enormous lengths to try to harness that power for their own benefit. After Margaret Thatcher was elected Prime Minister of Britain in 1979, she and her supporters accused broadcasters of 'treasonous' behaviour on several occasions – most notably during the Falklands war, but also with documentaries about Ireland and about right-wing infiltration of the Conservative Party. Yet Thatcher herself had been specially tailored for television; in the months before her election campaign she transformed her image by simplifying her hairstyle, changing her wardrobe and lowering her voice by an octave or so (she had to perform humming exercises to achieve the desired result). Her American counterpart, Ronald Reagan, was also an adept exploiter of the medium. As early as 1964 Reagan had been used in a fund-raising broadcast for Barry Goldwater; the cheques poured in. It was at that point that Republican managers began to think seriously of Reagan as a marketable political commodity. As Walter Cronkite says, 'There is no question that Ronald Reagan is a superb communicator, absolutely the best, better than Kennedy very probably.' Yet Reagan's election was ensured not only by his television successes but also by vigorous campaigning from the Moral Majority – a group of people who spend much of their time decrying the 'sinfulness' of television.

Ronald Reagan in 1968, denouncing anti-war protesters; Walter Cronkite considers him 'a superb communicator, absolutely the best'.

The Moral Majority are not content to criticise television from the sidelines. The organisation's President, Dr Jerry Falwell, is one of the growing number of 'electronic preachers'. Every Sunday he presents a show called *The Old-Time Gospel Hour* from his Thomas Road Baptist Church in Lynchburg, Virginia, where there is a television control room behind the pulpit. The programme is carried by hundreds of cable television channels in the United States, Canada and Australia. He makes little distinction between his roles as politician and pastor, often using *The Old-Time Gospel Hour* to attack the Soviet Union or praise President Reagan's increase in the defence budget.

Evangelical television has expanded apace in recent years. In March 1980 there were thirty-five American television stations which broadcast predominantly religious programmes, and since then the figure has increased at the rate of one station a month. One of the most successful TV preachers, Rex Humbard of Akron, Ohio, has said that 'I'm going to evangelise the whole world by electronics'. Another, Robert Schuller, has built a huge cathedral with 10,000 windows in Garden Grove, California, from where he transmits his weekly services to an audience of millions. One of his principal claims to fame is that he 'brought John Wayne to the Lord'.

The most systematic attempt to produce 'Christian television' has been made by the Christian Broadcasting Network (CBN), run by a former lawyer named Pat Robertson. Robertson's ambition is for CBN to become America's 'fourth network' and eventually to defeat the 'three Goliaths' of NBC, CBS and ABC. His network mimics the conventions of mainstream television, creating Christian chat shows, soap operas, cartoons and documentaries. Robertson has also installed an earth station through which CBN's shows are beamed around the world by satellite.

Robertson's programmes – and in particular his chat show, *The 700 Club* – have influenced viewers thousands of miles away from the United States, as have the other electronic evangelists. In the Philippines, for instance, Channel 7 in Manila shows at least seven American religious programmes every week, including broadcasts by Jerry Falwell, Rex Humbard and Pat Robertson. The channel's President, a born-again Christian named Menardo Jimenez, says that God has called on him to do something for 'his kingdom and his people'.

Narcisso Padilla is a wealthy Filipino businessman who has taken the message to heart. On 1 August 1977 he happened to watch *The 700 Club* on Channel 7, and he decided there and then to become an evangelical Christian. Shortly afterwards, when another Manila channel came on the market, he bought it with the intention of making programmes which would be 'uplifting to the soul'. Since then his plan has been constantly frustrated. He owns a fully-equipped studio and transmitter, he has hired staff, but the Telecommunications Commission has refused to issue him with a licence until it has President Marcos's signature. This has not been forthcoming. Padilla is not sure why Marcos has been so reluctant. It could be because Padilla's uncle is a political opponent of the President. It could be that the owner of Manila's other stations, Roberto Benedicto, has been lobbying against the proposal, unwilling to have his profits diluted by the newcomer. Whatever the reason, ever since the late 1970s Padilla has been sitting on the top floor of his fourteen-storey skyscraper (emblazoned with the words 'Glory to God') waiting for the elusive signature. Weary of negotiation, he has decided to leave the problem 'to the Lord'. But it seems that the Lord, supposedly omnipotent though he is, does not have the power to put a television station on the air. Only governments can do that – and it is not a right which they will easily relinquish.

Blessed are the peacemakers, for they shall be called the children of God.

TV bible-thumpers in USA. By March, 1980, thirty-five stations were devoting themselves to evangelism.

(Opposite) Wedded to the box – until death do them part?

"Here is The News."

On Monday 2 January 1950 there was a BBC TV news broadcast at 8 p.m. On Wednesday 4 January the BBC transmitted 'a repeat of Monday's edition'. Since then, television's ability to cover news has been transformed: events on the other side of the world – or even on the surface of the moon – can be shown 'live', as they happen. The newscasters themselves have become stars.

What is surprising, in retrospect, is how few people predicted that this would happen. When television was in its infancy most commentators agreed that the medium's future, if it had one, was as a purveyor of entertainment. As late as 1953, the recently-retired Chairman of the BBC, Lord Simon of Wythenshawe, felt confident that television news would never become a serious force. 'A great majority of items are of such a nature that they cannot, either now or ever, be shown visually,' he announced. 'Of those that could be shown on television the majority occur overseas, often in distant countries, and it will be a long time before television films can be flown from all over the world to London on the day on which they happen. Television newsreels will, of course, continue to develop and be of the greatest interest and attraction but there is surely not the least possibility that they will ever replace news on sound.'

Until the mid-1950s television news suffered from what Sir Hugh Greene calls 'the BBC radio mentality': it was sober, conservative and dull. The Corporation's official policy for television news, as laid down in 1954, was 'to state the news of the day accurately, fairly, soberly and impersonally. It is no part of the aim to induce either optimism or pessimism or to attract listeners by colourful and sensational reports. The legitimate urge to be "first with the news" must invariably be subjugated to the prior claims of accuracy.' One of the rules which was supposed to ensure this accuracy was that every story had to be backed up by two or three news agencies. On one occasion a BBC reporter witnessed the death of a famous speedboat racer on a Scottish loch; his report of the incident, sent just before the one o'clock news, was not used, because no news agency had yet confirmed it.

Sir Hugh Greene, who became director of news and current affairs in 1958, recalls that 'there was some sort of rule that news about the royal family had to come first. And there was a joke going round that the favourite opening for a television news bulletin would have been: "Yesterday, the Queen Mother did something or other."' Greene's first task was to rid television news of the influence of radio and to develop 'a television attitude'. A spur for his efforts was undoubtedly the success of commercial television and, with it, Independent Television News (ITN). Aidan Crawley, ITN's first editor-in-chief, had said that he intended to make the news 'human and

(Opposite page) The dramatic end of the Iranian Embassy seige in London, transmitted live on a Bank Holiday Monday in 1980, was one of the most memorable examples of 'real-time' news on television.

Neville Chamberlain returns to Heston from Germany in 1938 and becomes the first of many politicians to face the cameras at an airport.

alive'. On 4 September 1955, less than three weeks before ITN's first transmission, the BBC had shown its newsreaders' faces on screen for the first time; even then, however, the newsreaders were not named, for fear that this would jeopardise the bulletin's impartiality.

Aidan Crawley had decided that ITN would call its presenters newscasters rather than newsreaders; they would help to write their own scripts, and they would also act as reporters and interviewers. The people he chose for the job were selected primarily for their skill in communication, not their journalistic experience. Crawley thought of ITN as 'television's first popular newspaper'. As the *Observer* commented in 1957, 'ITN with deft flashbacks and live interviews with bystanders established their usual lead over the BBC's news department.'

One of the most notable differences between the two channels was in the conduct of interviews. The BBC continued to be deferential in the extreme ('I wonder, Prime Minister, whether you would care to say a few words to the viewers') but ITN's style was more probing and combative. An early example of this occurred in January 1956, only a few months after ITN's inception, when Aidan Crawley resigned in protest at the ITN board's refusal to give him an adequate budget and longer news bulletins. The Chairman of the Independent Television Authority, Sir Kenneth Clark, agreed to be interviewed by Robin Day on ITN's evening news. 'I had no option but to put questions as in any other news interview,' Day wrote later. 'Was Aidan Crawley right to resign? Did he [Clark] share doubts which had been expressed as to whether companies whose main business was to run light entertainment were the right people to provide news? What was his answer to press criticism of the ITA for being "weak-kneed" in controlling ITV? The interview continued on these lines for several minutes and overran the bulletin time.'

The BBC's remaining strength was that people were believed to turn to it at moments of crisis – a legacy of the importance of BBC radio during the Second World War. But by 1956 even this monopoly was endangered. When the Hungarian uprising was put down in October, only ITN managed to bring back news film from Budapest. During the Suez crisis, a month later, it was ITN that broadcast the first pictures of British and French troops landing at Port Said. ITN followed this success with another world exclusive in 1957, when Robin Day interviewed President Nasser in Cairo. Since diplomatic relations between Britain and Egypt were still severed, Nasser's comments generated enormous interest, especially as he expressed his willingness to resume Egypt's 'friendship' with Britain. For Day, too, the interview was a triumph, proving that the ITN style would be applied even to heads of state. When Day asked whether Nasser accepted Israel's right to exist, the President accused him of 'jumping to conclusions'. 'No,' Day replied, 'I am asking a question.'

Robin Day's exclusive interview with President Nasser in 1957 for ITN, filmed in a garden outside Cairo.

Christopher Chataway, the athlete who became ITN's first newscaster.

Day and his colleagues soon became celebrities, just like any other television performer. There was the glamorous young athlete, Christopher Chataway, who had held the world record for running the mile. There was Ludovic Kennedy, who attracted attention because of his marriage to Moira Shearer, the dancer. There was Reginald Bosanquet, who wore a toupee and slurred his speech; his cheeky smirk was said to drive female viewers wild with ecstasy. These

Reginald Bosanquet, the ITN newscaster with the slurred speech and the lop-sided grin, received huge quantities of fan mail from female viewers.

Nothing better illustrates the transformation of news-readers from journalists into celebrities than the career of Angela Rippon, a BBC newsreader who appeared on the Morecambe and Wise show and later presented her own programme with choreo-grapher Lionel Blair.

pioneers can, however, scarcely have guessed just how besotted the press would become with television reporters in later years. In the 1970s, when ITN's Anna Ford became engaged to another ITN journalist, the romance was reported on the front page of most papers; in 1983 (after she had left ITN), when she threw a glass of wine over a Tory MP at a cocktail party, she again became headline news. Even the BBC's newsreaders were treated as fit subjects for gossip columns. In 1976 the *Daily Mirror* devoted most of its front page to an 'exclusive' photograph of Angela Rippon in a split-thighed evening dress, recording a dance routine for the *Morecambe and Wise Christmas Show.*

Television news exploited the personalities of its presenters to compensate for the fact that many news stories take place without cameras being present, and some stories – a fall in the balance of payments, for instance – are not particularly 'visual' in any case. The American networks recognised this from the outset. NBC's first regular news programme, begun in 1947, was *Camel News Caravan* (so called because it was sponsored by Camel cigarettes). It was presented by John Cameron Swayze, a jovial character who would conclude each edition by 'hopscotching the world for headlines' – at which he would dismiss in a sentence all the international events that had occurred that day but had not been filmed. In NBC's early-morning show, *Today*, the showbiz element was even more predominant: the programme was presented by Dave Garroway and a performing chimpanzee named J. Fred Muggs.

Dave Garroway with the notorious chimpanzee J. Fred Muggs on NBC's Today show.

The problem with television news was that it refused to deal with any given subject for more than about a minute. It was terrified of boring its audience. As David Brinkley, NBC's longest-serving anchor man, once wrote: 'The news judgments that newspapers and wire services have developed over the generations may be fine for them, but not for us.' He argued that 'the basic reason we are different is that in a newspaper you can skip around, read what is interesting to you and ignore the rest; while on a news broadcast you have to take it as it comes, in order.'

The consequence of such an attitude was that television trivialised many important stories. Not everyone, however, was prepared to accept that this was inevitable; and so, alongside the chimpanzees, there grew a more intelligent offshoot of television news – the current affairs programme. Its purpose was to take only one or two items each week and cover them 'in depth'.

In the early days, at least, the personalities of the presenters were as important to current affairs programmes as they were to newscasts, but for a different reason. Whereas newscasters were prized for their informal manner or their skill at repartee, the hosts of more serious current affairs shows had to be seen as the embodiment of wisdom and authority. The most famous British example was Richard Dimbleby, who took over as presenter of *Panorama* in September 1955, when it was re-launched as a 'weekly window on the world'. Dimbleby's stature was such that when he broadcast an April Fool's Day film on *Panorama* in 1957, claiming that spaghetti grew on trees, thousands of viewers believed him. At the height of the Cuban missile crisis five years later, one woman was reported to have telephoned the BBC to say that she would not send her children to school the next day 'unless Mr Dimbleby can promise me that there will be no war'.

Dimbleby's American counterpart was Edward R. Mur-

Richard Dimbleby, the face and voice trusted by millions, interviews Prince Philip on Panorama *in 1961.*

Dimbleby was so authoritative that many viewers fell for his April Fool's hoax in 1957 on Panorama, *when he reported on the Swiss spaghetti harvest.*

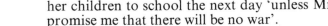

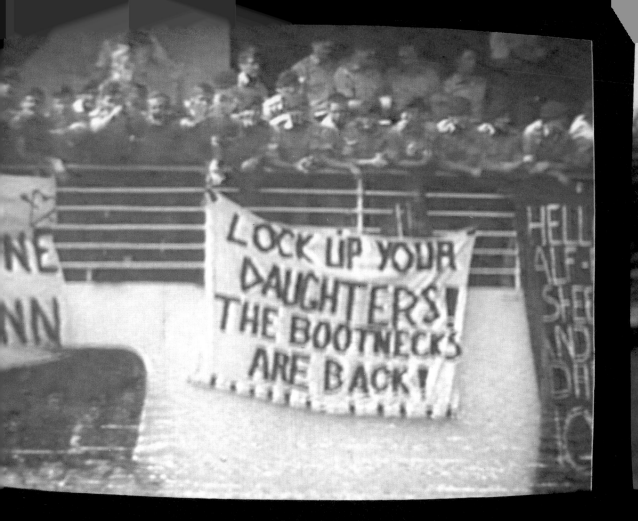

Edward R. Murrow's reputation was earned as a war-time correspondent in London for CBS Radio; as a television presenter in the 1950s he had remarkable editorial independence because of his friendship with CBS boss William S. Paley.

January 1957: Overlooking Pennsylvania Avenue from the roof of the Treasury building, Sgt Horace Freeman demonstrates how the Signal Corps will use a new 'Tela-Scout' portable TV camera and transmitter during Eisenhower's inauguration parade.

row, who is often described as the father-figure of television journalism. He had made his name during the Second World War as CBS Radio's correspondent in London, so he was already a highly respected figure when he initiated CBS Television's programme *See It Now* in 1951. On the first edition of *See It Now*, Murrow and his producer, Fred W. Friendly, arranged for live pictures of the Brooklyn Bridge in New York and the Golden Gate Bridge in San Francisco to be shown simultaneously on a split screen – symbolising their intention that the programme should be a truly national institution, as well as their determination to use the technological possibilities of television to the full.

The early years of *See It Now* were a traumatic time for the United States. Joseph McCarthy, the junior Senator from Wisconsin, was conducting a hysterical witch-hunt against 'Communists', a term which he defined rather broadly to include anyone of even mildly liberal views. Television newscasters had been wary of criticising McCarthy, not least because the networks themselves had succumbed to his influence by creating 'blacklists' of suspected Communists who were not to be allowed to broadcast.

Even Murrow took some time to summon up the courage to tackle McCarthy. When he did so, the effect was devastating. His first programme on the subject, broadcast in October 1953, was titled *The Case Against Milo Radulovich, A0589839.* It concerned an Air Force lieutenant who had been forced out of the service because his sister and father had been accused (by an anonymous informant) of reading 'subversive newspapers'. Much of the programme was composed of interviews with the lieutenant and his family, but it ended with a statement from Murrow himself, made directly into the camera: 'Whatever happens in this whole area of the relationship between the individual and the state,' he declared, 'we will do ourselves. It cannot be blamed upon Malenkov, Mao Tsetung or even our allies. It seems to us – that is, to Fred Friendly and myself – that it is a subject that should be argued about endlessly.'

Lieutenant Radulovich was reinstated as a result of the programme. Yet CBS was nervous about Murrow's new crusade. Murrow and Friendly had bought an advertisement for the programme in the *New York Times* with their own money because the network refused to pay for any publicity. 'They certainly weren't jumping and cheering that we did the programme,' Friendly says. 'And a week later somebody very high in the company said to me, "You may have cost us the network."'

It was only Murrow's reputation from the Second World War and his friendship with CBS's Chairman, William S. Paley, that enabled him to pursue the subject against the wishes of CBS's executives and sponsors. He collected all the footage he could find in which McCarthy made specific charges against 'Communists' in public office, and then interspersed these clips with the facts. The resulting programme, broadcast in March 1954, brought a predictable protest from Senator McCarthy, who described Murrow as 'the leader of the jackal pack which is always found at the throat of anyone who dares expose individual Communists and traitors'. But it was also, according to Friendly, the moment at which the American public began to see McCarthy for what he was: 'I think two things happened in that programme. You saw the McCarthy assassination and you saw Murrow rebuffing it. And you also saw a man with a presence of integrity –

November 1951: the first edition of See It Now *showed simultaneous live pictures of the Brooklyn Bridge and the Golden Gate Bridge, using coast-to-coast coaxial cable.*

Senator Joseph McCarthy in 1954, replying to Murrow – 'leader of the jackal pack'.

Murrow, remembered from the Battle of Britain, remembered as somebody who was a straight arrow, saying, "This man is a menace, and we have lots of things to worry about in this country but Communists-under-the-bed is not the biggest one. The biggest thing we have to worry about is guilt by association, and spying on each other, and what for lack of a better word we call McCarthyism." ' Friendly believes that 'the fact that a man of Murrow's stature could do that, did do that, made other people say, "We don't have to sit back and listen to McCarthy any longer – we can write about him, we can attack him." ' In 1955, the demolition job begun by Murrow was completed by McCarthy himself, when his wild and ranting performance during the hearings of his dispute with the army was televised. Both viewers and Senators turned against him; his spell was broken.

The techniques which Murrow and Friendly developed for current affairs television were adopted, in modified forms, elsewhere in the world. The British programme *Panorama*, for all its authority, still tended to avoid controversy and to interpret 'news' as meaning the actions of political leaders. Murrow, by contrast, had shown that ordinary people could be just as newsworthy. Much of the power of his programme on Lieutenant Radulovich had come from the fact that the subject of the film was a young man with whom viewers could identify; he might be anyone's son. ITN in Britain had allowed ordinary people into their news bulletins by using 'vox pop' interviews with members of the public, but the most significant breakthrough was made, surprisingly, by the BBC, which in 1957 started a daily magazine show called *Tonight*. As if recognising its debt, *Tonight* included an interview with Murrow in its first edition.

The conception of *Tonight* occurred because of the ending of a bizarre agreement known as the 'Toddlers' Truce', whereby both ITV and the BBC closed down for an hour between 6 and 7 p.m. so that parents could more easily persuade their children to go to bed. The job of filling this extra hour was given to Donald Baverstock, a young BBC producer who had visited the USA in 1956 and had returned with a powerful conviction that, compared with American output, BBC programmes were 'pretentious or boring – or both'.

Alan Whicker, the much-travelled and much-parodied British reporter, made his television debut on Tonight.

By a fortunate coincidence, *Tonight*'s birth happened at the same time as the death of *Picture Post*, a much-loved but uneconomic magazine. *Picture Post* had two characteristics in common with *Tonight* – an awareness that visual images could be as important as words and a belief in treating ordinary people without condescension. Baverstock took advantage of *Picture Post*'s demise by hiring some of its best journalists, including Fyfe Robertson, Trevor Philpott, Slim Hewitt and, later, Kenneth Allsop. He also took on Alan Whicker, a young foreign correspondent working for the Exchange Telegraph news agency. Among the film directors he employed were several who later became internationally famous, such as John Schlesinger, Jack Gold and Kevin Billington.

Fyfe Robertson, an idiosyncratic Scot (also much parodied), was another person to achieve national fame through Tonight.

It was a formidable team. Baverstock and his colleagues almost instantly hit on the style which was to win them an audience of 7 million viewers by 1958. Hard news was interspersed with quirky 'human interest' items. A discussion about nuclear war might be followed by an interview with a farmer whose hens were laying strangely-shaped eggs. One of the regular features was a topical calypso, written by Bernard Levin. The programme's anchor-man, Cliff Michelmore,

Cliff Michelmore, anchor-man, signed off each episode with the words 'And the next Tonight *will be tomorrow night'.*

became a national hero, described by one newspaper as 'the face that dogs and maiden aunts trust on first sight'.

An article in the *Observer* in 1958 pointed to the secret of *Tonight*'s success: the show had proved that 'politicians needn't be treated with awe, railwaymen with condescension'. And although many of the items were perhaps more whimsical than newsworthy, *Tonight* was not afraid of controversy. One of the earliest editions included an interview with a man who had just been released from police custody, having initially been suspected of murdering his nephew. 'BBC Television did an astonishing thing last night,' the *Daily Herald* reported. 'In an "interview" programme a man was asked: "What does it feel like to be a suspect in a murder case?"' One day later, however, the Corporation's executives decided that the interview had been rather too 'astonishing' for their taste: they issued a statement that the item 'should not have been broadcast'.

Tonight did have its limitations, the most obvious of which was that, as a 'magazine' programme, it did not feel able to report 'in depth' on any particular subject. As Alasdair Milne, Baverstock's co-editor, told an interviewer some years later: 'It seemed to us that the "drip on stone" technique would do far more good than a deluge of information. It's a lot to ask of an audience that they should give up a whole hour to listen to what you've got to say on, for example, the defence budget, which we dealt with in the early *Tonight* days. And quite right. Why the hell should anyone give up an hour to listen to the absurdities of the defence budget? They'll give up five minutes to listen to the man with the bent eggs or to watch the pretty girl.'

It was left to others to follow the more dangerous part of Murrow's example, that of crusading and investigative journalism. *Tonight* had presented many touching human stories, but it would never have devoted half an hour to the plight of, say, a British equivalent of Lieutenant Radulovich. If there had been such a person, his case would undoubtedly have been presented instead on Granada TV's *World in Action*; and Granada discovered, like Murrow, that such programmes require not only an ability to maintain the audience's interest for longer than five minutes but also a willingness to fight interminable battles with the powers that be. Ironically enough, the first *World in Action* to fall foul of the authorities dealt with defence spending, the very subject which Alasdair Milne considered to be of little interest. The Independent Television Authority banned the programme on the grounds that it was 'biased'.

This was hardly surprising. *World in Action* was the brainchild of Tim Hewat, a dynamic but abrasive Australian who had already earned notoriety as the producer of Granada's *Searchlight* programmes between 1958 and 1960. As *Contrast* magazine reported: 'Each programme took a single subject – Teenagers, The Comet, Suicide, Cruelty to Children, Dirty Food, Road Accidents – and banged at the central issue with the simple directness of a *Mirror* leader. Hewat was never so happy as when a *Searchlight* caused some sort of commotion.' Hewat's choice of subjects often seemed like a direct incitement to commotion: he was happy to tackle matters which had previously been taboo, such as artificial insemination and the Pill. At the end of the first series of *Searchlight*, Granada was officially reprimanded by the ITA, who claimed that every single programme had contravened the Television Act's ban on editorialising. Hewat was unmoved. He believed

Brian Inglis presented the first edition of Granada's What The Papers Say *in 1956; twenty years later he also presented the thousandth edition.*

Searchlight, 1959: for a programme about drunken driving, Tim Hewat arranged bodies in a London road to represent the number of people knocked down at that spot in the previous six months.

(Opposite) Man on the moon. James Burke was studio front-man for all the BBC coverage of the Apollo lunar landings.

Compared with the tabloid-style liveliness of Granada's Searchlight *and* World in Action, *Richard Dimbleby's* Panorama *seemed rather staid and old-fashioned.*

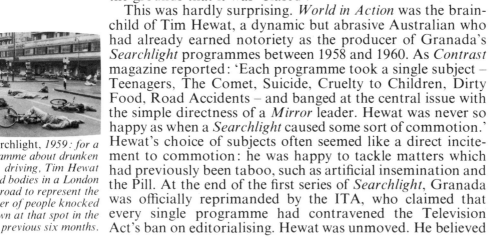

that 'objective journalism' was a myth. 'One goes into some subjects with a prejudice or a belief that one wants to see borne out on the screen,' he said. 'Conversely, one goes into other programmes without preconceived beliefs but in a spirit of inquiry and investigation. Having made the investigation, and being satisfied that it has been done thoroughly and fairly, then I think it is the responsibility of the producer to draw conclusions from the information.' This attitude represented a risky and radical new approach to television journalism, which was fenced about with rules demanding 'due impartiality' and 'balance'. Another interesting innovation was that *World in Action* did not use an on-screen reporter or a reassuring anchor-figure such as Murrow or Dimbleby; it stood or fell solely on the quality of its journalism.

Tim Hewat with Labour politician Barbara Castle before her appearance on Granada's election programme Marathon.

Hewat's buccaneering spirit was bound to cause friction with the ITA, supposedly the guardian of 'fairness'. In 1963 he produced four half-hour specials on Cuba (*Cuba Si!*) which provoked a letter from the Authority to Granada, complaining that 'we can't escape the conclusion that the four programmes taken together lacked impartiality and were in places slanted unfairly against the United States'. This was a harbinger of the trouble which was to beset *World in Action* in its dealings with government and the ITA (later the IBA) from the first series in 1963 to the present day. In September 1963 *World in Action* revealed the appalling living conditions of black people in South Africa and Angola (which was then a Portuguese colony), causing an inevitable protest from the ambassadors of the two countries. The ITA agreed that the programme had not been impartial, and decreed that in future all Granada's current affairs programmes should be vetted before transmission by the Authority's staff. In 1964 *World in Action* described the poor facilities available to British athletes who were training for the Olympic Games; the ITA refused to allow the programme to be broadcast, not least because Granada had not invited a government spokesman to give the 'official' view. The following year, the pharmaceutical industry complained to the ITA about a *World in Action* which had accused drug companies of overcharging. The ITA agreed with the complaint but Granada refused to apologise, and the argument rumbled on for the best part of two years without resolution.

The trial in Jerusalem of Adolf Eichmann, former Gestapo chief, for 'crimes against humanity' was shown exclusively on ITN in Britain in 1961.

Conflict between Granada and the IBA continued during the 1970s. In 1971 *World in Action* decided to make a film which would show that the Northern Irish 'troubles' were having an effect on Southern Ireland. Two of the interviewees were to be the Chief of Staff of the Provisional IRA and the President of Provisional Sinn Fein; the programme was banned by the Authority, who said that Granada was 'aiding and abetting the enemy'. In January 1973 the IBA delayed the showing of Granada's special investigation into the affairs of the corrupt architect John Poulson, who had bribed politicians in order to secure contracts; the IBA explained that *World in Action* had given 'too much emphasis to repeating and developing strictures . . . against named individuals'. In 1979 an interview with the Irish Republican Danny Morrison was not used by *World in Action* after a government minister had refused to appear on the same programme as Morrison. Two years later, when *World in Action* attempted to report on the 'propaganda war' in Ireland, the IBA insisted that it should delete pictures of a dead Republican hunger-striker; rather than obey, Granada withdrew the programme altogether.

Cuba Si! – *four documentaries made for Granada at the time of the Bay of Pigs.*

In 1976, World in Action *smuggled secret film out of the Soviet Union showing meetings of Jewish dissidents, including Anatole Scharansky.*

During the British election of 1983, World in Action *hired Walter Cronkite; for one of his reports he travelled to Greenham Common to interview peace women.*

For more than twenty years, *World in Action* has remained the most consistently original and daring of British current affairs series, not least because it has been defended by its parent company, Granada, against the buffetings of the IBA and politicians. The most famous example of Granada's support for the programme occurred in 1980, when the British Steel Corporation (BSC) won a court order requiring Granada to name the 'mole' who had leaked confidential documents from BSC. Granada continued to protect its source, even when the order was backed up by the Appeal Court and the House of Lords. Although BSC won the legal battle, it finally recognised that there was no point in pressing a demand which clearly would not be met.

Granada has also been helped by the admiration which it has won from other programme-makers and reporters. When Tim Hewat's film about defence spending was banned in the 1960s, part of it was promptly broadcast instead on the BBC's *Panorama*, thereby making the ITA look exceedingly foolish. The same thing happened in 1980, when the IBA vetoed a *World in Action* which disclosed corruption and incompetence on the part of British intelligence officers in Hong Kong. Parts of the offending film were shown on BBC-2's *Newsnight*, and *World in Action*'s allegations were reported at great length in the *Daily Mirror* and the *New Statesman*. It was another moral victory for Granada: how could a story that was acceptable to Fleet Street and the BBC be too 'sensitive' for ITV?

The boldness of *World in Action* has encouraged other British television companies to be more forthright in their coverage of current affairs. The London station, Associated-Rediffusion (which later merged with ABC to become Thames Television), received a barrage of protests when it alleged, in 1966, that police were habitually 'bending the rules' when dealing with suspects. A year later, the ITA ruled that *This Week* had been in 'obvious breach' of the Television Act for claiming that private airline operators were lax in their attitude to safety standards.

Even the BBC, which is always under pressure to avoid controversy because of its 'public service' function, has sometimes dared to defy the government. In 1972 it announced its intention of screening a long debate – two hours and fifty minutes – to be called *The Question of Ulster*, which would involve a number of British and Irish politicians. Although the proposal seemed tame enough, the Home Secretary of the day, Reginald Maudling, did his utmost to stop the programme being made. He came to the brink of invoking his power of veto over the BBC (the Corporation's licence allows the Minister, *in extremis*, to order the BBC not to transmit a particular programme), but Maudling eventually drew back from taking such an unprecedented action. He did, however, make public his opinion that *The Question of Ulster* 'can do no good and could do serious harm'. It turned out to be much less explosive; it was a harmless discussion programme, which attracted few viewers.

Seven years later the BBC was again under fire from a Conservative government for its treatment of Ulster. In July 1979 its late-night news programme *Tonight* (not to be confused with the early-evening *Tonight* of the 1950s and 1960s) broadcast an interview with a member of the Irish National Liberation Army, the group which claimed responsibility for the murder of Airey Neave MP. 'I am appalled it was ever transmitted,' Margaret Thatcher, the new Prime Minister,

Union leader Clive Jenkins (left) and former Foreign Secretary Lord George-Brown joined 15 'ordinary Britons' on a 3,000 mile bus trip across Europe for a World in Action *special, shown just before the 1975 referendum on EEC membership.*

(Following pages) The 'troubles' in Northern Ireland have provided many potent images: missile-throwing youths and flak-jacketed politicians as well as IRA members in black berets and black glasses. But have the images been used as a substitute for serious analysis of the conflict?

told the House of Commons, 'and I believe it reflects gravely on the judgment of the BBC and those responsible.' Worse was to come. Three months later a team from *Panorama*, filming in the Republic of Ireland, received an anonymous tip-off urging them to take their camera crew to the village of Carrickmore, just north of the border. There they found that the village had been sealed off by hooded IRA men, who were happy to be filmed. When news of the incident leaked out, three weeks afterwards, a Unionist MP accused the BBC of participating in 'a treasonable activity'. Mrs Thatcher was equally blunt: 'It is not the first time I have had occasion to raise similar matters with the BBC. Both the Home Secretary and I think it is about time they put their house in order.' The threat was enough to send the BBC's Governors rushing for cover. They announced that *Panorama* had failed to observe the rule that the BBC's Northern Ireland controller must be informed whenever a crew ventured into the province. *Panorama*'s editor was sacked – although he was later reinstated when his union threatened to go on strike. The programme itself was never shown.

BBC staff who were alarmed at what they saw as capitulation to the government were slightly reassured some years later, in 1984, when the BBC showed that it could sometimes withstand official pressure. The *casus belli* this time was a *Panorama* programme which alleged that racists and neo-fascists had infiltrated the Conservative Party. The party's Chairman, John Selwyn Gummer, made frequent and angry demands for an apology; but on this occasion, at least, the BBC declined to oblige.

All these incidents suggest that governments are firm adherents to the theory that people believe what they see on television news and are influenced by it. Whether this theory is correct or not is a matter of constant debate, but there is some evidence to support it. John Lewis, who was Martin Luther King's assistant during the great civil rights campaigns of the late 1950s and early 1960s, is convinced that it was the television coverage of the agitation which made possible the passage of the Civil Rights Act of 1964 and the Voting Rights Act of 1965. 'It was a great story, a story that needed to be told, and you had all the necessary ingredients there for television,' he says. 'I think people got mad when they saw people being tear-gassed or attacked by men riding on horses or being beaten as they tried to march to Montgomery, Alabama. Those images created a sense of urgency and said to the American people – we must act, and act now.' This opinion is shared by Nicholas Katzenbach, who was President Kennedy's Attorney-General: 'The most dramatic incident that I can recall was when Dr King was marching in southern Alabama,' he says, 'and was then attacked by a bunch of Ku Klux Klan, people with cattle prods and night sticks and hoses. It was a really disgusting event, and I think probably that as much as any other single event led to the passage of the 1965 Act.' The campaign was also assisted by Martin Luther King's understanding of the practicalities of television: he always ensured that his rallies ended in time for the networks to meet their evening news deadline.

The effect of all this was not lost on King's opponents. 'White racists in the South looked upon the television reporters and the cameras as being the real enemies,' John Lewis recalls. 'It was very dangerous for a cameraman to be covering a civil rights effort in the South, and on many occasions, particularly during the early 1960s, during the

The American civil rights movement gained extensive television coverage, including the struggle in 1957 to integrate Little Rock, Arkansas.

Thanks to the brave efforts of Czechs operating mobile transmitters, the outside world was able to watch as Russian tanks rolled into Prague in 1968.

Freedom Rides; I saw a camera crew's camera taken and smashed.' The cameramen themselves were often beaten up before the Freedom Riders. Some television stations in the South refused to carry any film of the civil rights protests and one station, WLBT in Jackson, Mississippi, eventually had its licence revoked because it had persistently ignored the whole issue, and had kept black people off its other programmes.

Fear of the potency of television images has manifested itself all over the world. One of the causes of the Soviet invasion of Czechoslovakia in 1968 was the increasing honesty of Czech news programmes under the liberal regime of Alexander Dubcek. This trend had actually begun before the 'Prague Spring'. Under its radical Director-General, Jiri Pelikan, Czech television was already showing a regular one-and-a-half hour programme in which people were able to challenge Ministers directly in the studio. By the spring of 1968, government censorship of news on television had been abolished altogether. This, together with the other flowerings of the Prague Spring, was a development which the Russians could not allow to continue; in August the tanks rolled in. The invasion produced some of the most memorable news pictures ever seen on television, as Czech cameramen rushed their film to secret mobile transmitters whence it was beamed across the border to Austria. Since Austrian television could be picked up in many parts of Czechoslovakia, viewers around the country were able to watch their own nation being invaded, much to the annoyance of the Russians. Once the invasion was completed, of course, strict censorship was re-imposed.

Censorship of news is by no means the sole preserve of the Soviet bloc. Only three months before the invasion of Czechoslovakia, France came within an inch of revolution during *les événements* of May 1968; yet for much of the time French viewers were no better informed about their national crisis than the Czechs were about theirs. The French government had always exercised tight control over television. The broadcasting organisation, ORTF, came under the umbrella of the Ministry of Information, where an 'Interministerial Liaison Service for Information' met daily to discuss what ought to be covered in the news programmes. French television had produced some distinguished current affairs series – *Cinq colonnes à la une* (Five Columns on Page One), *Panorama* and *Zoom* – but these had concentrated almost exclusively on the safe topic of foreign affairs. A study of *Cinq colonnes à la une* in 1965 – the year of a Presidential election in France – revealed that of the fifty-six subjects it had covered only three were connected with French politics.

When strikes and student riots erupted in May 1968, ORTF at first made light of the crisis and refused to allow the students to state their case. After a few days, television reporters defied their management by providing fuller and more sympathetic coverage. Matters came to a head when the weekly *Panorama* proposed to screen a studio debate which would include student leaders. Only minutes before the programme was due to go on the air, officials from the Ministries of Information and Education arrived at ORTF's headquarters and ordered that the discussion should not be shown. In the following week two other programmes were stopped in the same fashion. All but twenty-three of ORTF's journalists voted to go on strike. For the next five weeks, as France underwent one of the greatest upheavals in its history,

Television coverage of the near-revolution in France in May 1968, provoked a strike by journalists at the French channel ORTF, who complained that the government's view was being given undue prominence.

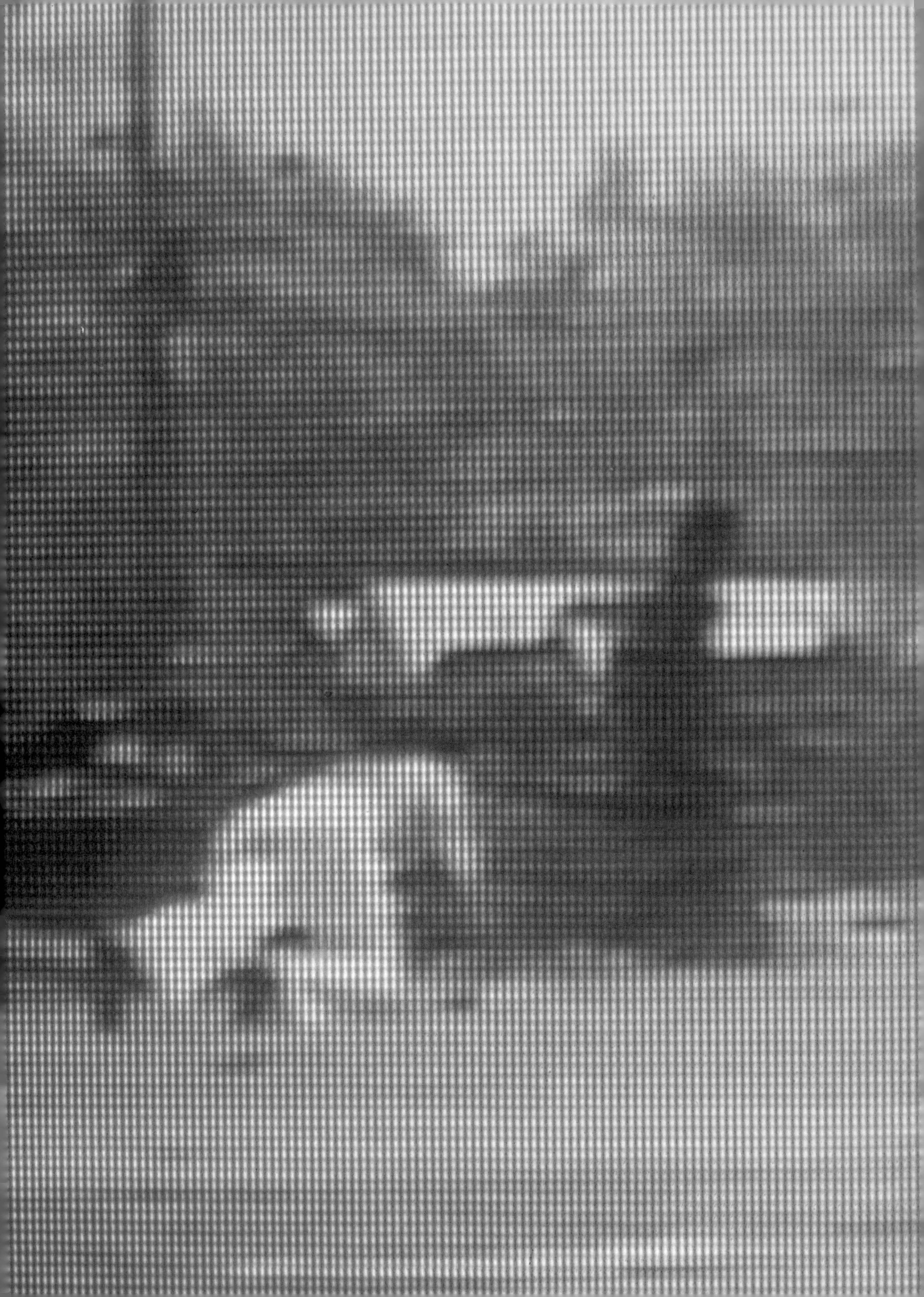

The assassination of American television journalist Bill Stewart in Nicaragua in June 1979 was influential in turning opinion in the US against Somoza's corrupt regime; after their victory, the Sandinistas built a memorial to Stewart.

ORTF had only brief news bulletins produced by a skeleton staff. By July, de Gaulle had triumphed and the strike had folded; fifty-nine journalists were sacked, and another forty were transferred to obscure jobs in the provinces.

When Georges Pompidou was elected to succeed de Gaulle in 1968, he promised to reform ORTF. Since then, however, television news in France has still been bedevilled by charges of bias and manipulation. In 1974 ORTF was abolished, to be replaced by three 'autonomous' television organisations – TF1, A2 and FR3. But although these were theoretically commercial companies, the government was the only shareholder; the state's monopoly of broadcasting was thus maintained. Whenever a new government has been installed, there has invariably followed a comprehensive change of personnel at the top of these companies, bringing in supporters of the new regime. As Pompidou himself said in 1970: 'Being a journalist in ORTF is not like being a journalist anywhere else . . . ORTF is the voice of France. You who write the news must always keep in mind that you are not speaking for yourself. You are the voice of your country, and your government.' After the election of a socialist President, François Mitterrand, in 1981, all senior directors in French television were fired and replaced by socialist appointees. In November 1981 there were protests from Gaullists when, for the first time in twenty-three years, two Communists were employed as journalists on the main channel; their appointment had been made over the heads of programme editors after a 'direct intervention' by the Communist Party's press spokesman.

The year of 1968 is considered to have been a crucial one in the history of television news, not merely in France and Czechoslovakia but also – and perhaps most importantly – in the United States. It was the year in which Walter Cronkite reported that the Vietnam war could not be won and Lyndon Johnson announced that he would not stand for re-election, thus sparking off a fierce debate as to whether television news was causing America to 'lose' the war. It is an argument that has continued ever since.

August 1965: American marines set fire to a Vietnamese village with a cigarette lighter in full view . of Morley Safer and his camera crew from CBS.

One point that is often overlooked is that until the Tet offensive of 1968, American television coverage of Vietnam had been remarkably docile, taking statements from the U.S. Administration at face value. There had been a few honourable exceptions – but only a few. In August 1965 CBS's Morley Safer filmed a group of marines 'punishing' the village of Cam Ne, which had been suspected of harbouring members of the Vietcong: a marine set fire to a thatched roof with a cigarette lighter and within minutes the whole village had been razed. Some civilians were burnt alive when the Americans turned flame-throwers on them. The fact that Safer's camera crew was allowed to film all this was in itself proof of how uncritical television coverage had been: it had simply not occurred to the marines that pictures of their activities might be used 'negatively'. They apparently assumed that Safer's commentary would explain that this was yet another heroic action by brave troops who were eradicating 'the Cong' and saving Vietnam from Communism.

In fact, Safer's report was fairly restrained, but the horrific film told the story. After its transmission on CBS's evening news, many viewers rang to protest at the station's 'disloyalty' to 'American boys'; others realised for the first time that the version of the war which they had hitherto been given was a lie. Frank Stanton, the President of CBS, received a phone call from Lyndon Johnson early the next morning:

Lyndon Johnson said that CBS's reports from Vietnam were a betrayal of the American flag.

'Frank, are you trying to fuck me?' Johnson asked, adding that 'yesterday your boys shat on the American flag'.

Pressure from the government persuaded the networks to resume their old-style coverage, though in 1967 CBS did summon up the nerve to broadcast a special programme called *Morley Safer's Vietnam*. For most of the time, however, the networks found Vietnam an embarrassment, something they would rather avoid. In 1966 Fred Friendly resigned as President of CBS News when, against his wishes, the network stopped its live coverage of the Senate Foreign Relations Committee's hearings on the war and put on instead old re-runs of *I Love Lucy* and *The Real McCoys*. CBS's management said that they had abandoned their transmissions from the Senate on purely commercial grounds – advertisers wanted day-time programmes which would attract higher ratings – but the decision was nevertheless symptomatic of a feeling that Vietnam was not all that important when compared with soap operas and comedy shows. The effect of television's unwillingness to probe more deeply into the facts of the war was demonstrated by a *Newsweek* survey in 1967 which found that 64 per cent of Americans had had their support for the war *strengthened* as a result of watching news programmes; only 26 per cent said that television had made them more uneasy about America's involvement in Vietnam.

Yippy protests at the 1968 Chicago convention: 'the whole world is watching'.

In 1968, however, the tide began to turn. Americans had previously been led to believe that the war could easily be won because the Vietcong was not an effective fighting force; the Tet offensive showed this to be false. Walter Cronkite's famous report from Vietnam was supplemented by a succession of ghastly images, such as the film of a young Vietcong suspect having his brains blown out at point-blank range by South Vietnam's police chief, Nguyen Ngoc Loan. 'It was not until 1968 that people at the grass roots here in this country got all that much affected by media views,' says Dean Rusk, the former Secretary of State. 'Finally I think they came to the conclusion that if we could not tell them when this war was going to be over then we might as well chuck it. I think that was the critical time.' Rusk points out that it was the first war to be fought on television in people's living rooms every day. 'One can reflect upon what might have happened in World War II if the Anzio beach-head and the Battle of the Bulge and Dunkirk had been on television and the other side was not using it. I think the effect could have been very profound. So I think we need to do a good deal of thinking about whether or not an armed conflict can be sustained for very long if the worst aspects of it are going to be reflected on television every day.' Rusk draws the conclusion that 'there may have to be certain kinds of censorship'.

A shot that echoed around the world: a young Vietcong suspect has his brains blown out by police chief Nguyen Ngoc Loan.

Not everyone accepts that television helped to end the Vietnam war. Some surveys have suggested that by being exposed to film of battles night after night, viewers actually developed a tolerance for the war. Michael Arlen, the *New Yorker*'s television critic, argued that the combat scenes had been 'diminished in part by the physical size of the television screen, which, for all the industry's advances, still shows one a picture of men three inches tall shooting at other men three inches tall'. The British war correspondent Phillip Knightley wrote: 'When seen on a small screen, in the enveloping and cosy atmosphere of the household, some time between the afternoon soap-box drama and the late-night war movie, the television version of the war in Vietnam could appear as just another drama, in which the hero is the correspondent and

After Vietnam, military chiefs believed that hostility to the war had been fuelled by television pictures; hence the restrictions on television film from the Falklands a decade later.

everything will come out all right in the end.'

Nevertheless, American generals were sure that television had had a decisive influence, and their opinion was heeded by military men elsewhere in the world. At a seminar in London organised by the Royal United Services Institute in 1970, Air Vice-Marshal Stewart Menaul said that television had 'a lot to answer for' in having caused 'the collapse of American morale'. Another speaker, Brigadier F. G. Caldwell from the British Ministry of Defence, said that, after the American experience in Vietnam, if Britain went to war again 'we would have to start saying to ourselves, are we going to let the television cameras loose on the battlefield?' By the time Britain did go to war again, in 1982, the question had been answered resoundingly in the negative: no television film of fighting in the Falklands was transmitted until the war was over. The Ministry of Defence claimed that pictures could not be sent for technical reasons, because of insuperable difficulties with satellites, but both the BBC and ITN believed that these problems could have been overcome if the Ministry had wanted to do so. Sir Frank Cooper, who was Permanent Secretary at the Ministry during the Falklands conflict, admits that 'we'd have been very worried' if live film had been shown: 'It would have caused a good deal of problems.' He says that the Ministry was frightened of the power of pictures: 'Both the spoken word and the written word, in a situation of conflict, seem to be more measured and less graphic than pictures are. Pictures convey the realities of war to a degree which I think nobody speaking or writing could ever possibly convey, however skilled they are.' It seems likely that this was the real reason for the slowness in sending film back from the Task Force to Britain. The average delay was seventeen days, and some film took as long as twenty-three days to reach London.

Television journalists accompanying the troops were therefore reduced to sending voice reports, for all the world as if Britain was still living in the Golden Age of sound radio. They were also hampered by constant interference and censorship from the 'minders' who had been sent by the Ministry to keep an eye on them. When Michael Nicholson of ITN tried to report on the sinking of HMS *Sheffield* he was confronted by a minder 'absolutely outraged at what we wanted to do. He said, "Didn't you realise that you were with us to do a 1940 propaganda job?" – you know, Tommy over the top giving the Jerry a black eye. That's really what they expected us to do.' Nicholson says that the officers commanding the Task Force had obviously learnt from America's experience in the 1960s: 'Time and time again they'd say, "We're going to keep a watch on you because we saw what you fellows did to the Yanks." And of course the Vietnam syndrome was immensely powerful. It was no use trying to argue to the military that it wasn't the British press or the French press or the American press that lost the war in Vietnam, it was the American military.' One senior officer told Nicholson: 'If I'd had my way I'd have told nobody anything until it was all over and then I'd have told them who won.'

Just as the British took note of Vietnam, the Americans learned from the Falklands. When the United States invaded Grenada in 1983, the only film of the struggle was that provided by the Pentagon; network journalists were not allowed on to the island until the shooting had died down.

Governments' fear of the power of the television camera

(Opposite page) During the Balcombe Street seige in London in 1975, the IRA gunmen inside the flat were surrounded not only by the police but also by television cameras, whose pictures were watched by the gunmen themselves.

Ian McDonald, a previously unknown press officer at the Ministry of Defence, became a television celebrity with his daily performances during the Falklands War; his announcements were made all the more dramatic by the plodding monotone in which he delivered them.

is in many ways understandable. All too often in television newscasts the amount of enlightenment provided is in inverse proportion to the dramatic quality of the film. Pictures of a young man being shot in the head by a Vietnamese policeman may be visually arresting, but what do they tell viewers about the origins and the complexities of a far-off war? As Phillip Knightley has written, years of television coverage of Vietnam 'left viewers with a blur of images consisting mainly of helicopters landing in jungle clearings, soldiers charging into undergrowth, wounded being loaded on to helicopters, artillery and mortar fire, air strikes on distant targets, napalm canisters turning slowly in the sky, and a breathless correspondent poking a stick microphone under an army officer's nose and asking, "What's happening up there, Colonel?"'

Morley Safer once said that sensationalism is inherent in television news, 'because you're not talking about it, you're showing it'. Reuven Frank of NBC News agrees: 'Television news has the power to transmit the experience itself rather than information about the experience.' It is a prisoner of the medium. When American marines in Beirut were blown up by a bomb-packed lorry at the end of 1983, a producer in the CBS newsroom exclaimed proudly: 'This week we have brought grief into American homes – fast.' Sure enough, the network had shown the bodies of the dead marines being flown back to America for funerals with full military honours. What it had done less successfully was to explain why the marines had been in Beirut in the first place. Serious and lucid analysis of that kind would involve the use of a 'talking head' – something that most news producers shun for fear of boring the audience.

The history of television news is thus peppered with memorable but uninformative – and sometimes misleading – footage of exciting events. When Ronald Reagan was shot in 1981, film of the incident was broadcast within six minutes; but the commentary that went with it floundered in hopeless ignorance, stating that the President had not been hit (he had) and that his press secretary was dead (he was actually wounded). Moments later the networks allowed Alexander Haig, the Secretary of State, to give a live address in which he announced that 'as of now, I am in control here in the White House'. It was gripping television, but it also gave a thoroughly inaccurate impression.

Violent death or injury have always appealed to the producers of television news. The first assassination of a politician to be shown on television occurred in October 1960 when the leader of the Japanese socialist party, Inejiro Asanuma, was stabbed to death by a young right-winger at a public meeting. The main Japanese station, NHK, had been videotaping the meeting for transmission later that afternoon, after a broadcast of a Japanese baseball game. With surprising restraint, when word of the assassination reached NHK's studios, the channel's controllers decided to let the game finish before showing Asanuma's bloody demise. The film was then screened over and over again. 'For a week – a month – afterwards there was hardly any other topic of conversation anywhere in the country,' one NHK producer recalls. 'And as a result there were many voices raised demanding that violence be driven from the television screen, and there was a lot of discussion in the world of journalism and the mass media concerning our attitude to the extreme Right.'

Japanese television seems to have a remarkable knack of being in the right place at the right time. The first satellite

When Japanese socialist leader Inejiro Asanuma was stabbed to death by a young right-winger at an election meeting in 1960, a recording of the incident was shown over and over again to a stunned Japanese audience.

link from the United States to Japan was inaugurated on 23 November 1963; it was due to be a twenty-minute broadcast, consisting largely of a message from President Kennedy to the Japanese people. Less than an hour before the transmission, the Japanese heard that Kennedy had been shot in Dallas. Instead of hearing Kennedy's speech, the huge Japanese audience saw live reports on the aftermath of the assassination.

The first satellite broadcast in the other direction, from Japan to America, took place in March the following year. The Japanese Prime Minister, Ikeda, was to send a message of greetings to the Americans, but on the day before the broadcast the American Ambassador to Tokyo was shot dead. The Prime Minister scrapped his original speech and used the link to apologise to the United States; this was later described as the first example of television diplomacy.

Televised assassinations have become a depressingly regular feature of life over the past twenty years – so much so, indeed, that it is something of a rarity for a public figure to be shot when the television cameras are not present, as happened to Martin Luther King. One can discern a familiar pattern: news of the assassination is flashed on to the screen, followed by film a few minutes later; there is then an hour or more of chaos, with the newscasters unable to say whether or not the victim is dead and who the assailant was. The paucity of information leaves viewers with confused emotions. All they can do is watch the incident in slow motion again and again while waiting for a proper account.

Death on camera: the assassination of Robert Kennedy in California, June 1968.

CBS was the first American network to broadcast the news that John Kennedy's motorcade had been shot at, in the early afternoon of 22 November 1963. Walter Cronkite made the announcement in sound only, as the newsroom cameras had to be warmed up for ten minutes before they would work. 'My first reaction was "Good God!" – for humanity, for American people, for John Kennedy,' he recalls. 'I didn't have any idea of course in the first moments that he was actually hit or how badly he might have been hit. And my second reaction was: we have got a terrific story, we have got to get mobilised. I was a little disappointed that it took us that long to get the cameras hot and running. But the fact that we were on the air was satisfying; we were first, and as a news feat that was good.'

George Wallace, Governor of Alabama, was shot during his presidential campaign in 1972; he has been confined to a wheelchair ever since.

In dealing with the more spectacular terrorist incidents, too, television has often managed to generate more heat than light. In 1975 millions of Americans watched live coverage of a shoot-out in Los Angeles between police and members of the Symbionese Liberation Army who were holed up in a house. During the transmission, television journalists often reported a rumour (started by the FBI) that the heiress Patty Hearst was in the building. It turned out to be untrue. The man who directed the broadcast, Bill Eames, said afterwards: 'We always try to check out the bits of information we get, but in a Real-Time situation there is no time.' British broadcasters had similar difficulties at the *dénouement* of the Iranian Embassy siege in London, which was carried live at peak viewing time on 5 May 1980. Smoke was seen pouring from a front window of the embassy: had the terrorists let off a bomb, or had the building been stormed by British troops? A man wearing a balaclava appeared on a balcony: was he a terrorist or a member of the Special Air Service, the British army's most secretive corps? The BBC's commentator had no idea. ITN's reporter suggested that the explosions had been set off by the captors, and the rescue attempt had therefore been

bungled. As the novelist John le Carré wrote: 'For those few minutes, for however long it took for the wheel to turn, millions of deeply concerned British men and women, glued to their television screens, shared a false trauma of national humiliation . . . In those intense few minutes we, the public, were mini-hostages, ignorant of practically everything that was going on before our eyes.'

In circumstances of such confusion and excitement, television often allows itself to be manipulated. In 1975 a group of IRA gunmen were trapped in a flat in Balcombe Street, London, with an elderly couple whom they had taken hostage. The police knew that the IRA men were watching television reports in the flat; cameras from ITN and the BBC were therefore positioned where they would show that the police had the flat surrounded and that there was no chance of escape. As ITN's foreign editor wrote later: 'All branches of the media gave the story massive coverage, but only within the strictly defined limits of cooperation with the police in their aim of securing the release of the hostages and the capture of the gunmen.'

Michael Nicholson of ITN recalls an occasion which proved that guerrillas could be just as adept as the police in exploiting television's desire for pictures. Palestinian guerrillas had hijacked an aircraft at Dawson's Field in Jordan, and Nicholson was covering the event with a local freelance cameraman; when the hostages were released Nicholson told the cameraman that he would have to leave at once in order to send his film back to London in time for the evening news. The cameraman begged him to stay for a moment. 'And so I stood with him and he started to run his camera and within ten seconds the aircraft blew up. We're used to cameramen switching off at the wrong time and this guy switched on at the right time, so I said, "How did you do that?" And he said, "Because I'm one of them." He was a Palestinian. Unknown to us he'd been working with them all the time . . . It was a publicity exercise, and he was part and parcel of it.' The Palestinians had their propaganda coup, and ITN had a world exclusive film.

However much the producers of news programmes might wish to fill their broadcasts with pictures of exploding aeroplanes, police shoot-outs and attempted assassinations, they are confronted by an inconvenient fact: there are some news stories which have to be reported, because they are manifestly important, but which are utterly 'non-visual'. In some cases the problem is easily solved: a report about arms talks, for instance, can be illustrated by shots of missiles and mushroom clouds. Sometimes, however, the straining for visual effects drives producers into the higher realm of absurdity. Dick Salant, the former head of CBS News, used to tell his staff, 'In the beginning was the word. Don't be afraid of words.' Not all his colleagues heeded his advice. 'I'll give you an example of the kind of thing I think is so bad in allowing pictures to interfere just for the sake of having pictures,' Salant says. 'One of the networks' evening news within the last year had a lead story about the first month in which the cost-of-living index stayed flat. That was big news and it was a legitimate lead story. The economics reporter was doing a sound professional job. His opening line was: "Not since 1976, the year of the American Bicentennial, has there been a flat cost-of-living index." Important point, good. But they went away from a picture of the correspondent and they showed the Statue of Liberty at night on the Bicentennial

Dawson's Field, Jordan, 1970: PLO hijackers blow up a plane and ITN gets exclusive pictures.

(Previous page) Thirty-eight kings, heads of state and Islamic leaders attending the Islamic summit in Mecca in 1981 were accompanied by an equally international collection of camera crews.

celebration with a bunch of fireworks, just because it was a spectacular picture that happened in Bicentennial year. Now I challenge anybody to watch that and not just remember the fireworks and the Statue of Liberty rather than what the correspondent was saying.'

Salant's story is by no means an isolated example. When another network reported on the economic difficulties of Mexico, the economics correspondent began by saying that the Mexican peso had become less and less valuable, and was going down in the same way as divers jumping off 100-foot cliffs in Mexico. With the inevitability of cliché, this comment was illustrated with film of . . . Mexican divers jumping off cliffs. It is a perennial vice of television news that reporters have to write their stories to fit the editors' pictures.

Gimmickry of all kinds has flourished in American news programmes during the past fifteen years. In the 1950s and 1960s, networks regarded news as something of a public duty rather than a money-spinner, but by the early 1970s it became what Americans call a 'profit centre', as important a weapon in the ratings war as a soap opera or a game show. If a network could make its news more attractive to a mass audience it would win more viewers; and if it could do that, it could increase the prices charged to advertisers for thirty-second spots. The order went out from television executives: news had to be popular.

The impetus had come, in fact, from local stations, whose rivalry in their own particular region was as intense as the national struggle between the networks. The trend-setter was *Eye-Witness News*, a local programme put out by stations owned and operated by ABC. It used a simple formula: plenty of sports reports; even more weather forecasts; a little news, kept as 'soft' and 'visual' as possible; and interminable jokey banter between the anchor-people and the weather-man. Indeed the weather forecaster was often the star of the show. In his book *The Newscasters*, Ron Powers quotes a typical exchange between weather-man John Coleman and the anchor-men on *Eye-Witness News* in Chicago:

The inescapable powder-puff: (above) French politician Jacques Chirac is made up before being interviewed on Actuel 2 *in 1974: (below) in the same year, Soviet war hero Colonel Boris Solovei gets the treatment before a TV appearance in Paris.*

Los Angeles station KABC TV is one of many to use the formula of Eyewitness News *(sometimes derided as* Eyewitless News*), including a jokey weatherman in an absurd bow-tie.*

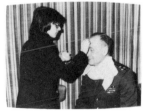

> *Joel Daly:* Well, what kind of cat-and-mouse games do you have for us in the weather, John?
> *Coleman:* I'd be willing to discuss the weather, Joel, if I knew that nursery rhyme, 'Ding, dong, bell . . .'
> *Daly:* 'Pussy's in the well.'
> *Coleman:* Go on.
> *Daly:* I don't remember the other . . .
> *Coleman:* I never heard that nursery rhyme, did you, Mike?
> *Mike Nolan:* Oh yeah, I heard it.
> *Daly:* That's right. 'Who put him in?'
> *Coleman:* Who?
> *Daly:* Little . . . Johnny . . . Coleman! (*general laughter*)
> *Coleman:* Aw, now, cut that out. Well, I'm sure we're not experts on nursery rhymes, but I am reasonably well informed meteorologically at this moment, and a one-word comment would be, YAH-HOOOOO!

This kind of inanity became known as Happy Talk news, and stations around the country hired 'news consultants' to come in and convert their programmes to Happy Talk.

Newscasters had always been celebrities, of course; even such sober figures as Ed Murrow or Walter Cronkite had been nationally famous. But the notion of the newscaster as showbiz personality was something new. Anchor-people were

Becky Luce, prepubescent anchorperson, checks her script before going on the air with Kids' News *for Sun Prairie cable TV viewers.*

Cabinet Minister Norman Tebbit ended controversy over the showing of possibly intrusive TV news pictures of his dramatic rescue after the Brighton bomb in 1984. Without the TV lights his rescue would have been severely hampered. Later that morning live TV coverage of the Tory Party conference continued.

being hired not for their journalistic prowess but for their entertainment value. In fact, many of the new anchor-people had no journalistic experience at all. In 1979, when CBS's station in Los Angeles hired a sportscaster named Brent Musburger as its anchor-man, the management explained their choice thus: 'He's a real upbeat person.'

Newscasters were hired and fired with great frequency as executives sought the right 'personality mix' for their news shows. In 1976 Barbara Walters achieved international stardom when she left NBC's *Today* programme to present ABC's evening news on a five-year contract worth $1 million a year. 'I'm really depressed as hell,' said Dick Salant of CBS when he heard of the move. 'This isn't journalism – this is a minstrel show. Is Barbara Walters a journalist or is she Cher? In fact, maybe ABC will hire Cher next. If this kind of circus atmosphere continues and I have to join in it, I'll quit first.' Today, he is still depressed. 'Happy Talk news, much to our distress, was very successful,' he grumbles. 'I can see that circulation is important – you've got to have circulation, there's no use in talking into a barrel down a rainpipe at nobody, you are serving no purpose. But where I go off the track is where it becomes so important that it affects not only how you present the news, but your choice of news stories. So when there is a sacrifice of important news for the sake of interesting and titillating news I'm very distressed and worried.'

CBS, to its credit, tried harder than most to resist the tide of trivia. With its show *60 Minutes* it proved, as *World in Action* had done in Britain, that a news programme could deal with serious issues and still be popular. The specialities of *60 Minutes* were investigative journalism – what producer Don Hewitt described as exposing people 'doing things in dark corners they shouldn't be doing' – and aggressive interviewing, mainly conducted by Mike Wallace. By the end of the 1970s the programme was regularly topping the ratings, beating even *M*A*S*H* or televised football games. In the first week of December 1980 *60 Minutes* came a disappointing second in the ratings; in mitigation it could point out that the show which had toppled it was the episode of *Dallas* in which J.R. was shot. By 1981 *60 Minutes*, broadcasting for just one hour a week, was making a weekly profit of $1,500,000; a thirty-second commercial during the programme cost $175,000. Despite this astonishing success, however, most other news shows continued to avoid serious journalism. The lure of sex, fun, weather and disaster stories was irresistible.

Part of a videotape, made with a hidden camera, which was used at the first 'Abscam' trial in 1980, showing Congressman Michael Myers accepting $50,000 from an undercover FBI agent.

The United States prides itself on its freedom of the press – and, by extension, of its television news. It is true that news broadcasts are relatively free from direct interference by the government. However, they are constantly pummelled by pressure from other quarters, notably advertisers and network executives desperate for high viewing figures. It is not surprising that more authoritarian countries feel resentful that most international criticism of television news is directed at them. As one Soviet broadcaster puts it, 'The trouble with you in the West, you show too many fires and murders on TV.' It would be hard to disagree. The editor of *Vremya*, the main Soviet news programme, argues that 'We show many more stories about America than they show about the Soviet Union.'

Soviet news is the exact reverse of its American counterpart. There are no clowning weather forecasters or buffoonish anchor-people; instead, it has cultivated the art of extreme seriousness. The emphasis is on 'positive' news, such as advances in agriculture or industry. This can seem excessively dull to an outsider, but the *Vremya* reporters usually manage to display great enthusiasm for their task. *Vremya*'s correspondent in Uzbekistan, Irismat Abdukhalikov, waxes rhapsodic about his unceasing reports on the production of grapes, cotton, grain or meat: 'As a journalist,' he says, 'I'm in the thick of events and I have direct contact with the immediate producers of all these items of our wealth, and you can't fail to be amazed, you can't fail to be thrilled by the industriousness of this people.' Soviet journalists make no apology for the fact that television news is strictly supervised by the state. 'Sometimes when I speak with Americans I say, you do it your way, we do it our way,' says *Vremya*'s editor. 'You want us to be like you, but we don't want you to be like us. That's it. The head of the TV and radio is himself a member of the government, so why should we try to be democratic, to be critical of the government? There are other ways to criticise shortcomings.' According to Gosteleradio, *Vremya*'s nightly newscast at 9 p.m. is watched by 228 million people.

April 1977: escaped train-robber Ronald Biggs, speaking by satellite from Brazil, appears on BBC news to plead for a royal pardon, saying that he's done nothing dishonest since his jailbreak in 1965.

Gosteleradio's Vice-President says that 'we are not pretending that we are independent from the Party or government. We are dependent. We are serving them and we are proud of them.' Hence the main purpose of the 'positive' news stories is to do a propaganda job for the government. Television news is exploited in the same way throughout Eastern Europe and much of the Third World.

April 1984: an American participant in the Geneva disarmament talks sits in a Washington studio, where he is questioned by journalists from several European countries by satellite link-up.

Nevertheless, the difference between 'censored' news in dictatorships and 'free' news in the Western democracies may not be as vast as we are sometimes led to believe. Certainly *Vremya* has never told the Soviet people what Russian troops are doing in Afghanistan, but there are many aspects of American foreign policy on which viewers in the United States are just as poorly informed, what with the cavortings of the celebrity newscasters and the determination to keep every news item as brief as possible. Even British television, which has traditionally provided one of the best (or least bad) news services in the world, has begun to succumb to the attractions of showbiz. In June 1984 the BBC announced that it was terminating its show *Sixty Minutes*, thus ending a twenty-five-year commitment to having some sort of current affairs programme in the early evening – a tradition which had begun with *Tonight*. One might think that the producers of television news would be able to steer a course between the official uninformative tedium of *Vremya* and the free-for-all, uninformative frolics of Happy Talk; yet for most of them the challenge seems to be impossibly difficult.

DALLAS POLICE DEPT.

6306

DRAMA

Soaps and Classics.

Several times a week, 400 Californians are invited to the Preview Theatre on Sunset Boulevard, Hollywood. Their job is an awesome one: they are to watch pilot programmes of next season's television shows. Each member of the audience has a little black box with a dial calibrated for five possible reactions – Very Good, Good, Fair, Dull and Very Dull.

Before they can begin their work, the viewers themselves have to be tested by watching an old *Mr Magoo* cartoon ('Mr Magoo goes skiing'). 'We use the Magoo as a control,' says David Castler, Director of the Preview Theatre, 'because having used that Magoo every time we've opened the doors of this theatre we know how every audience should respond, and by watching them respond up here [in the control room] we can determine if this is a typically responding audience.' Woe betide the viewers if they do not react as they should. 'We have had a couple of instances where the Magoo has indicated the audience is responding very atypically,' Castler says. 'We had a situation the night that John Kennedy was assassinated; we had a situation the night that Martin Luther King was assassinated. In both cases the Magoo reacted in a very atypical manner. Those evenings we just did not carry on with the test. We did the session but we didn't use any of the data.'

If the audience passes its Magoo test, it can settle down to give its verdict on the new dramas for the networks. Castler admits that there is always considerable nervousness in the control room: 'A lot of people have a lot resting on this. There are the creative people, the actors, the actresses, the producers, the network people – it gets very tense.' If the whole audience keeps its dials turned to 'Very Good' throughout the performance, the network will probably commission a whole series of the programme for the following season. If the audience gives an unequivocal thumbs-down, the show will probably never be seen again. What is more common, however, is for the networks to alter a show to take into account the audience's specific reactions. Castler has an electronic chart on his wall with a breakdown of the viewers in the theatre by age and gender. If the men in the audience turn their dials to 'Dull' whenever a particular female character appears on screen, she will be written out of the script.

By flicking their dials, these 400 people decide what millions of Americans will or will not see in their living rooms in a few months' time. Indeed, their responsibility is even greater than that, since American dramas are bought by dozens of countries around the world. If the 'typically responding' Californians lend their approval to a new police series, for instance, there is every chance that viewers from Manchester to Manila will be watching that series before too long.

It is a process which seems guaranteed to deaden the creative spirit of any talented author or producer, and the pro-

Dallas *is the epitome of modern television drama in the US and around the world.*

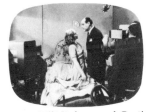

Lilli Palmer and Cecil Parker in Little Ladyship, *televised by the BBC from the Strand Theatre, 5 March 1939.*

Basil C. Langton (on floor) Oliver Burt and Ernest Milton in Rope, *televised from Alexandra Palace, 8 March 1939.*

(*Opposite*) *Sue Ellen (Linda Gray) looking appropriately like a convict: if simple nastiness were an offence, the rest of the* Dallas *cast would probably join her.*

ductions which emerge from it bear witness to this. 'I don't watch television drama,' says J. P. Miller, the veteran American scriptwriter. 'I can't stand it. It's too bad.' Miller is in a good position to notice the changes over the past thirty-five years, having started writing for television in the 1950s, a period which is now referred to in the United States as the Golden Age of television drama. It was a time of 'anthology series' such as *Philco Television Playhouse*, *Kraft Television Theater*, *Goodyear Television Playhouse*, *Studio One*, *US Steel Hour*, *Robert Montgomery Presents* and *Playhouse 90*, in which, week after week, the networks would broadcast original plays. There was an extraordinary flowering of talent. Many little-known actors and actresses in New York first attracted national attention by appearing in these dramas, including Rod Steiger, Joanne Woodward and Paul Newman. The anthology dramas also provided opportunities for directors (John Frankenheimer, Sidney Lumet, Arthur Penn) and playwrights (Paddy Chayefsky, Rod Serling, Reginald Rose, Gore Vidal). These directors and writers were given – in the early days, at least – an artistic freedom which is unknown in American television today. They flourished. Moreover, contrary to the myth which is sometimes put about today by network executives, these plays were popular. In December 1954, for instance, four of the top ten shows in the ratings were anthology dramas.

Considering that the plays were transmitted live, it is remarkable how many of them have endured in the memory without the benefit of continual repeats (although it is true that some were later made into movies). A brief selection of highlights from the mid-1950s would include Rod Serling's *Requiem for a Heavyweight* and *Patterns*, Reginald Rose's *Thunder on Sycamore Street* and *Twelve Angry Men*, Gore Vidal's *Visit to a Small Planet* and Paddy Chayefsky's *Marty*. Transmitted in 1953, *Marty* set the tone for many of the dramas that were to follow, with the naturalism of its setting in the Bronx and the street-talking realism of its dialogue; it dealt with the difficult love affair between a butcher (played by Rod Steiger) and a schoolteacher (Nancy Marchant). As Rod Steiger commented afterwards: 'People from all over the country and all different walks of life, from different races and religions and creeds, sent me letters. The immense power of that medium!'

Another memorable drama from the Golden Age was *Days of Wine and Roses* by J. P. Miller, whose account of the play's creation provides a good illustration of the informality of television in those days, unencumbered with Preview Theatres and the other paraphernalia with which the networks now equip themselves: 'I was walking down the street one day in New York and I bumped into Fred Coe [producer of *Playhouse 90* for NBC]. He said, "You're just the guy I want to see . . . I'm going to do three *Playhouse 90*s and I want you to do one of them." I said no way, forget it. I am not going to write anything for anybody for I don't know how long; I'm going to be a fisherman. He says, "Nonsense, listen, I want you to think about it . . . and if you change your mind, I want to do something really strong – alcohol, or whatever. You think of it but if you get an idea, call me – you've got the slot." I said, "Thanks a lot Fred, but forget it." And somehow the word alcohol stuck in my mind. That night I was lying in bed and I started thinking about my drunken uncle, everybody has a drunken uncle . . . And I thought of one particular scene in which he came home one Christmas Eve and tore up the

Rod Serling's Requiem For a Heavyweight, *one of the best known plays of the American 'golden age', starred Jack Palance, Keenan Wynn and Ed Wynn.*

Twelve Angry Men *by Reginald Rose, transmitted as a* Studio One *drama in 1954, later became a successful feature film.*

Christmas tree; we were all living together during the Depression. I had a thing about that, and somehow or other a story started coming to me.' There and then – at one in the morning – Miller telephoned Coe. 'I said I want to do a story about a love affair between two people who drink a lot. A nice young man and a nice young woman. When they drink a lot they fall in love, they have a lot of fun drinking, and slowly the bottle becomes more important to each than each is to the other. And the bottle that brought them together separates them. Fred says, "I love it. Write it."'

The fact that these plays were transmitted live gave them an extra tension. Most of the actors and actresses worked on Broadway rather than in Hollywood, since the TV studios were in New York, and they were therefore used to delivering their lines without the chance of a second take. Nevertheless, there was quite a difference between performing in front of a few hundred people in a theatre and acting for an audience of millions; even the most experienced performers were sometimes seen to vomit with fear just before transmission.

J. P. Miller's Days of Wine and Roses, *starring Cliff Robertson and Piper Laurie, was a* Playhouse 90 *production.*

When something did go wrong in live drama, the whole country knew about it. John Frankenheimer, who directed *Days of Wine and Roses*, tells an anecdote which encapsulates the risks inherent in this form of production. It was in the days when he was still ('thank goodness') an assistant director: 'We had Lee Marvin playing a private detective and the director decided that he would end on a shot of Lee Marvin and begin on a shot of Lee Marvin in a phone booth for the next scene. I pointed out to the director that this was highly impractical for the simple reason that Lee Marvin was already on the set – how was he going to get to the phone booth? Well, I was told to mind my own business . . . The director decided that he was going to save face and show me, this upstart, that he was able to do all this. "All right Lee," he said, "what you do here at the end of this scene is put your cigarette out in that ashtray and we'll pan down to the cigarette and you get out of the set and run over to the phone booth." Lee said, "Look, I can't make it," and the director said, "We'll fix it – we're going to put the phone booth on a dolly with wheels on it and we're going to put it right here next to the set; and you just get up from here, run into the phone booth and that's that." Well, it was great if you like shots of smouldering cigarettes in ashtrays, because we hung on it for about 15 to 20 seconds in the dress rehearsal and we got Lee into the phone booth. Now the director forgot a couple of things: he forgot about the adrenalin that happens on live television, and he forgot that the studio in which we were doing this show was at a slight angle and we were up at the top of it. Well, on the air we panned down to the ashtray. The cigarette was sizzling and Lee, because he was on the air, got this terrific burst of adrenalin and he hit that phone booth at about twenty miles an hour, whereupon the phone booth proceeded to go right across the studio very slowly. We were panning this phone booth across the studio past the cameras – we even panned past one actress who was completely naked, changing for her next scene – and of course you couldn't hear anything that Lee was saying because the boom was still where we left it. So he was talking a mile a minute and we were panning and it came to an end when the phone booth hit the wall at the end of the studio.'

It was the very unpredictability of live drama that was one of the causes of its downfall. The networks decided that drama ought to be recorded (a development made possible by the

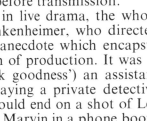

Paddy Chayefsky's Marty, *starring Nancy Marchant and Rod Steiger, was made for* Goodyear Television Playhouse *in 1953 and influenced a generation of television dramatists.*

The ultimate accolade for a soap opera: the Queen and Prince Philip visit Coronation Street *and chat to the fictional characters who are real to millions.*

Charlton Heston and Felicia Montealegre starred in the Studio One *production* Of Human Bondage.

arrival of videotape), after which 'a lot of things just didn't have the same spontaneity, the same urgency', according to Frankenheimer. But this was not the only reason for the end of the Golden Age. The change to recorded drama came about partly because of the expense of these live productions: sets, actors and producers had to be paid for, yet the result of their work could be seen only once – if it was repeated, the play had to be staged 'live' all over again. If drama was recorded, the networks could show it again as often as they wished and sell it to other television companies elsewhere in the world, thus receiving a better return on their investment. Moreover, the Golden Age unhappily coincided with Senator McCarthy's witch-hunts; both the sponsors and the networks began to feel uneasy about the social realism of so many of the dramas. Intimidated by the McCarthyites, whose publications *Red Channels* and *Counterattack* listed 'Communist infiltrators', networks and sponsors compiled their own black-lists of suspect writers, actors and producers. Some of the grandest talents of the Golden Age were forced out of the television business.

There was another reason for the demise of live drama, possibly the most important of all: the networks moved their production centre from Broadway to Hollywood, and the thoughtful honesty of such men as Chayefsky and Serling was replaced by the values of Tinseltown. The networks had been wooing the main film companies for some time, since they believed that Hollywood understood how to produce 'mass-audience programming'. At first, the film moguls had been unreceptive. 'Hollywood saw television as the enemy and was fearful of TV because it was killing off movie theatres and drawing off the movie audiences and replacing the movies as a mass entertainment medium,' says Les Brown, one of America's leading television historians. 'But around the mid-to late-1950s, Hollywood began to see its survival in television.'

The first network to establish a foothold on the West Coast was ABC, the youngest of the three, which had come into existence only because NBC had been ordered by the courts in 1943 to dispose of one of its two networks; it had sold the weaker of the two, the 'blue' network, which then became the American Broadcasting Company. For its first ten years ABC was always the most impoverished and the least imaginative of the three television networks. It also achieved the lowest ratings. In 1953, however, it persuaded Walt Disney to produce a weekly series called *Disneyland*, which swiftly went to the top of the ratings when it began the following year. It was a profitable venture for Disney, since ABC paid him handsomely and allowed him to plug his films on *Disneyland*. Other Hollywood studios realised that there was money to be made in the new medium. In 1955 Warner Brothers became the first of the major film companies to sign a deal with a network – ABC again.

Walt Disney broke ranks in Hollywood by signing a deal with ABC in 1953; other film studios soon followed Disney's example.

It was an impressive *volte-face*. Jack Warner, the head of the company, was so hostile to broadcasting that he would not even allow a television set to be included in a scene in any Warner Brothers movie. 'Nobody watched television in Warner pictures at that point, nobody,' says William Orr, the first TV producer at Warner Bros. 'But our business had been going down in the theatres, and eventually it was a matter of "If you can't beat 'em, join 'em". So we did. I was placed in charge one Friday afternoon – much to my surprise, because at that time you only went to television on the stop-over to

Devil's Island.' Jack Warner agreed to produce adventure dramas for ABC under the generic title *Warner Bros Presents*, consisting almost entirely of Westerns, such as the series *Cheyenne* and *Colt 45*. Before long, the old type of television drama – original single plays – had all but disappeared from American screens, never to return.

Warner Brothers' first television success was Cheyenne, *starring Clint Walker as frontier scout Cheyenne Bodie.*

This development was not confined to the United States. In any country with a powerful movie industry, when the film companies choose to work with television they change the form of TV drama utterly. The traditions of the theatre – a limited, enclosed set – are abandoned, to be replaced by the language of film. The emphasis of television drama is changed, to put it bluntly, from emotional action to physical action. Many people working in television had always feared that this would happen. The former head of BBC TV in Britain, Maurice Gorham, wrote in 1949: 'It seems to me a fortunate thing for television that Hollywood did not see its possibilities at the start and swamp it with second-rate pictures until a television set became no more than a home substitute for a flea-pit theatre showing half-forgotten films. Despite all its difficulties, television has at least had the chance to grow up in its own way.' His celebration was premature: television had hardly reached puberty when it was indeed 'swamped' by Hollywood and its values.

Japan, like America, enjoyed a brief Golden Age of television drama which was killed off by the TV stations' demands for programmes of action and adventure. It lasted from about 1958 to 1963, and its first and most famous production was *I Want To Be a Seashell*, directed by Yoshihiko Okamoto for the commercial channel TBS. Okamoto had some difficulty in finding anyone to write the script – 'many outstanding writers were still of the opinion that television was a very poor medium,' he says – but he eventually won the cooperation of a screenwriter called Hashimoto Shinobu. The hero of the story was to be a young Japanese man sitting in a condemned cell awaiting execution for having shot American prisoners of war on the order of his senior officers. Okamoto's original proposal was that the man should be 'an aged nationalistic engine driver of the Japanese National Railways, or a very radical young man who had just returned from the war. These people were the lowest ranks of labourers in Japan, but Mr Hashimoto chose that the hero should be a barber – somebody even more popular and typically Japanese.'

The last gasp of anthology drama was Playhouse 90*'s lavish two-part version of* For Whom The Bell Tolls *in 1959, starring Jason Robards and Maria Schell.*

The production was technically innovative, too. The first half-hour of the play, showing the barber's actions up to the moment of his arrest, was recorded on videotape; the next hour, in which the hero ruminated in his cell, was transmitted live. Before being taken to the gallows, the young barber told his family, 'I wish I were a seashell in the depths of the sea . . . a seashell can't be conscripted, knows nothing of war, needs not fear for his family's future.'

I Want To Be a Seashell was unusual in a number of ways. Its hero was a commoner; and it referred to the taboo subject of Japan's involvement in the Second World War. 'It brought back powerful recollections for everybody,' Okamoto says. 'The minute it finished, telephone calls came pouring in. What everybody was saying was that they recalled the hard times of war, the deaths of their fathers in the war, the fact that their fathers were also executed as B or C Class war criminals, and they said that they understood for the first time where responsibility for the war lay, for until then they had wondered

The cast of The Grove Family, *Britain's first TV soap opera, pictured in 1954. Front row (left to right): Mr Grove (Edward Evans), Grandma (Nancy Roberts), Mrs Grove (Ruth Dunning); back row: Daphne (Margaret Downs), Pat (Sheila Sweet), Jack (Peter Bryant) and Lennie (Christopher Beeny).*

why their own fathers should have had to be killed. Everyone spoke with great enthusiasm on the telephone, saying that they would never take part in any more wars.'

The other leading director of Japan's Golden Age was Katsumi Oyama, who, like Okamoto, worked at TBS. He, too, was determined to bring ordinary working-class Japanese characters into dramas. In 1962 he directed *Young Man*, which was set in a car factory. 'I wanted to depict very realistically the problems faced by Japan's young people at the time,' he says. 'It was the time of high economic growth, when the economy was beginning to flourish. Young people were coming from the provinces into factory work in large numbers. I wanted to depict the worries that those young people had, and the problems they were facing.' In the same year, he followed *Young Man* with *Bilbilili Sings*, a slightly surreal drama set in an office building where a baby was constantly crying. 'It's rather similar to the situation with *Young Man*,' Oyama says. 'In the 1960s people collected in towns at a very rapid pace . . . The office block was a sort of symbol of this phenomenon.'

Yoshiko Sakuma and Toshiyuki Nishida in Onna Taikoki, *an NHK drama which won a large female audience by emphasising women's roles.*

The single play in America was snuffed out by a combination of political pressure from McCarthy's supporters and the economic imperatives of networks seeking a mass audience; Japan's Golden Age came to an end for very similar reasons. Okamoto says that in the early 1960s many programmes were stopped as a result of political pressure: 'After *Seashell* I made a drama called *ABCDEFG* . . . in which the post-war Japanese Liberal Party – the conservative party – appropriated money for political funds from private financial institutions. There was a certain amount of political intervention. *Seppuku*, by Hashimoto Shinobu, had been suppressed and had never seen the light of day at all. An anti-war programme called *Only Child*, which I produced at RKB Mainichi broadcasting station in Kyushu, was also suppressed.' Okamoto eventually felt obliged to resign. 'I am a person who is only interested in dramatising social problems – the sort of problems people are facing. That's how I first got into drama,' he says, but in the early 1960s 'it gradually became impossible to produce what I really wanted to produce.'

Katsumi Oyama believes that the main reason for the death of the Golden Age was the obsession with ratings: 'Everything is measured in numbers. Rather than the content of a programme, it is evaluated in terms of how many people watched it.' Although he agrees that the decline of serious drama is 'a pity', he thinks there have been compensations: 'There is some merit in the fact that – since everything is measured in terms of audience ratings – there has been a popularisation of drama; it has become possible for drama to be watched by large numbers of people   drama with a high entertainment content.'

Natalya Fatayeva in The Black Cat, *a Soviet television series of the early 1980s.*

The one place where television plays were not abandoned in the 1960s was Europe. Soviet television to this day continues to devote much time to serious drama, although most of this takes the form of outside broadcasts from theatres. The amount of drama specially written for television is small.

The country which, more than any other, has continued to nurture original drama is Britain. Until 1952, when Michael Barry became head of drama at the BBC, television in Britain had been dependent on classic stage plays. Barry spent his entire first year's budget for commissioning new scripts – £250 – on one man, a young short-story writer called Nigel Kneale. Within a year he had written *The Quatermass*

Experiment, a six-part serial about a three-man spaceship which returns to earth, whereupon one of the crew turns into a vegetable monster and starts destroying London. It was stunningly produced by Rudolph Cartier, although many of the special effects which so terrified the viewers were achieved with little more than string and sealing wax. 'We had a photo cut-out of Westminster Abbey seen from below the arches,' Cartier recalls, 'and Nigel Kneale, the author himself, had a glove with some vegetables on the fingers, and he made the Thing descend on it. On the television screen everything looked all right, of course, but nothing to compare with now – today it would be the real Westminster Abbey and a real monster.' The serial was such a success – Cartier thinks the viewers were hungry for something more modern than Dickens – that it was followed by two more six-parters, *Quatermass II* (1955) and *Quatermass and the Pit* (1958).

The imposing visage of Big Brother from the BBC's live production of Orwell's Nineteen Eighty-Four, *transmitted in December 1954.*

Emboldened by the first *Quatermass*, Kneale and Cartier began work on an even more ambitious project – a television adaptation of George Orwell's *1984*. The budget was high by the standards of the time, but Cartier still found it restricting: 'All the production – two hours – including copyrights, artists, sets and costumes was limited to £3,000. I was supposed to use discs for the music, and I said one can't do it . . . somebody must write some good music.' Cartier commissioned John Hodgkis to compose and conduct a score, at a cost of £300. 'This £300 was not in the budget – I had endless fights with the financial bosses to get live music to accompany *1984*.'

October 1955: Quatermass II, *sequel to* The Quatermass Experiment, *starred (left to right) Monica Grey as Paula, Hugh Griffith as Dr Pugh and John Robinson as Quatermass.*

The play was first transmitted at 8.30 on Sunday 12 December 1954. Within minutes, the BBC's telephones started ringing: 'There were hundreds, perhaps a thousand phone calls to the BBC,' Cartier recalls. 'Half of them said it was horrible – why have a horror movie on a Sunday night?' Over the next couple of days four motions were tabled in the House of Commons by Conservative MPs who accused the BBC of unnecessarily frightening the audience. The furore died down when Prince Philip came to the defence of the Corporation in a speech at the Royal Society of Arts. 'The Queen and I watched the play and thoroughly enjoyed it,' he was reported to have said. When it was repeated on Thursday 16 December – 'live' again, of course – it attracted the biggest television audience since Queen Elizabeth II's coronation.

Two scenes from Nineteen Eighty-Four: *(top) Peter Cushing as Winston Smith, Yvonne Mitchell as Julia; (below) Keith Davis, Hilda Fenemore and Pamela Grant as the repellent Parsons family.*

The fuss caused by *1984* was understandable, for Cartier's production was breathtakingly powerful. When a telerecording of it was shown at the National Film Theatre in London many years later – in 1984 itself, in fact – the drama did not look dated at all. Cartier was helped by the calibre of the performers, notably Peter Cushing as Winston Smith and Yvonne Mitchell as Julia, but he also managed to avoid the jerkiness of scene changes which sometimes marred live drama; in between live scenes he subtly interspersed filmed segments. He says that '*1984* was particularly difficult because it had so many sets – twenty-eight sets – and five or six film sequences which couldn't be shown in the studio. So we arranged that the film sequence would come between the main sequences to give us time to move the artists from one set to another; and as we were doing this we also had to move the cameras.'

Cartier does not regret the passing of live drama, 'because it was a considerable strain on the artists and the producer and on the whole studio to know that it goes out the moment it's done; but it gave a particular little bit extra to the quality of the acting because the actors, knowing that it cannot be

(*Following pages*) The Prisoner, *starring Patrick McGoohan, was arguably the most enigmatic series ever transmitted, but it won a devoted following; to this day, the show's fan club meets regularly.*

A discussion between two designers, Jack Kine and Tom Taylor, who worked on special effects for Quatermass II.

repeated, gave their best.' Certainly this is evident from the performances in both *Quatermass* and *1984*. Imaginative though they were, however, these productions – one a science fiction story, the other a vision of the future – did not deal with everyday concerns and ordinary people. They were far removed from the kind of social realism which was then at its zenith in the United States – what Paddy Chayefsky once described as 'the marvellous world of the ordinary'.

Fittingly enough, that kind of drama was brought to Britain by someone from across the Atlantic, albeit a Canadian rather than an American. In 1958 ABC, one of the new commercial companies which made up the ITV network, appointed Sydney Newman to run its *Armchair Theatre*. Newman was a former head of drama at the Canadian Broadcasting Corporation who had also worked for NBC in America. He believed that television plays in Britain ought to reflect the nation's social changes. His productions for *Armchair Theatre* 'were going to be about the very people who owned TV sets – which is the working class'. *Armchair Theatre* was transmitted on Sundays – in direct competition with the BBC's traditional Sunday night play – and the contrast between the two soon became apparent. The BBC's plays were, for the most part, 'safe' and conventional, while ABC was using some of Britain's most promising young directors – Philip Saville, Wilfred Eades, Ted Kotcheff – on plays by writers such as Harold Pinter and Alun Owen, who addressed themselves to 'the marvellous world of the ordinary' with the same lack of condescension which had marked the American Golden Age. They also proved that serious drama could attract a mass audience: between the autumn of 1959 and the summer of 1960, for instance, *Armchair Theatre* was among the top ten programmes in the ratings for thirty-two weeks out of thirty-seven.

A veteran American producer, Franklin Schaffner, once pointed to 'the essential difference between the East Coast and West Coast writer. An East Coast writer comes in, sits down, and says, "I've got an idea." Then he tells you his story. A West Coast writer comes in, sits down, and says, "What do you want me to write?" ' Schaffner used the comparison to demonstrate the difference between the Hollywood attitude to television drama, which eventually triumphed, and the freedom given to scriptwriters in New York during the Golden Age. As we have seen, this freedom enabled them to produce several small masterpieces, such as J. P. Miller's *Days of Wine and Roses*. When Sydney Newman came to London, he treated his writers in much the same way. He first approached Alun Owen, for example, after admiring a play of his at the Lyric Theatre, Hammersmith.

Alun Owen's No Trams to Lime Street, *an* Armchair Theatre *presentation in 1959, starred Jack Hedley and Billie Whitelaw; both Whitelaw and Owen subsequently won awards from the Guild of TV Producers and Directors.*

'He got in touch with my agent and asked if he could come along to see me,' Owen recalls. 'He said, "I saw your play, Owen, very good – why don't you write for television? If Shakespeare was alive today, Owen, that's what he'd be writing for." So I said, "Yes, fine," and he said, "Well, what would you like to write?" Sydney was talking about the changing face of Britain at this time – that was the sort of thematic line of his series – and so I said, "Well, things are changing all the time. I mean, when I go back to Liverpool, it's changed: the overhead railway's gone and there are no trams to Lime Street." He said, "You've got your title." ' And so it was that Alun Owen wrote his first television play, the evocative *No Trams to Lime Street*. It was about three sailors who go back to Liverpool for a night on the town and discover, in Owen's words, that 'things were in a state of flux. The trams had gone, the buses had come, the cobblestones were being ripped up and people's attitudes were being ripped up and ripped off and changed.'

It was significant that both Sydney Newman, the producer, and Ted Kotcheff, the director of Owen's plays, were Canadians. They were therefore baffled by the English tradition of using, say, middle-class actors from the south of England to play the parts of working-class characters from the north. The tradition was being challenged in the cinema at roughly the same time by films such as *Room at the Top* and *Saturday Night and Sunday Morning*, which were unequivocally working-class. In television, it was *Armchair Theatre* that broke the convention. Alun Owen recalls that the casting director for *No Trams to Lime Street* had lined up a number of Irish actors to play the parts of Liverpudlians, 'and Ted Kotcheff said, "They don't sound very Scouse to me," and she said, "Ah, well, no, you couldn't possibly play love scenes with a Scouse accent," to which I said, "How do you think all those bloody babies get born?" . . . Because Ted had no preconceived British attitudes we were able actually to do something. Neither Ted nor Sydney had this sort of inhibition about class and accent.'

Alun Owen was also responsible for another of *Armchair Theatre*'s best-remembered productions, *Lena O My Lena*, in which Billie Whitelaw gave a stunning performance as a straight-talking female factory worker falling in love with a young student who comes to work in the factory. Once again, Owen had to contend with middle-class prejudices about what working-class people should look like, images formed by countless plays and films in which working-class men all wore mufflers and caps. 'I remember having an argument when this wardrobe mistress came up and said, "Could I have the cast for a moment to get the mufflers and caps?" – literally! "My life!" I said, "haven't you heard about Burton's? We dress differently nowadays" – but then she was in a different world from us.'

The other commercial stations tended to prefer transferring stage plays to the screen rather than commissioning original drama. Even so, their choice of plays was much more enterprising than that of the BBC. Granada, for instance, transmitted John Osborne's *Look Back in Anger* (which the BBC had decided was 'not suitable for a television audience'), Harold Pinter's *The Room*, and two plays by Arthur Miller, *Death of a Salesman* and *All My Sons*. But it was *Armchair Theatre* that most irritated the BBC.

Hugh Greene, the BBC's Director-General, solved the problem adroitly in December 1962 by simply 'poaching' Sydney Newman from ABC and effectively inviting him to continue *Armchair Theatre* under another name, *The Wednesday Play*. 'What I felt,' Greene says, 'was that people had to be shown the unpleasant side of life. One must get away from the middle-class "Who's for tennis?" type of drawing-room drama to show the problems of poverty, lack of housing and what have you. And one could only bring about change, and change in people's minds, by shocking them, by showing them things that they didn't necessarily like to see but ought to know about.'

Shaun Sutton, who worked at the BBC, wrote later that Newman 'burst into the BBC Television Centre like a hurricane. Timing his entrance when television incomes were rocketing and the money flowing, he at once created a drama

The first Wednesday Play *was* Alice *by Dennis Potter, based on the Lewis Carroll stories; later productions were more realistic.*

(Following pages) August 1963: the cast of Z-Cars *in a read-through of their scripts.*

group out of a drama department, splitting the output into Plays, Series and Serials . . . Most important of all, by his creation of a separate Plays Department, he underlined the importance of the single play.'

For the rest of the decade, the BBC produced a succession of original plays which were memorable and often shocking. Two of the most famous were Nell Dunn's *Up the Junction*, a brutally honest account of life in South London, and Jeremy Sandford's *Cathy Come Home*, in which a young woman loses both her home and her family. The scenes in which Cathy's caravan burns down, and her children are taken away from her, were all the more harrowing because they were filmed in the style of a documentary. Ken Loach, who directed both plays, says that they were 'a reaction against studio-based television and drama'. The increased sensitivity of 16mm film and the greater mobility of cameras made this kind of location filming possible.

Up The Junction, *Nell Dunn's down-to-earth picture of South London, starring Vickery Turner and Tony Selby.*

Original television plays have continued to be produced ever since, but in the past fifteen years they have been fewer, as many writers have broadened their horizons beyond the 'single play' and the broadcasting organisations seem to have lost their initial enthusiasm. Nevertheless, a number of high-quality dramas were seen in the 1970s and early 1980s. In 1978 the BBC screened Dennis Potter's six-part drama *Pennies From Heaven* about a travelling sheet-music salesman of the 1930s who is unfaithful to his wife and is later charged with murder. At frequent intervals during the action, characters would suddenly break into song, miming to old melodies of the period. It was an audacious device, but it worked. An equally improbable idea was used to great effect in Potter's play *Blue Remembered Hills* (1979), about a group of children playing and fighting together on a summer's day in 1943: the parts of the seven-year-old children were all played by adult actors.

Janine Duvitski and Helen Mirren played the parts of children in Dennis Potter's Blue Remembered Hills *(1979).*

It was also in the 1970s that Mike Leigh produced his 'improvised' dramas (*Nuts in May*, *Abigail's Party*, *Who's Who*) which were not scripted but 'evolved' by a collaboration between the director and the cast. 'Political' plays were still shown, too, in which writers such as David Edgar and Trevor Griffiths provided a socialist analysis of the Right in Britain while working within the conventional forms of televised drama. In his series *Bill Brand*, Griffiths also examined the conflicting pressures – public and private – on a young Labour politician.

In Mike Leigh's Nuts in May *(1976), Alison Steadman as Candice-Marie and Roger Sloman as Keith inflicted their songs on fellow-camper Ray (Anthony O'Donnell).*

Nevertheless, after the excitement of the 1960s, the 1970s seemed to be 'the censorship decade', according to Kenith Trodd, producer of many dramas for both the BBC and ITV. One example was the BBC's banning of Trodd's production of *Brimstone and Treacle*, a Dennis Potter play about a disturbed girl and the devil. 'It was notorious for two reasons, I think,' Trodd says. 'One, that it was killed after the thing was completely made, and also that it was the work of Dennis Potter, who remains probably the most celebrated, the most talented and the best known of television dramatists.' Other plays to be banned included Roy Minton's *Scum*, which gave a violent picture of life in a borstal, and Ian McEwan's *Solid Geometry*, in which the opening scene showed a penis pickled in a jar.

These acts of censorship may have been occasioned by simple prudery, but they were indicative of the broadcasting authorities' periodic nervousness about social and political controversy in televised drama. The people who actually

(Opposite) Cathy Come Home, *broadcast in November 1966, brought about the creation of the housing charity, Shelter; it featured (left to right) Sean King as Sean, Ray Brooks as Reg, Stephen King as Stephen and Carol White as Cathy.*

Bob Hoskins and Cheryl Campbell starred in Dennis Potter's Pennies From Heaven *(1978), which was later made into a Hollywood movie.*

Patricia Hayes played the title role in Jeremy Sandford's Edna The Inebriate Woman, *transmitted in October 1971.*

Glenda Jackson, haughtily regal as Elizabeth R *(1971).*

Andre van Gyseghem played Judge Robert Quigley in Law and Order *(1978), G. F. Newman's controversial series about crooks, cops, briefs and screws.*

(Opposite) Leonard Nimoy as Mr Spock in Star Trek *...'to boldly go where no man has gone before'... but NBC executives were only bold enough to make a mere seventy-eight episodes, never realising its potential. At the last count* Star Trek *is seen on one hundred and forty stations in the USA, and in forty-seven other countries world-wide.*

write and produce these dramas deny that they are particularly influential, although there have been one or two famous instances of the power of television plays: Shelter, the pressure group for the homeless, was founded as a result of *Cathy Come Home*. Kenith Trodd admits that 'there was a period when I and some of the people I was working with, including writers like Jim Allen and directors like Ken Loach, did actually believe that if you had a play on a Tuesday night which was about the strike in the Liverpool docks, on Wednesday morning every port – not just Liverpool port – could be idle.' Today he thinks that that belief was an 'extremely romantic delusion'. His opinion now is that television drama can influence individuals in the way they lead their lives, but not society as a whole. He gives a rather alarming illustration: 'When *Pennies From Heaven* was on the air I was just astonished at the number of people who, often quite aggressively, would accuse me or Dennis Potter of changing their lives. I remember somebody came into a party and said, "You're the man who ended my affair." I said, "Well, I don't think we've actually met until now," but what she meant was that her boyfriend had been so traumatised identifying with Arthur Parker in *Pennies From Heaven* that he'd walked out and left her.'

What seems to trouble television companies and many viewers, however, is not influence such as this but the allegedly misleading influence of the 'drama-documentary' (also known as drama-doc, docu-drama and faction), a form in which a dramatic production is used to convey a vivid sense of reality. The makers of such programmes are often accused of 'blurring the line between truth and fiction' and thereby confusing the viewer. The accusation is a selective one. No one described Shakespeare's *Richard III* as a 'drama-doc' when he was writing it, even though it contains recognisable historical characters. Nor has the tag of drama-doc ever been applied to many television productions which have been based on genuine people or events – *Edward VII*, *Edward and Mrs Simpson*, *The Six Wives of Henry VIII*, *Nancy Astor* or *Elizabeth R*.

Why the fuss, then? Charges of 'blurring the line' between fact and fiction seem to be made mostly against those dramas which are thought to be subversive in one way or another. In 1975, for instance, controversy erupted when the BBC screened *Days of Hope*, a four-part drama about working-class politics between the Great War and the General Strike in 1926. The scriptwriter, Jim Allen, said shortly afterwards that 'it appears that whenever we make a film where working men are articulate and intelligent, and where you show them at work up to their necks in clay or down the pit like moles, it's no longer art. But if you make a film about Sandhurst or a public school, you can generate as much documentary realism as you like.'

There were more right-wing protests in 1978 after the showing of G. F. Newman's *Law and Order*, a four-part drama which portrayed policemen on the take, bent lawyers and brutal prison officers. The Prison Officers' Association banned the BBC from filming inside its jails for a year after the programme went out. Yet all the characters in *Law and Order* were fictional.

What causes trouble, then, is drama which exploits documentary techniques to achieve a realistic tone, even if all the incidents and people in it are fictitious. Ken Loach admits that with *Cathy Come Home* he was trying to capture the style

Two of many 'historical' costume dramas: (top) The Six Wives of Henry VIII *(1970), with Keith Michell as Henry and Rosalie Crutchley as Catherine Parr; (below)* Edward VII *(1975), with Timothy West in the title role and Annette Crosbie as his mother, Queen Victoria.*

of a *World in Action* programme. On the other hand, there have seldom been complaints about straightforward dramatic reconstructions of historical events. While dramatists have tried to ape the techniques of current affairs documentaries, journalists in television have been borrowing some of the traditions of drama to tell stories for which traditional *World in Action* methods would be inadequate. In Britain, Granada Television has pioneered this form. Its products have included *The Man Who Wouldn't Keep Quiet* (1970), based on the diaries of the Soviet dissident Grigorenko; *A Subject of Struggle* (1972), a dramatisation of the Red Guard trials during the Cultural Revolution; *Three Days in Szczecin* (1976), a reconstruction of the Polish shipyard strike; *Invasion* (1980), which dealt with the crushing of the Prague Spring in 1968; and *Strike* (1981), a dramatised account of the Gdansk strike of the previous year which had given birth to Solidarity. A booklet published by Granada in 1980 restated the 'Woodhead Doctrine' for these drama-docs (named after Leslie Woodhead, who had produced most of them): 'The aim of a dramatised documentary is to re-create as accurately as possible history as it happened. No invented characters, no invented names, no dramatic devices owing more to the writer's (or director's) creative imagination than to the implacable record of what actually happened. For us, the dramatised documentary is an exercise in journalism, not dramatic art.'

But even 'exercises in journalism' can fall foul of the authorities. In April 1980 ITV screened Antony Thomas's film *Death of a Princess*, a dramatised version not only of the execution of a Saudi Arabian princess for adultery but also of Thomas's own trawl through the rumours surrounding the story; the character of Thomas appeared in the programme, played by an actor like everyone else. What caused the trouble, however, was not just Thomas's interesting embellishment to the drama-doc technique but his implicit criticism of the Saudi Arabian moral code. It was reported that Britain lost £200 million worth of business with Saudi Arabia as a consequence of the film, and the Foreign Secretary, Lord Carrington, was sent scurrying off to the desert to make amends. He described *Death of a Princess* as a 'bad film' in which 'some incidents were clearly based on innuendo and rumour. The new formula of mixing fact with fiction, dramatisation masquerading as documentary, can be dangerous and misleading.'

Antony Thomas's Death of a Princess *caused such a rupture between Britain and Saudi Arabia that the Foreign Secretary, Lord Carrington, had to apologise personally to the Saudi leaders.*

The United States has also produced some highly successful 'faction', but little of this has aroused the kind of controversy generated by *Death of a Princess*. One exception was *The Day After*, ABC's $7 million drama about the effects of a nuclear attack on an American town, which was transmitted in November 1983. It was denounced by right-wingers for being anti-nuclear propaganda, but what was slightly lost in all the arguments about the film's politics was the fact that its dramatic qualities were almost non-existent. As *Time* magazine commented: 'Political immediacy is just about all *The Day After* has going for it. By any standards other than social, it is a terrible movie.'

Roots *followed Alex Haley's family through the generations: (above) the new-born Kunta Kinte is held by Cicely Tyson; (below) young Kunta Kinte, played by Levar Burton (centre), is sold into slavery.*

Most American 'factions' have avoided political controversy by stressing that their chief intention is to provide a gripping drama rather than an exercise in journalism. This was certainly true of *Roots*, Alex Haley's factually-dubious story of his search for his forebears in Africa, or *Washington Behind Closed Doors*, a thinly-veiled picture of life inside

CBS's Helter Skelter *was a dramatised account of the gruesome activities of Charles Manson's 'clan'.*

Nixon's White House, with Jason Robards playing a doomed President. Another case in point was CBS's *Helter Skelter*, a two-part dramatisation of the story of the Charles Manson clan and their murder of Sharon Tate. It was written, surprisingly enough, by J. P. Miller, the author of *Days of Wine and Roses*. He is in no doubt about where he stands in the debate on docu-drama and faction: 'There is no such thing as docu-drama . . . It's either a documentary, and it's true, or it's a drama, and it's not true. When you say docu-drama, you're saying it's a documentary that's been dramatised; that's just drama . . . What they call a docu-drama is really a historical drama. It's the dramatisation of actual events. But I don't care how true the scene is, the minute you put an actor in there saying those lines that Charlie Manson said, it's no longer a documentary, it's a drama, because it's a different person, different inflection. I wrote the words, Charlie Manson didn't really say them . . . What you have to do is give the impression that it's real – but you have to do that with all dramas, don't you?'

Not necessarily. As T. S. Eliot wrote, human kind cannot bear very much reality. It was the verisimilitude of plays such as *Days of Wine and Roses* which helped to speed the demise of the Golden Age. Serious drama may have won awards and praise from the critics, but sponsors and network executives long ago decided that what the public wanted was not social realism but entertaining escapism. And the public got it, in an unbroken line of descent from *Cheyenne* to *Dynasty*. The history of popular drama on television may not be as intellectually edifying as the history of original plays by Pinter or Chayefsky, but it is probably more important to the cultural role of the medium.

It began with the Western, right from the day when Warner Brothers became the first major studio to sign a production agreement with an American network. The choice of genre was partly influenced by the fact that it was popular with cinema audiences and there was every reason to suppose that it would be equally appealing to the viewers at home. But there were other factors as well. Westerns were safely uncontentious; they were also likely to be highly profitable for the film company, since it could smuggle plenty of standard Western footage from its old movies into the supposedly 'made-for-TV' series. 'Warner had made myriads of Westerns, and so when we would do *Cheyenne* we would cleverly integrate a lot of stock film from our own company,' William Orr explains. 'We'd get a couple of cattle and have Cheyenne ride in the back lot and shoot up over a cattle's horn; then we'd go back to the stock film. He looked like he had 10,000 head of cattle with him all the time.'

The first series of *Warner Bros Presents* for ABC, in 1955–6, consisted of three different dramas used in rotation – *King's Row*, *Casablanca* and *Cheyenne*. But *Cheyenne* proved so popular that the other two were soon phased out. It starred the previously unknown Clint Walker playing the part of frontier scout Cheyenne Bodie. William Orr describes how the new star was born: 'Norman Walker came over and filled the room. He was 6 foot 5 inches and about 240 pounds at the time. We were making tests for *Cheyenne* and we'd elected to go with new people, make our own star. So we tested Norman at the time – I'll call him Clint from now on, since we named him Clint – and Clint being massive and a quiet man to start with, he was not a flamboyant personality . . . So we had him play it fairly monosyllabic and he became

Cheyenne's success inspired film companies to produce dozens of other Westerns for television, often using up 'stock film' of cattle, horses and cactus-strewn locations.

Wagon Train *(top) featured Robert Horton and Ward Bond;* Sugarfoot *(below) starred Will Hutchins and Tom 'Sugarfoot' Brewster.*

(Following pages) Before its transmission, The Day After *attracted attention for its 'controversial' theme of nuclear destruction; after transmission, most comment was devoted to pointing out what a poor drama it was.*

the kind of typical Western hero who does the right thing all the time, wears the white hat.' Orr adds that 'most of our shows in those days had the old-fashioned morality play going for them because that's what was happening in films in those days due to censorship'. The black-and-white morality of the Western was perfectly in keeping with the atmosphere of the time, with a Cold War internationally and a search for enemies of the state at home. Clint Walker thus became the prototype for dozens of stoic gunslingers who did what a man had to do on American television screens over the next few years, rewarding virtue and punishing evil. Other film companies were quick to follow Warner's example by going into the mass-production business for television, among them Twentieth Century Fox, MGM and Columbia.

The barrage of Westerns during the second half of the 1950s and the early 1960s was unstoppable – *Maverick, Colt 45, Wyatt Earp, Gunsmoke, Sugarfoot, Lawman, Frontier, Wagon Train, Tales of Wells Fargo, Adventures of Jim Bowie, Wanted – Dead or Alive, Have Gun – Will Travel, Rawhide, Bonanza, The Virginian, The High Chapparal, Laramie*, and so on and on. By the end of the 1950s a dedicated television viewer would have been able to watch more than thirty Western series in prime time *every week*. A CBS executive once suggested that the only thing which differentiated most of these shows from one another was the size of the gun: Steve McQueen, in *Wanted – Dead or Alive*, had a sawn-off shotgun; Chuck Connors, in *The Rifleman*, had (as you might expect) a rifle; Richard Boone, who played the freelance troubleshooter in *Have Gun – Will Travel*, had a revolver in a holster with a chess knight on top of it. Steve McQueen was not the only future star to appear in these Westerns. In *Maverick*, James Garner – who starred in *The Rockford Files* many years later – played the part of Bret Maverick, an inveterate gambler. The young Clint Eastwood appeared in *Rawhide* as Rowdy Yates, a Texas rancher. In the first years of *Gunsmoke*, Dennis Weaver – who later became better known for *McCloud* – took the part of Chester, deputy to Marshal Matt Dillon of Dodge City (who was played by James Arness). Lorne Greene achieved enormous fame through his portrayal of Ben Cartwright, the rock-solid head of the family in *Bonanza*, assisted in his tasks at the Ponderosa Ranch by his even more heavyweight son, Hoss (Dan Blocker). Although the Westerns were good at producing their own stars, however, they were not so successful when used as vehicles for existing stars. Henry Fonda appeared as Marshal Simon Fry in *The Deputy*, which was taken off after two years.

Many of the series were of impressive longevity. *Rawhide* ran for seven years, *Cheyenne* for eight and *The Virginian* for nine. The undisputed champions were *Bonanza*, which notched up fourteen years with NBC, and *Gunsmoke*, which was transmitted by CBS for an incredible twenty years, between 1955 and 1975.

Since these series were on film, rather than 'live', they could be sold abroad. Thus began America's long colonisation of the world's television screens. The foreign earnings from these sales represented pure profit to the film companies, who could therefore afford to charge ridiculously low prices – as little as $1,000 for a one-hour episode. In countries such as Canada and Australia, indigenous programmes all but disappeared from view: why bother to spend large sums of money on a home-produced drama when an American telefilm could be had for a tenth of the cost? In Third World

Steve McQueen (top) and Clint Eastwood (middle) were almost unknown when they started appearing in, respectively, Wanted – Dead or Alive *and* Rawhide*; Henry Fonda was already an established Hollywood star when he was given the part of Marshall Simon Fry in* The Deputy *(below).*

countries which had introduced television, it was the same story. 'The content of our programmes at that time was overloaded in favour of foreign programming,' says Chief Segun Olusola, a former head of Nigerian Television. He adds, with some understatement: 'Not all of the *Bonanzas* and *Wagon Trains* of that period were particularly good and balanced in favour of black people, in favour of the Third World. This was the time when it was the fashion to beat down all black people – Indians will always lose, that kind of thing.' Another worry was that many Africans apparently believed that the Westerns were accurate representations of life in modern America, complete with rearing horses and stetson-clad sheriffs. 'What they saw on television, they held to be almost the truth,' says Chief Olusola. 'That was unfortunate.'

When the appetite for Westerns started to diminish, in the 1960s, the networks and film companies had a simple solution: they increased production of that even more enduring cornerstone of popular television drama – the crime series. In the 1960s and 1970s crime drama achieved the same kind of dominance which had been enjoyed by Westerns in the late 1950s, but even in the earliest years of American television it had been a regular feature on the schedules. The first episodic series of this sort was *Man Against Crime*, begun by CBS in 1949, which starred Ralph Bellamy as special investigator Mike Barnett. Writers on the series were instructed that 'somebody must be murdered, preferably early, with the threat of more violence to come'. Bellamy himself 'must be menaced early and often'.

For the first three years of its existence, *Man Against Crime* was transmitted live from CBS's studios at Grand Central Station in New York. To ensure that the programme ran to time, writers were instructed to include a 'search scene' near the end of each episode, in which Bellamy would hunt for a crucial clue. His search could be shortened or extended almost indefinitely when the show was on the air, so that it always finished punctually.

In 1952 *Man Against Crime* abandoned live production; episodes were filmed in advance instead. This may have been caused by the appearance of a rival action drama, *Dragnet*, which had been on film since its inception in December 1951 on NBC. *Dragnet* was created by Jack Webb, who also starred in the show as Detective Sergeant Joe Friday of the Los Angeles Police Department (the series was supposed to be based on the Department's actual case histories). Friday was not a character who wasted his words. 'My name's Friday – I'm a cop' was his usual way of introducing himself. One of his regular catchphrases was a plea for 'just the facts, ma'am'. *Dragnet* was immensely popular, running for 300 episodes between 1951 and 1958 and another 98 when it was revived in 1967. It was also the first American drama series to be sold to British television.

Film companies were not yet cooperating with television when *Dragnet* began, but the Hollywood settings were a foretaste of what was to come when agreement was reached with the networks three years later. By 1957 film studios were churning out crime series with almost as much enthusiasm as they were devoting to Westerns. The two genres were not all that dissimilar: both presented a simple, Manichean view of the world, whether it was divided into cops and crooks or cowboys and Indians. Out they poured – *Racket Squad*, *Official Detective*, *Suspicion*, *M Squad* and countless others. Even Broderick Crawford, who played a traffic policeman in

Dragnet *starred Jack Webb as Det. Sgt Joe Friday (left) with Ben Alexander as Officer Smith.*

(*Following page*) Brideshead Revisited, *successful on both sides of the Atlantic, made stars of Anthony Andrews and Jeremy Irons as well as starting a craze for teddy bears.* Boys From the Blackstuff *starred Bernard Hill as Yosser Hughes, whose plea 'Gissa job' became a national catchphrase of the unemployed.*

Highway Patrol, managed to fit in plenty of crime-fighting between his admonishments about road safety and his introduction to the jargon of police radio ('Ten Four – and out'). *Naked City* was filmed in the streets of New York, and included ordinary passers-by as extras.

Over the next twenty-five years, producers of crime series tried just about every conceivable variation on a rather limited theme. The hero had to be given some quirk which would distinguish him from the heroes of every other action drama. There were blind investigators (*Longstreet*), overweight investigators (*Cannon*), scruffy, working-class investigators (*Columbo*), suave millionaire investigators (Amos Burke in *Burke's Law*), bald investigators who sucked lollipops and said 'Who loves ya, baby?' (*Kojak*), one female investigator (*Police Woman*), a pair of female investigators (*Cagney and Lacey*), three female investigators (*Charlie's Angels*), an ex-criminal turned investigator (*The Rockford Files*), a Vietnam veteran turned investigator (*Magnum PI*), a cowboy on assignment as an investigator in New York (*McCloud*), investigators in an exotic setting (*Hawaii Five-O*), buddy-buddy investigators (*Starsky and Hutch*) – the list could be extended indefinitely. In 1967 NBC introduced an investigator confined to a wheelchair, in *Ironside*. No gay investigators have turned up yet, but they will.

The hero of a crime drama did not have to be a police officer or a private detective. He could be a lawyer, as Raymond Burr demonstrated in *Perry Mason*, a courtroom drama which ran for eight years from 1957, in which Perry Mason invariably got the better of District Attorney Hamilton Burger. There was also a number of medical dramas which attracted high ratings; as network executives cheerfully explain, the dramatic potential of doctors is almost as great as that of the police, since they are constantly involved in life-or-death crises.

One distinctly above-average series in which lawyers were the heroes was *The Defenders*, which was created for CBS in 1961 by Reginald Rose (author of *Twelve Angry Men*). It featured a father-and-son team of attorneys, played by E. G. Marshall and Robert Reed, who took up important but delicate issues such as abortion, black-listing and capital punishment. Herbert Brodkin, who produced the series, says that his intention was 'to do an entertaining series about the reality of life in New York from the real point of view . . . I think we were able to tackle some difficult subjects and do them quite well. We had marvellous writers, we had marvellous directors and we had New York actors. And we didn't have anyone to tell us that what we were doing was incorrect or wrong.' It lasted for 132 episodes, ending in 1965. '*The Defenders* almost changed the face of television,' Brodkin says. 'It was then that something called *Beverley Hillbillies* came along, and some others like it, and that changed it right back.' The networks gratefully retreated from the dangerous reality of *The Defenders* to their preferred diet of cop shows, which were to become increasingly violent.

But violence has its problems. 'The problem is,' says Les Brown, former TV critic of the *New York Times*, 'that the audience gets very sophisticated about these things, and it's a short order. If you've done violence and you've done quite a lot of it in the course of a week, then the audience doesn't find that very violent any more. You've already done that, so you've got to escalate the violence. You have to get more and more until the people start to scream – that is, decent people

'Who loves ya, baby?' Telly Savalas was the shaven-headed, lollipop-sucking hero of Kojak.

Perry Mason: *William Talman played District Attorney Hamilton Burger, who was (almost) always outwitted by Raymond Burr as Mason.*

Just good friends: (top) Paul Michael Glaser and David Soul in Starsky and Hutch*; (below) Kate Jackson, Farrah Fawcett and Jaclyn Smith as* Charlie's Angels.

The Untouchables *featuring Keenan Wynn and Robert Stack, was generally reckoned to be the most violent television series ever made.*

Before The Defenders *could quite change the face of television, 'something called* The Beverley Hillbillies *came along . . . and changed it right back'.*

out there start to scream, and that's happened a few times. And then they come down hard on the networks and the producing companies.'

This first occurred in the early 1960s. Crime series had become more and more violent, reaching some kind of apogee with ABC's *The Untouchables*, first broadcast in 1959, which dealt with organised crime in the 1920s. It starred Robert Stack as the chief of the Federal Special Squad (nicknamed 'the untouchables' because of their incorruptibility during Prohibition). It is usually described as the most violent series ever shown on television. '*The Untouchables* was supposed to be violent, damn it,' the show's producer, Quinn Martin, once snapped. It won a large audience, but it also attracted the attention of those people who were becoming concerned about violence on the screen. A group in Los Angeles which monitored prime-time television in November 1960 found that in one week the networks had transmitted 144 murders, 143 attempted murders, 52 justifiable killings, 14 druggings, 12 jailbreaks, 36 robberies, 6 thefts, 13 kidnappings, 6 burglaries, 7 cases of torture, 6 cases of extortion, 5 cases of blackmail, 11 planned murders, 4 attempted lynchings, a massacre in which hundreds of people were killed, another mass murder and three shoot-outs between gangs. When Newton Minow was appointed by President Kennedy in 1961 to chair the Federal Communications Commission, he told the National Association of Broadcasters that he considered American television to be 'a vast wasteland' in which could be found 'game shows, violence, audience participation shows, formula comedies about totally unbelievable families, blood and thunder, mayhem, violence, sadism, murder, western bad-men, western goodmen, private eyes, gangsters, more violence and cartoons . . . Gentlemen, your trust accounting with your beneficiaries is overdue. Never have so few owed so much to so many.' Minow added a stinging *coda*: 'I understand that many people feel that in the past licences were often renewed *pro forma*. I say to you now, renewal will not be *pro forma* in the future.' The networks were so alarmed by Minow's threat that they cleaned up their acts – but not for long. Once the hue and cry had died down they returned to their old ways, which included the 'escalation of violence' as described by Les Brown. Senator Thomas Dodd held public hearings into television violence in 1961; he began as an implacable foe of the networks, but he suddenly performed an abrupt about-turn on the subject, and ordered that his report should not be published. It was later revealed that he had accepted lavish gifts from a number of television companies.

Every so often since then, the networks have temporarily 'toned down' the action in their shows when there has been an unusually loud public clamour about the effects of violence on television – after the assassination of President Kennedy in 1963, for instance, and after the deaths of Martin Luther King and Bobby Kennedy in 1968. When Bobby Kennedy was shot, several hundred leading actors and scriptwriters took advertisements in a number of papers, announcing that 'we will no longer lend our talents in any way to add to the creation of a climate for murder'.

But the television companies' public promise to reduce the level of violence in their dramas was never more than half-hearted. 'Please murder the baby tastefully' and 'Please see that the lady is raped without offending accepted decorum' were two (genuine) continuity notes given by networks to their

The Defenders *tackled sensitive subjects and, in the words of its creator, 'almost changed the face of television'.*

Newton Minow of the FCC found television full of 'blood and thunder, mayhem, violence, sadism, murder'.

131

producers in the 1970s. To appease the anti-violence groups who kept a tally of the number of murders in crime series, a few statistical adjustments were made: if a script called for ten people to be shot in a particular episode, the producer might reduce the number to two. By way of compensation for the smaller amount of physical action (punch-ups, shoot-outs and so on), producers increased the prevalence of what one might call 'mechanical violence' – explosive car chases accompanied by an exaggerated soundtrack of screeching tyres, which were *de rigeur* in the movies after *Bullitt* and *The French Connection*, also became a permanent feature of cop shows such as *Starsky and Hutch*.

(Opposite) In Minder, *lovable rogue Arthur Daley (George Cole) often had to be extricated from trouble by the flying fists of minder Terry McCann (Denis Waterman).*

There was a continuing and unresolved debate about how much influence televised violence really had on the minds of the viewers. Sometimes newspapers would seize on a case in which a youngster explained that he had committed a murder after seeing it done on television. But others dispute that television has that much effect, including some criminals themselves. 'If I'm going to rob a bank, there's going to be violence,' says David Peterson, who has been in San Quentin jail for the past ten years, having been convicted of first-degree murder. 'But I don't need television to rob a bank. If I'm going to go and rob a bank, I'm going to rob it. I ain't going to sit and wait for a television picture to come and see how they do it. I'm going to use my own ideas and go. I don't think violence on TV has done anything really to push violence.'

At the end of the 1970s, in fact, the violent cop shows did begin to disappear – not so much because of the work of pressure groups as because networks felt they had exhausted the seam. They also discovered that it was possible to achieve high ratings without festooning the script with multiple killings or car smashes. The most successful police series of the early 1980s was *Hill Street Blues*, a witty and amiable show set in a police station with a 'heavy ethnic mix'. Its first series, in 1980, was notable for eschewing the action stunts which had hitherto been thought essential. It won the record number of nine Emmy awards. In later series of *Hill Street Blues*, the car crashes began to creep back in, but the programme was still distinguished from its predecessors by its 'natural' filming style (hand held cameras, unsynchronised dialogue) and by the fact that its characters were presented as credible human beings. It was a far cry from *Charlie's Angels* or *Starsky and Hutch*.

Hill Street Blues, *a refreshing break with the tradition of violence and screeching car tyres, won Emmies galore.*

Concern about the influence of action dramas has not been confined to America. In Britain, the chief constable of Merseyside, Kenneth Oxford, once remarked that 'when the *Starsky and Hutch* series was showing, police on patrol duty were adopting sunglasses and wearing their gloves with the cuffs turned down. They also started driving like bloody maniacs.' As early as 1960, the BBC had issued a set of rules which stated that violence, if used, 'should arise naturally from the story'. If it was inserted 'extraneously' or for 'depraved' effect ('this happens with many of the "private eye" and police series which come from the United States'), it would be rejected outright. The rules added that no sequence should 'dwell upon the more gruesome and bloody physical aspects of a combat', and soundtracks should not 'magnify the impact of violence, e.g. the breaking of bones, the cracking of a skull or jaw'. The ITA issued similar guidelines in 1964. Yet at that time British programmes were, in any case, remarkably free of 'gruesome and bloody physical' combats.

'Evening All': George Dixon, played by Jack Warner, was the embodiment of the genial old British bobby – rather too genial for some tastes.

Cause for celebration: on 19 September 1964, Dixon finally wins his sergeant's stripes and is congratulated by woman police sergeant Jean Bell (Patricia Forde).

Rupert Davies, portrayal of the pipe-smoking French inspector, Maigret, was praised even by Simenon himself.

The first British police drama, *Dixon of Dock Green*, was as gentle as any sucking dove. Its hero, Police Constable George Dixon (later elevated to Station Sergeant), was played by the genial Jack Warner, who introduced each episode with the words 'Evenin' all'. He was as soft-hearted a bobby as ever filled out a charge sheet.

Dixon of Dock Green was the creation of Ted Willis, whose inspiration for the series came not from *Man Against Crime* or other action dramas of the early 1950s, but from the plays of the Golden Age, such as *Marty*. 'Paddy Chayefsky showed me how to do it, it's as simple as that,' says Willis (who is now a member of the House of Lords). 'He said that there is no such thing as "ordinary people" – everybody is extraordinary in their own way.'

There was no native tradition on which Willis could draw. 'You have got to remember that prior to Dixon there had really been no serious police series on television,' he says. 'Dixon actually went behind the scenes in police stations. I spent six or eight weeks at a police station in Paddington Green, riding round in police cars, sitting behind the counter, talking to policemen; and I decided that I would do a series and it would be non-violent. It would concentrate on marriages being more important than murder, but at the same time would have a documentary quality.'

It may have seemed an unlikely formula for success, and it was certainly not one that would have been accepted by an American network – marriages more important than murders, for heaven's sake – but the BBC liked it and so did the audience. It lasted for twenty-one years, from July 1955 to May 1976, during which time 367 episodes were shown. However, only a few years after it began it was already under fire from certain critics, who argued that it presented a much too rose-tinted picture of the police force. 'I think *Dixon* did run out of steam and become a bit tired and cosy,' Willis concedes. Part of the trouble was the personality of Jack Warner himself, who, try as he might, could never come over as anything other than a friendly, twinkling, avuncular fellow. The police, at least, appreciated the public relations job which he was doing on their behalf. When he died in 1981, his coffin was borne by officers from Paddington police station, where Ted Willis had done his original research. A tribute from Scotland Yard described him as 'a charming character who served the Metropolitan Police and public so well . . . His warmth and understanding of the problems of London's PCs will long be remembered with affection.' What the Yard neglected to add was that in his later years Warner had come to think of himself as a real policeman (as many viewers believed, in fact), and was often to be found pottering around the streets of London in his uniform.

The *Dixon* view of the police was challenged in 1962 with the arrival of *Z Cars*, a much less blinkered series, set on Merseyside. 'I got a bit fed up with the idea that all the critics were beginning to say that *Dixon* was too cosy and *Z Cars* was the up-and-coming thing,' Willis admits. 'So I got hold of Allan Prior, an old friend of mine who was writing for *Z Cars*, and I borrowed a script from him. There was a very violent scene in it where Barlow had a juvenile delinquent in his office and he was shaking the life out of this lad and saying, "Now, if you don't talk I will . . ." and so on. I took that scene word for word and gave it to Jack Warner and put him in an office with a juvenile delinquent. And whereas Stratford Johns kept saying "Come on!" Jack Warner would say,

"Now come on," and it came out as cosy as if I had written it. I realised then that there was no way you could change Jack.'

It was the unreality of *Dixon of Dock Green* that caused Troy Kennedy Martin to create *Z Cars*. 'I was in bed with mumps,' he recalls, 'and really to pass the time I kept monitoring these police messages on the VHF; and the impression I got of the police was quite different from that that was coming over in *Dixon of Dock Green*. So I began to think about these rather young policemen who appeared to be a bit out of their depths. I began to think that perhaps there was a series in tackling it from the point of view of people and of law and order, but in a way which showed that the police weren't actually able to get to grips with it.' He developed his idea with people schooled in the documentary tradition, notably Elwyn Jones and Robert Barr.

Inspector Barlow (played by Stratford Johns) and Sergeant Watt (Frank Windsor) were thus portrayed as fallible characters. The series showed that policemen, like other men, did not always achieve what they wanted, argued with their wives, sometimes bent the rules. Within two months of the show's first episode in 1962 it was attracting an audience of 14 million; it ran until 1978. It also produced a spin-off, *Softly, Softly*, which revealed what happened when Watt and Barlow were moved to the Regional Crime Squad; this, too, was very popular, lasting for ten years between 1966 and 1976.

Frank Windsor (Watt) and Stratford Johns (Barlow) took their characters from Z-Cars *to its successor,* Softly Softly.

Troy Kennedy Martin himself was not so happy with what happened to his idea, and he left *Z Cars* three months after its first transmission. 'It pulled back,' he explains. 'It lacked a kind of critical edge . . . For instance, in the first six episodes we were already showing that crime, to a certain extent, did pay; and policemen were saying, "You know we don't catch all the people, lots of them get away with it." But this was against part of the code at that time, which one wasn't allowed to transgress. At the end of the episode the criminal had to be arrested.' Eventually, he believes, it became a series about television itself, with the power struggles in the police bureaucracy reflecting those at the BBC: 'Senior policemen barging and plotting against each other were senior producers actually, trying to take over parts of the administration.'

Troy Kennedy Martin illustrates his conviction that the series succumbed to timidity with a story about G. F. Newman – who, many years later, was to write *Law and Order*, the most hostile drama about the police ever screened on British television. 'He needed some money and he said could I introduce him to anyone who knew anything about police series, so I sent him to see the *Z Cars* and *Softly, Softly* people at Television Centre,' Kennedy Martin says. 'His story would be for *Softly, Softly* so he starts by saying, "Well, Sergeant Watt takes this bribe of £500," and he was shown the door within a minute.'

Roger Moore (later to become James Bond) starred in The Saint, *a series of hour-long thrillers based on Leslie Charteris's novels, starting in 1962.*

Like their American colleagues, producers of crime drama in Britain have usually tried to make each hero somehow 'different' from all the other heroes of the genre, even if this involves nothing more than the shameless use of a gimmick such as Kojak's lollipop. ITV's first crime series, in 1955, was *Colonel March of Scotland Yard*, in which the title character (played by Boris Karloff, eccentrically enough) had only one eye; the other was covered with a black patch. Since then British viewers have been treated to a one-armed investigator (*Mark Saber*), a snuff-taking investigator (Chief

Superintendent Tom Lockhart in *No Hiding Place*), a Parisian investigator (*Maigret*, the highly successful adaptation of Simenon's stories, which starred Rupert Davies), investigators of the Victorian era (*Sergeant Cork*, *Cribb*), a Dutch investigator (*Van der Valk*), an investigator working for a local radio station (*Shoestring*), an investigator in an exotic setting (*Bergerac*), and – although not until 1980 – female investigators (*The Gentle Touch* and *Juliet Bravo*).

During the 1960s there were also several series featuring spies and intelligence officers, a genre which was in vogue in the United States at the same time. Les Brown thinks that this may have been because television is a mirror of society: 'The year that Nixon was running for President against Hubert Humphrey, he was running on a law-and-order platform, and nine of the ten top-rated shows were law-and-order shows – that is, they were police shows or Westerns or something with a goody and a baddy, and the lawman prevailed. So that told you something about the mood of the country.' In support of this theory one can adduce the fact that the age of space travel in the 1960s brought with it such popular series as *Dr Who* and *Star Trek*. *Dr Who*, about a man who travels through the galaxies in a police telephone box defeating strange-looking foes, was started in 1963 as a children's programme, but millions of adults also watched its Saturday afternoon transmissions. In *Star Trek*, which began in 1966, Captain Kirk (William Shatner) and his pointy-eared assistant Officer Spock (Leonard Nimoy) both gained a cult following as they roamed the heavens in the Starship *Enterprise*.

It is not hard to see what events might have sparked off the craze for spy series in the mid-1960s. In the United States, the public was learning that the Bay of Pigs had not been the first occasion on which the CIA had employed 'dirty tricks'; meanwhile British people were at last discovering the truth about the penetration of their intelligence services by Soviet agents such as Kim Philby. An additional influence was the international popularity of James Bond films. Most of the spy dramas on television, like the Bond movies, did not take themselves too seriously: how *could* one take seriously apparently wicked organisations with such preposterous names as THRUSH or KAOS? The first of the American series was *The Man from UNCLE* (which stood for United Network Command for Law Enforcement); week after week, agents Napoleon Solo (Robert Vaughn) and Ilya Kuryakin (David McCallum) saved the world for freedom by fighting the menace of THRUSH. After that, the deluge: *The Girl from UNCLE*, *I Spy*, *The Man Who Never Was*, *Get Smart*, *Mission: Impossible* and *It Takes a Thief*.

By far the most entertaining of the British spy series of the time was *The Avengers*, produced by the commercial television company ABC. Patrick Macnee played the debonair Old Etonian John Steed who carried out assignments for his corpulent intelligence controller, known merely as 'Mother'. The bowler-hatted Steed was assisted by a succession of women who were expert in the martial arts – Cathy Gale (played – often in black leather outfits – by Honor Blackman), Emma Peel (Diana Rigg), and Tara King (Linda Thorson).

The Avengers was never attacked for its violence, since the show was so obviously a spoof (and the violence was, in any case, most elegantly executed). In the late 1970s, when British television directors were picking up the American trend to all-film drama, the creator of the series, Brian Clemens, produced a much tougher spy drama named *The*

(Opposite) Emma Peel (Diana Rigg), in typically exotic dress, accompanied by the eternally debonair John Steed (Patrick Macnee) in The Avengers.

Kanako Higuchi, Yuko Tanaka and Ken Ogata in Edo Porn, *an aptly-named Japanese production.*

Professionals in which Bodie and Doyle, agents of CI5, had no compunction about shooting to kill. Unleavened by the wit which had redeemed *The Avengers*, the programmes were fiercely criticised. In his defence Clemens could argue that *The Professionals* was merely reflecting the facts of the time; after all, it was well known that the SAS operated in a similarly unrestricted fashion. One episode, indeed, was almost a carbon copy of the SAS's actions when they stormed the Iranian Embassy in 1980.

The other British series of the 1970s which was denounced for its violence was *The Sweeney*, a brutal drama about the work of the Flying Squad starring John Thaw as Inspector Jack Regan and Denis Waterman as his sidekick, George Carter. The series was criticised for showing the police swearing, getting drunk, taking bribes and beating up suspects; *The Sweeney*'s defenders pointed out that the current inquiries into police corruption were revealing that such behaviour was common in the force. However, it was noticeable that when *The Sweeney*'s producers looked for a show to succeed it as a vehicle for Denis Waterman, they chose *Minder*, a softer and jokier drama. *Minder* was something of a rarity in that its heroes were villains. To defuse the possibly subversive implications of this idea, the heroes in question – Arthur Daley (played by George Cole) and his 'minder' Terry McCann (Denis Waterman) – were made into essentially lovable, small-time crooks who seldom managed to hang on to the proceeds of their capers; more victims than villains, really. Other new crime series in the 1980s, such as *Juliet Bravo* or *The Gentle Touch*, indicated that British television was beating a retreat from the harsh 'realism' of *The Sweeney* and choosing instead to produce a modified and updated version of *Dixon of Dock Green*, or perhaps *Z Cars*.

The people who produced the earliest episodic dramas in British television, such as *Dixon*, were fortunate enough to be working in a sheltered environment. Unlike Canada, Australia and many other nations, Britain restricted the number of American series which could be imported. There was no specific quota: the Television Act of 1954 merely required ITV to provide a 'proper proportion' of programmes of 'British origin and performance', which was also the policy of the BBC. (In 1965 the ITA did rule that, between Mondays and Fridays, no more than two of the five programmes in the 8 p.m. to 9 p.m. slot could be American, but this was withdrawn in 1967.) Nevertheless, both ITV and the BBC enforced an informal quota which prevented the schedules from being swamped by cut-price American cop shows and Westerns, and provided room for the development of a British tradition of popular drama.

One country which was even more successful than Britain at resisting the American invasion of the 1960s was Japan. It too was enabled to establish its own television drama. But it had had a narrow escape: for a period in the late 1950s Japanese stations gratefully accepted anything the Americans could send them – *Laramie*, *Highway Patrol* and dozens of others, all dubbed into Japanese. By 1960 there were forty-five foreign programmes being shown every week, almost all of them American.

The boom ended in the 1960s, as Japanese programme-makers began to assert themselves. Hollywood police dramas were replaced by the form which has been immensely popular ever since – *samurai* drama. It was not a new form, of course. *Samurai* movies had been watched by large audiences since

Slave Girl Isaura: *a highly popular novela about white slavery in the nineteenth century.*

1910, and they drew on the even older traditions of the *kabuki* theatre, whose plays were full of stories about wicked and violent men. An essential ingredient of the historical *samurai* films was the *chanbara* – violent but stylised sword-fighting. As Japanese producers realised, this could be used to make television dramas which would be just as gory and exciting as *The Untouchables*, and much more acceptable to the Japanese people's cultural palate.

There are two distinct types of *samurai* drama on Japanese television. The first, which is the type favoured by NHK, Japan's public television station, is based on well-known historical tales. The second type, which is to be found on the commercial channels, uses the conventions and themes of *samurai* but updates them, taking its plots from stories in the newspapers. The most obvious example of this modernised *samurai* is *Underground Executioner*, which has been produced by Hisashi Yamauchi for the Ashahi Broadcasting Corporation since 1972. The hero, a man called Mondo Nakamura, is an utterly incompetent police officer who is mercilessly bullied at home and ridiculed by all his acquaintances; in secret, however, he carries out a one-man vigilante campaign on behalf of the poor, conducting ritual killings of evil men.

Yamauchi claims that his series meets a serious need. 'The Japanese worker is very biddable, and works very hard – I really think he does work hard – and he's loyal to his company. But he is often angry – not with the company as a whole, but with his immediate superior or someone a little above that. On occasion he will go to a pub for a drink and complain. But even though he may grumble, there isn't much of a tradition of arguing with his superiors. He obeys them. But there is a sense of frustration, and he puts his department chief or whoever in the place of the villain [in a *samurai* drama] and gets rid of his frustrations that way.' Yamauchi believes that 'in the hearts of the Japanese there is a sort of combativeness, a desire not to be beaten, the admiration for the bravery of the small man overthrowing the powerful'. He says that *samurai* drama also acts as an antidote to feminism: 'The Japanese man today is much weaker than he was; there are now many women who do nothing but assert themselves.' In *samurai*, however, women are modest and retiring while men are brave.

Yamauchi becomes angry if anyone suggests that *Underground Executioner* depends on gratuitous violence. 'People call this series "murder drama",' he expostulates, 'but on average he only kills about three people per episode. But in other, so-called "respectable" historical dramas, they kill thirty or forty people.' In any case, killing is obligatory in *samurai* dramas: 'To the Japanese audience, a historical drama without sword-fighting is like tea without milk, or beer that's gone flat . . . I don't think there is anything brutal about it.'

Samurai dramas are aimed at a male audience. For the women, there is what the Japanese call 'home drama' – soap opera, in other words. As in America, many of the home dramas are transmitted during the day and watched almost exclusively by housewives, but quite a few of them are made for prime-time viewing as well. Ben Wada, one of NHK's most distinguished drama directors, moans that 'we now have a situation where we have nothing but domestic dramas. I think that is very regrettable.' Regrettable, perhaps, but unalterable. Unlike Western soap operas, which could

Stephanie Turner playing Inspector Jean Darbly in the BBC's Juliet Bravo, *one of two British series of the early 1980s which focused on female police officers (the other was* The Gentle Touch).

The Daleks remained a constant enemy, but Dr Who himself was played by several actors over the years; among the best-known are (from top) William Hartnell, Jon Pertwee, Tom Baker and Peter Davison.

'Beam me up, Scotty': boldly going where no man had ever gone before, the crew of the Starship Enterprise in Star Trek *were all engagingly down-to-earth characters in spite of their extra-terrestrial setting.*

The Man From UNCLE, *the most popular American spy series of the 1960s.*

theoretically run for ever, Japanese home dramas are finite; they reach some sort of conclusion, but usually only after scores of episodes. And as soon as they finish, there are plenty more to take their place.

A typical home drama series was *A Wandering Life*, which began in 1977. In the first few episodes the background to the plot had to be established: the heroine, Ryoko, is a poor seamstress who marries into a rich family and is bullied by her mother-in-law. Unable to bear the constant scorn and taunts, Ryoko leaves home to go a-wandering, bereft and penniless. The ratings soared when the series reached this point. As Ian Buruma notes in his book *The Japanese Mirror*, 'One really has to suffer to be popular in Japan.' Buruma also points out that the average Japanese heroine is 'a passive victim of fate', which Ryoko certainly is. All that keeps her spirits intact as she suffers is the memory of Minoru, the son she left behind. The series reaches a crescendo when her ex-husband stands for Parliament and she is blackmailed by a man who threatens to expose her and ruin her husband's career. She kills the blackmailer – not out of loyalty to the husband but because she cannot endure the thought that her son Minoru might learn of her wretched condition. She is duly charged with murder. The defence lawyer who is assigned to her by the court turns out to be her grown-up son. There is a tearful reunion, at which Minoru utters the closing word of the series: 'Mother!'

The same theme of female suffering and fortitude dominated the most popular home drama of all, *Oshin*. Its heroine is born at the turn of the century to a family of tenant farmers in north Japan. At the age of seven she is sent into effective slavery to work for a merchant family who will pay her with one sack of rice per year. There is a long-drawn-out scene of her departure from her parents, replete with tears and screams. In the new master's household Oshin is given just a couple of radishes and a few grains of rice at the end of the day; to compound the misery, the regular maid bullies her ceaselessly. By this stage the ratings for the series had reached a record 60 per cent; the more she suffered, the more they rose. In the 1920s the great Tokyo earthquake occurs just as she is trying to build her own dress business; her home and her business are ruined, forcing her to become a servant once again. When she becomes pregnant, she loses the baby as a result of having to work for long hours in a paddy field.

Oshin does eventually live happily ever after. Her tale provided the sales pitch for a whole industry of merchandise – Oshin dolls, Oshin *saki*, Oshin rice. A statue was erected in her honour. Japanese politicians all felt obliged to comment on the significance of her story: the Education Minister remarked, rather bizarrely, that the moral of it all was that children should be respectful to their parents (on the grounds that it turned out all right in the end). Even President Reagan referred to her when he visited Tokyo, noting that her 'tenacity and great hard work' had brought her success.

Japanese home dramas are no more implausible and heart-tugging than soap operas the world over. It is a form which seems able to command a huge audience however ridiculous the plot and exaggerated the acting. What matters is that viewers should be willing to maintain their suspension of disbelief even when the stories inhabit the furthest realms of fantasy. 'The people of Brazil believe in miracles,' says Daniel Filho, a leading Brazilian director of *telenovelas*, the wildly popular Latin American type of soap opera. He lists some

Callan ran for 52 episodes from July 1967 and starred Edward Woodward (left), who was shabby, sympathetic but cold-blooded.

John Thaw played it rough as Inspector Jack Regan in The Sweeney; the title from Cockney rhyming slang (Sweeney Todd = Flying Squad).

Highway Patrol, starring Broderick Crawford, was typical of the American shows which dominated Japanese screens in the late 1950s.

(Opposite) Richard Chamberlain made his name in the long-running soap Dr Kildare; more recently he played the part of an amorous Catholic priest in The Thorn Birds.

of the ingredients of a successful *telenovela*: 'First of all, there must be a couple of lovers. So the boy meets the girl, and they are going to be losing and meeting, and losing and meeting, until the end of the *novela* when they meet forever. One of them must be rising in class – in some *novelas* it is the girl, in some the man who is rising – because this keeps the American dreams, the capitalist dreams. Everybody feels, "If that happens to them, it can happen to me. So I can be a rich guy." So it is called the opium of the public.'

Regina Duarte in Malu, Woman, *Daniel Filho's novela which had the unique distinction of being bought by British television.*

Not everyone falls for this dream. People living in the *favellas*, the slum areas, often complain that the *novelas* hardly acknowledge their existence. As one slum dweller in Rio de Janeiro says, 'I think they should show what *favella* life is like. We have lots of difficulties here, like the water problem.' Another comments that *novelas* film 'the nicer things – scenes with more beauty. If they showed images from the *favella* it wouldn't interest people. It must be that.' Daniel Filho agrees. He once made a *novela* about people dying from pollution. 'Maybe you can do something very strong in television, but only for an hour, or maybe five chapters in a week,' he says. 'But for six months, to have someone every day saying "I am dying, I am dying" – people say, "Come on, die fast and let's see another thing."'

Brazil, Mexico and Puerto Rico now dominate the trade in *telenovelas*, supplying them for stations throughout Latin America and beyond (Italy and Portugal, for example). The form originated in Mexico and Cuba, in the 1950s. The early *novelas* lasted for between fifteen and twenty episodes, transmitted live on alternate days with a small cast. As the British author Jeremy Tunstall has written, 'Any search for cheap programming to build audience loyalty could scarcely fail to arrive at the formula of a serial drama with a tiny cast and minimal studio set. The key point about the *telenovela* is that it originates from a need to fill time (including day-time) cheaply – and this in turn arises from transposing multi-channel all-day commercial TV from a rich country to a much poorer one.'

Venezuela and Argentina were the next countries to adopt the *novela* as a cheap audience-puller. The introduction of videotape in the early 1960s transformed the *novela* from a perishable good, confined to the country where it was produced, into something that could be recorded and sold abroad; and the arrival of videotape coincided with Brazil's conversion to the *novela*. Brazil has been active in the market ever since, mainly because the Brazilian network Globo is by far the largest and richest in Latin America. From the mid-1960s the character of the genre changed from the old Cuban melodramas to the *novela* as it is to this day – an account of the aspirations of the urban middle class in Brazil.

There were a few exceptions. One of the most successful novelas of all time was *Simply Mary*, a girl's rags-to-riches story not unlike that of the Japanese *Oshin*. In the 1960s it was sold to every Spanish-speaking country, and at one stage attracted an even bigger audience than the World Cup.

The average *novela* runs for more than 100 episodes, but the style and subject matter vary slightly according to the time of day at which it is to be shown. At 6 p.m., Globo TV will show a *novela* which is suitable for children as well as adults – something like *Slave Girl Isaura*, in which a white slave girl is treated as a daughter by her mistress, falls in love with a young man and goes off with him to seek her freedom. The 7 p.m. and 8 p.m. *novelas* can be slightly more daring, dealing with murder, love and money. By 10 p.m., even political battles and corruption can be mentioned.

Novelas are often little more than glossy escapism, in which well-heeled characters pursue their careers against a background of nightclubs, wine-bars and yacht marinas. Just occasionally, however, some semblance of reality has managed to intrude in recent years, particularly in 'serial dramas' which have fewer episodes than full-blown *novelas*. *Malu, Woman* was as popular as any other *novela* yet the series dealt with the problems of a divorced woman (played by Regina Duarte, Daniel Filho's wife) honestly and humorously.

Significantly, *Malu* was the first *telenovela* to be screened in Britain, albeit on the so-called 'minority' station, Channel 4. With the exception of American hits such as *Dallas* and *Dynasty*, soap opera on British television has always been home-produced. It began in April 1954 with *The Grove Family*, so named because it was transmitted live, twice a week, from the BBC's studios at Lime Grove. During its three-year run, the show's characters – particularly long-suffering father Grove and grumpy but lovable Grandma Grove – were taken to the viewers' hearts. Any particularly surprising development in the script was reported by the press as if the Groves were real people.

Christopher Beeny, a mere boy when he appeared in The Grove Family, *later turned up in* Upstairs Downstairs *as Edward the footman.*

Noele Gordon starred as Meg in Crossroads *from its inception in 1964 until she was dropped in 1981.*

This was a foretaste of what was to happen with Britain's two most successful and long-running soap operas, *Coronation Street* and *Crossroads*. Both the companies who make these programmes, Granada and ATV (later Central TV) respectively, have always received hundreds of letters addressed to the fictional characters, offering criticism or advice along the lines of 'You need to get yourself a man, Bet Lynch'. Whenever a popular character has been 'written out' of the series – as happened to Meg Mortimer of *Crossroads* in 1981, or Len Fairclough of *Coronation Street* in 1983 daily newspapers have reported the story on the front page.

Coronation Street is the longest-running soap opera in Britain, having been transmitted twice a week since December 1960. It is also the most popular. Almost every one of the 2,400 episodes has been at or near the top of the ratings. Its success seems to depend on a subtle mixture of fantasy and reality. The settings are palpably unreal, a nostalgic evocation of the kind of northern working-class community which in reality was destroyed by the age of slum clearance and tower blocks in the 1950s and early 1960s. These developments somehow passed *Coronation Street* by: it still consists of a row of old terraced houses with a pub and a corner-shop. The characters who have inhabited this world, however, have been strongly delineated: Ena Sharples, the curmudgeonly old lady; Albert Tatlock, the even grumpier old man; Bet Lynch, the brassy blonde barmaid with a heart of gold; Stan Ogden, the bone-idle window cleaner who is forever sneaking off to the pub to escape chastisement from his forceful wife Hilda, seldom seen without a set of curlers in her hair; Annie Walker, the genteel landlady constantly looking down her nose in horror at the riff-raff who drink in her 'establishment'. The show has been assailed by some critics for failing to address itself to the 'real world' – race relations, mass unemployment and so forth. But the viewers don't seem to mind: the interaction between the powerful characters is more than enough to keep 16 million people glued to their sets every Monday and Wednesday. For one

Weddings are always a grand occasion in Coronation Street: *three of the most publicised have been (from top) Ken Barlow and Deirdre Langton, Len Fairclough and Rita Littlewood, Eddie Yeats and Marion Willis. The bottom picture shows the street's most argumentative couple, Stan and Hilda Ogden.*

A very different and more liberated picture of young people was provided by Channel 4's Brookside, *set on a private housing estate in Merseyside.*

week in 1983, the tabloid press filled its pages with little else but discussions on whether Deirdre Barlow would leave her husband Ken for the smooth-talking factory manager Mike Baldwin. She didn't.

Crossroads, which is set in a motel in the Midlands, has always had to play second fiddle to *Coronation Street*. It attracts a smaller audience and it is derided by the critics for its creaking scripts and wooden acting. When it started, in 1964, it was broadcast on five evenings a week, but this was later reduced to four and then (in 1980) to three. In 1981 ATV's executives took the drastic decision that quality would be improved by the departure of the show's central character, Meg Mortimer, who had been played by Noele Gordon ever since the first episode. Unmoved by a 'Save Meg' campaign, the scriptwriters arranged for her to sail away on the QE2 to a 'new life' in Australia.

The Guiding Light *has run, first on radio and then on television, for more than 40 years.*

The true home of the soap opera is the United States. It originated on US radio in the 1930s, taking its name from the fact that these narrative dramas were sponsored by a soap company. The attraction was obvious: it could be used to fill hours of broadcasting time very cheaply, yet it also grabbed a large audience, enabling radio stations to charge high advertising rates. When television arrived, soap opera seemed especially suitable for the new medium since the cumbersome cameras of the time were able to film only intimate dramas, with a minimum of physical movement.

Some of the day-time soap operas which were introduced in the early 1950s have been running ever since. Both *Love of Life* and *Search for Tomorrow* have been on the air since 1951. *The Secret Storm* lasted from 1954 to 1974.

The addictiveness of the soaps is as impressive as their longevity. From a shopping precinct in suburban Los Angeles, a company called 'Soaps By Phone' offers a twenty-four-hour service to any of its subscribers who may have missed an episode of one of the thirteen regular day-time dramas. Karen Anthony, the firm's director, says that 'it started one afternoon when I'm stuck on the freeway system at 2.15 in the afternoon, and I'm frustrated because I'm not going to get home in time to see my favourite soap opera. And so I think: if only there was a place to call tonight, then I wouldn't have to be frustrated.'

Dorothy Green and Robert Colbert play wife-and-husband Jennifer and Stuart Brooks in CBS's The Young and the Restless, *a perennial day-time soap.*

She now employs a team of young graduates who write a sixty-second précis of the highlights of each episode; this is then read on to a tape, which can be heard over the telephone by anyone who pays the subscription fee of $12.50. The plot summaries produced at Soaps By Phone give a flavour of the unceasing emotional crises and entanglements which characterise American soap opera: 'On Friday's *The Young and the Restless* on CBS Paul and Andy are hired by Kevin to investigate the mysteries surrounding Rick's first wife. Digging through old newspapers, part of the mystery is unravelled when it appears that Rick's wife Melissa drowned in a scuba accident off the coast of Mawi. However, the plot thickens as an accidental death theory leaves too many unanswered questions. Back in Geno City, Rick and Nicky bask in the afterglow of a passionate night of lovemaking. When Nicky questions Rick's past he becomes angry and swears that he has never been married. Tracy is still in a coma and Danny still refuses to leave her side. However, prompted by a call from Lauren, Professor Sullivan rushes to Tracy's side, and for the first time Tracy opens her eyes. On *As the World Turns* on Friday, also on CBS, Franny stalls Kirk's sexual advances claiming to be unprepared to commit herself physically to her boyfriend. However, Franny is concerned that if she doesn't sleep with Kirk he'll seek sexual favours elsewhere. Steve convinces Witt that Craig is responsible for the McCall coin heist and Witt vows to teach Steve a lesson that he will never forget . . . As David arrives with wife on arm he and Sally shockingly glare across the room at each other and Sally walks out of the room thoroughly upset. Mark has regained consciousness and asks to speak to Stacy. Stacy stands by his side and listens to Mark professing his love for her. She becomes very upset as she knows that she must tell him the truth about her and Jamie . . .' And so it goes on, day after day, year after year.

Mary Hartman, Mary Hartman: *a surreal, affectionate pastiche of soaps.*

Defenders of these programmes argue that, risible though they may seem, day-time soap operas tackle 'real' and sensitive issues which are seldom aired in prime time. It is easy enough to parody the baffling complexities of the plots – *Mary Hartman, Mary Hartman* and *Soap* have done so – but one of the staff at Soaps By Phone firmly asserts that 'they talk about relevant topics'. Karen Anthony agrees: 'I escape for a few hours a day into these story-lines, and a lot of the subject matters they deal with I can relate to personally; some of the problems that they deal with on the shows, I'm having myself.'

Day-time soaps were the first televised dramas to incorporate into their plots such topics as lesbianism, venereal disease, mastectomies, alcoholism, drug addiction and other taboos. The emotional frankness of the day-time dramas is undoubtedly related to the fact that their audience is almost exclusively female: network chiefs are firm believers in the theory that men don't like to watch emotional scenes. What the male viewer wants, in the networks' opinion, is stories about power, sex and money.

What he gets is just that. Its name is *Dallas*, the ultimate soap opera, which is an utterly different creature from its day-time cousins. Lee Rich, the executive producer of *Dallas*, happily admits that 'I don't think it has any social significance. I think it's just being entertained. That's the business we're in, the entertainment business, and that's what *Dallas* is – entertainment for people.' It began quietly in 1978, with just five episodes, as the story of a feud between two wealthy Texan families, the Ewings and the Barnes, who were connected by marriage. But by 1980 its popularity had soared. In November 1980 it was watched by an estimated 83 million Americans, giving it a record 76 per cent share of the television audience.

One of the main reasons for its success was the character of J. R. Ewing, played by Larry Hagman (who was previously best known as the 'master' in *I Dream of Jeannie*). In May 1980, in the last episode of that season's series of *Dallas*, J.R. was shot by an unknown hand. Viewers then had to wait for six nail-biting months before the next series revealed who had done it. Since J.R. had antagonised almost all of his business associates, relations and lovers at one time or another, it could have been virtually anyone. In the event, the culprit turned out to be his sister-in-law and former mistress, Kristin.

Lee Rich was once quoted as saying that '*Dallas* is crap, but it's good crap'. He claims that the phrase was taken out of context. 'I said that *Dallas* is what it is and we don't pretend it to be anything more than it is, but it's done with a great deal of style and a great deal of class,' he explains. 'We can't

Before Dallas, *Larry Hagman was best known as the 'master' in* I Dream of Jeannie *(top); today he is famous as JR (below), whose shooting kept viewers around the world on the edge of their seats.*

be in the business of determining the American public's taste. They have the wrong taste, we've gotta cater to it.' He also believes that critics are far too pompous about the show: 'We do not take ourselves seriously. It's done with a great big wink.'

The good life: Dallas *is criticised by the East German authorities for being 'to the advantage of very rich people'.*

Following the show's success a number of inferior imitations appeared, such as *Knots Landing* and *Dynasty*, but none has achieved the international penetration of *Dallas*. It has been seen in more than ninety countries, often in a locally-dubbed version. Dominic Paturell, the Parisian actor who has dubbed the part of J.R. for French television since the first episode, originally thought that the show wouldn't catch on because it was too American. 'I was wrong,' he admits. 'I think there is everything in *Dallas* – beautiful women, sex, heartbreak, cancer. Everything is there.' The actor who dubs for J.R. in Italy, Antonio Colonello, believes that 'this violent impact with reality, so purely, violently anti-rhetorical, is far beyond the good habits of the Italians. It has had a notable impact on the Italian audience, because the viewers were tired of the angelic, saintly character of our heroes, surrounded by the scent of sanctity. They wanted to see the other side of the coin – the diabolical side.' *Dallas* has even been seen in Eastern Europe, where many viewers are able to receive transmissions from the West. One might have thought that Communist countries would have bought *Dallas* for themselves and presented it as an exposé of the wickedness of American capitalism, but in fact they seem to fear its influence. 'I consider it as a very perfect, conventional, business-like, propagandist, cleverly-made series, which is unfortunately very capable of effecting a manipulation of the consciousness of the viewers – a manipulation of consciousness to the advantage of the imperialists, in the broad sense – to the advantage of very rich people,' says Margaret Schumacher, the head of drama for East German television. 'And because of that, it is immensely dangerous, because this series is designed so that the minds of millions of people who are beginning to think, or have not yet learned to think things through, are manipulated into quite a wrong attitude of mind.' She adds ruefully that 'we are attempting by other means to get close to our viewers, but unfortunately we find the effectiveness of this series is also very great in this country'.

The success of Dallas *inspired several imitations, of which the most popular was* Dynasty, *a torrid saga of treachery and passion starring English actress Joan Collins as 'super-bitch' Alexis Carrington.*

Larry Hagman himself says he honestly doesn't know why *Dallas* has attracted viewers in so many countries ('It's not popular in Japan,' he points out). The nearest he comes to advancing a theory is to say that 'I think everyone has an uncle or an employer or someone who is like this character and seems to get away with it. It's the general plan. World-wide hatred – it's wonderful.'

Some countries have tried to reproduce the ingredients of *Dallas* in a native version. In France, it has given rise to *Château Vallon*, planned as a fifty-two-hour serial about the cavortings of a family which owns a daily newspaper. 'They are rich,' says Serge Friedman, the producer of *Château Vallon*. 'So, roughly, the story is the story of the ten people of that family and their love story – their ambitions, their fights and the fights also of other families in this city.' He agrees that this is like *Dallas*, 'but we could also say that *Dallas* is like Balzac' – an idea which would undoubtedly boggle the mind of Lee Rich.

Dallas is merely the most extreme example of America's domination of the world's television screens, something which is often described by the recipients as cultural imperialism. William Shatner, who played Captain Kirk in *Star Trek*, tells an anecdote which illustrates just how far American culture can reach. 'We were in some deserted village in the wilds of the Caspian Sea, and I was sitting in a restaurant eating chicken kebabs,' he recalls. 'And this waiter came up. Of course he didn't speak any English, and the man was as remote from civilisation as you can get in the world. And he said, "Captain Kirk?" It was bizarre.'

A common complaint is that American imports have stunted the growth of indigenous drama. Father James Reuter, a Jesuit priest who produced many dramas for television in the Philippines in the 1950s and 1960s, says that the Filipinos love acting, and in the early days there was a great deal of native drama broadcast in Manila. Today, however, Philippines TV is stuffed with foreign programmes, primarily American soap operas. 'It is escapism,' Reuter says. 'It takes the mind of the people off the present situation. They [the authorities] don't want anything that will get people thinking about the way things are right here right now. If a drama comes from London or New York or Hollywood, it's just far enough away not to rock the boat, and that's why it's safe.'

Happy to cover the globe with its own output, the United States has been notably unwilling to accept any trade in the other direction. But some dents have been made in the armour. Lew Grade of ATV sold the Americans action series such as *The Persuaders* and *The Saint* in the 1960s, winning the Queen's award for export in the process. Starting with *The Forsyte Saga* in 1969, American television has also bought a succession of British serial dramas, including *Upstairs Downstairs* (a saga of life in an Edwardian house with plenty of servants, created by Eileen Atkins and Jean Marsh), *Rumpole of the Bailey* (John Mortimer's gruff but kind-hearted barrister), *Brideshead Revisited* (Granada's dramatisation of Evelyn Waugh's novel), and many others. But the commercial broadcasters' scepticism was demonstrated by the fact that these were bought by public television rather than one of the large networks. As David Victor, the creator of *Marcus Welby MD*, said of the British serials, 'There was no follow-up for the next season. The secret of a good series is that you must be able to see episode 35 or 49 before you begin.'

Jean Marsh and Angela Baddeley were exported successfully from Britain to America in Upstairs Downstairs, *the classic saga of Edwardian class differences.*

Leo McKern immortalised Horace Rumpole, the kind-hearted, Wordsworth-quoting barrister, created by John Mortimer, who is himself a barrister as well as a playwright.

The Forsyte Saga, it is worth noting, was also sold to Soviet television, most unusually for a Western drama. 'My wife really loves Russian classics,' says Konstantin Kuzakov, head of drama at Gosteleradio, 'and she loves English classical literature. *The Forsyte Saga* – well, that production didn't impress me particularly, but for her it was the pinnacle of art.'

Two BBC-2 productions which helped start the nostalgia boom: (top) Kenneth More as Jolyon in The Forsyte Saga; *(below) Philip Latham as Plantagenet and Susan Hampshire as Glencora in* The Pallisers.

Although the British costume-drama serials were shown in America only by public television (and even it felt obliged to preface each episode with an 'introduction' from some quintessential Englishman such as Alistair Cooke or Robert Morley), they did influence the networks, who overcame their fear of finite serials to invent the most significant new form in American drama of the last ten years, the blockbusting 'mini-series'. ABC started the trend in February 1976 with its twelve-hour adaptation of Irwin Shaw's novel *Rich Man, Poor Man*, which followed the lives and loves of two brothers, Tom and Rudy Jordache (played by Nick Nolte and Peter Strauss), from the Second World War to the 1960s. It was a huge ratings success.

The other networks joined in, and the next eight years witnessed a positive avalanche of mini-series, usually based on best-selling novels. A 'non-fictional' exception was *Roots*, ABC's twelve-hour dramatisation of Alex Haley's search for his ancestors, which was transmitted over eight successive nights in January 1977. It was actually a mixture of fact and fiction, showing how Haley's forebears were transported from the Gambia into slavery in the United States. 'We knew *Roots* was going to be a challenge to the American people, they were going to have to take a lot of blows watching it, they were going to be the guilty one, the aggressive one,' says David Wolper, the executive producer of *Roots*. 'I tried to use black Americans who were familiar to the American television audience, blacks who were on other television shows . . . so it wouldn't be too threatening to them.'

One critic dismissed *Roots* as 'middle-brow *Mandingo*', but Wolper took this as a compliment. 'American television *is* middle-brow,' he says, 'and I wanted to make a subject that was important in a middle-brow way so a large audience could appreciate it, understand it and get something out of it. I mean, people actually turned off basketball games in bars around the United States and put on *Roots* because they wanted to learn and they wanted to learn on their terms – they wanted a terrific drama, excitement and stars.'

ABC's decision to screen *Roots* eight days running was taken out of caution. Ratings in America are calculated on a week-by-week basis, and networks think in terms of who 'won' a particular week. 'ABC was a little nervous about it so they put on all the shows in one week so if it was a disaster they'd get rid of it all in one week and they'd lose that week,' Wolper says. As it turned out, the decision to transmit it on consecutive nights was one of the main reasons for the success of *Roots*. Wolper explains: 'People would get up in the morning, would go to work and talk about what they saw last night, and if you didn't watch *Roots* you were out of a conversation. So when you went home the second night you said, I'd better watch *Roots* otherwise I've nobody to talk to tomorrow morning.' A slight exaggeration, perhaps, but it is certainly true that what began as an expression of timidity has become a convention, and nearly all mini-series are now broadcast on consecutive nights. *Roots* had proved the pulling power of a one-week *blitzkrieg* by becoming the most popular drama in American television history: the last episode was watched by 80 million people, a record which stood for almost four years until *Dallas* came along.

The only other mini-series to deal with a sensitive subject – again in a middle-brow way – was NBC's *Holocaust*, a four-part drama about Hitler's extermination of the Jews, which won the biggest television audience of 1978. As with *Roots*, some critics complained that *Holocaust* transformed import-ant and ghastly passages from history into up-market soap opera. But when the serial was shown in West Germany its effect was traumatic, causing young Germans to think seriously – in many cases for the first time – about the actions of their parents' generation.

For the most part, however, mini-series have been the television equivalent of a fat paperback, concentrating on tales of towering passion set against a historical background, such as *The Captains and the Kings*, *Aspen*, *Studs Lonigan*, *The Winds of War* and *The Thorn Birds*. In many ways they *are* little more than expensive soap operas, but they break with the dramatic conventions of modern American tele-

Terence Rigby joins Alec Guinness, the inscrutable spymaster George Smiley, in Tinker Tailor Soldier Spy.

The Far Pavilions, *based on M. M. Kaye's romantic novel, was sold in advance to Home Box Office in the United States – a sign of things to come.*

vision in one respect. Both soap operas and prime-time series (whether *Starsky and Hutch* or *Marcus Welby, MD*) cannot afford to allow their leading characters to develop, since the shows are made with the intention of running indefinitely. In a mini-series, on the other hand, there is a clearly defined beginning, a middle and an end (as in a conventional play or novel), enabling characters to change, mature or die as the serial proceeds. It is for this reason that some television writers who lament the passing of the Golden Age are excited by the possibilities of the mini-series, even if they believe that its potential has not yet been properly exploited. J. P. Miller, author of *The Days of Wine and Roses*, describes the mini-series as 'the one hope of television drama'.

As *The Forsyte Saga* inspired the American mini-series, it is hardly surprising that British television should have continued to produce lavish historical drama serials. (The term 'historical' is almost as confusing as 'drama-documentary', since it means merely that the dramas are set in the past, not that the people or incidents in them are based on fact.) There has been a plethora of nostalgic dramas with a royal theme, such as *The Six Wives of Henry VIII*, *Edward VII*, *Edward and Mrs Simpson* and *Lillie Langtry*. There have also been dramatisations of novels, of which the most distinguished are *I Claudius*, *Brideshead Revisited* and *The Jewel in the Crown*. It would probably be unfair to describe these as 'mini-series' in the American sense of the word. But there is no doubt that in the next few years some producers do indeed hope to beat the Americans at their own game. In 1983 Central TV pulled off a remarkably cheeky coup by producing the seven-hour mini-series *Kennedy* and selling it to NBC in the United States, to be shown on the twentieth anniversary of the President's assassination. The cast was American, including Martin Sheen as John F. Kennedy and Blair Brown as Jackie, but the scriptwriter, producer and director were all British. In 1984, the British independent production company Goldcrest made a mini-series out of M. M. Kaye's novel *The Far Pavilions* for Channel 4 in Britain but also sold it to the Home Box Office cable network in the US. The American audience was clearly foremost in Goldcrest's mind when they produced the series: the role of the Indian princess Anjuli, for example, was incongruously played by Amy Irving, a well-known actress in the United States.

If other British television companies follow these examples, the inevitable consequence will be that even less drama will bother to deal with the subjects provided by contemporary Britain. There is little enough of it already. A recent series which swam against the tide of nostalgia and historical re-creations was Alan Bleasdale's five-part drama *Boys From the Blackstuff*, transmitted by the BBC in 1982, which showed the lives of a group of unemployed workers on Merseyside. '*Blackstuff* has certainly been a persuasive eye-opener to those of us who live in the protected isolation of London, where the soul-destroying impact of long-term unemployment goes largely unnoticed,' wrote the right-wing *Daily Mail*, while the Communist *Morning Star* described the drama as 'an invaluable, compassionate record of the ugly social impact of unemployment'. At the Edinburgh Television Festival in 1983 Jonathan Miller said that *Boys From the Blackstuff* was a work of art fit to be compared with James Joyce's *Ulysses*. The unemployed themselves showed their appreciation by turning the words 'I can do that; gissa job' – which had been the haunting refrain of the show's main

Kennedy *(1983), a mini-series on an American theme, shown on American television and using an American cast, was actually made by a British company, Central Television.*

character, 'Yosser' Hughes – into a national catchphrase.

Blackstuff was indeed a phenomenon. One of the reasons why the appearance of the series caused so much comment was that it was such a rarity. By the 1980s, most television drama seemed to have lost touch with real life, perhaps finding it too painful to contemplate. The 'marvellous world of the ordinary', which Paddy Chayefsky and others had depicted so brilliantly many years before, had become almost invisible.

Learning from the Box.

It was a Scotsman, John Grierson, who coined the word 'documentary'. In the 1930s and 1940s he and his colleagues at the GPO Film Unit (later the Crown Film Unit) created films about 'real life' that were just as enthralling as any fictional drama. Yet television was slow to adopt the tradition invented by Grierson, largely because early television programmes were all 'live', whereas the documentary technique involved weeks – perhaps months – of filming, followed by an equally long period of editing, in which numerous fragments of film would be shaped into a coherent whole.

When television did begin to use film, in the 1950s, documentaries could at last appear on the small screen. One of the first major figures was Denis Mitchell, whose televised documentaries for the BBC in the late 1950s included *Morning in the Streets*, *Night in the City* and *In Prison*. Mitchell was fascinated by what Paddy Chayefsky called 'the marvellous world of the ordinary'; but unlike Chayefsky, who portrayed this world through drama, Mitchell preferred to allow people to speak for themselves. He was particularly interested in the rhythms and vocabulary of everyday speech, and before moving into television he had produced some remarkable 'sound documentaries' for BBC radio, for which he had stood on street corners with a tape recorder (or disc recorder at first). 'I'd fallen in love with the human voice,' he says. 'It wasn't what they said so much as how they said it . . . Actors can't do it – we've tried. You can't reproduce it, the passion and the sadness imprisoned.'

When he started working for television, Mitchell again sought to capture the passion and the sadness. What distinguished his work from the documentary films of the 1930s was that it was less stylised; it lacked a script or an intrusive narrator. 'I don't plan films,' he says. 'I've never used a script in my life. I just hope for the best, and sometimes it works.' His films were not intended to hammer home any particular message. Of *Morning in the Streets*, he says: 'I suppose it was an honest film in that it didn't start trying to say people are lovely, people are wicked – I just said here are some people in Salford.' *Night in the City* was a gloomier film, showing what happens in the hours of darkness. As with all Mitchell's documentaries, the most memorable moments were completely unplanned. 'There was one man who really came out of the shadows, he saw me sitting around on a bomb site,' Mitchell recalls, 'and he said, "I have got to tell somebody, I'll tell you: I killed somebody." And he told me how he killed him, and I used that part of the film, the relevant bit, in this film about desolation. The next thing was that half the police force were on the phone, saying "Give me a description of this man." Fortunately I couldn't.'

In the 1960s Mitchell was hired by Granada Television,

Natural marvels: Dieter Plage photographing a small frog in the Okavango Swamps, Botswana, for Anglia's Survival *(1972).*

Animals have been popular with television producers (and audiences) from the earliest days: penguins were a particular attraction in Friends From The Zoo *(1937).*

where he joined forces with his old BBC colleague Norman Swallow to produce documentaries such as *A Wedding on Saturday*, an impressionistic account of a wedding in a Yorkshire mining village, which won an Italia Prize in 1964. 'I chose a wedding for two reasons,' Swallow says. 'Firstly because it gave the programme a shape, a structure. And also because of course a wedding and the build-up to a wedding is an emotional occasion and people were therefore feeling personally emotional . . . they're more likely to tell the truth, to be less worried and even, I think, to be less aware of our cameras.' To prevent the participants from being camera-conscious was no small achievement, since the documentary was shot on videotape, which required enormous cameras. The advantage of tape was that Swallow could shoot for one hour continuously, whereas with film the magazine had to be changed every few minutes. But there were disadvantages, too. 'We had a crew of twenty people and the equipment was so large that, although we had intimate chats with people in the mining village in their kitchens, we couldn't get our equipment into the kitchens. So there was an element of fake, in that we built their kitchens in a room belonging to one of the local pubs. I don't think it mattered because you saw their faces most of the time – it didn't stop them telling the truth, so I wasn't particularly worried about it. But I suppose in a sense it was a half-lie.'

Your Life in Their Hands, *which took viewers inside operating theatres, ran from 1958 to 1964 on the BBC and was revived in 1982.*

Another of Mitchell's productions was *The Entertainers*, directed by John McGrath, a documentary about club entertainers in the North of England which recorded both their public and private lives. When shown a preview of the programme in April 1964, the Independent Television Authority insisted on the removal of one sequence, lasting only about three seconds, in which a young striptease performer bared her breasts on stage. Granada refused to delete the scene – 'I'm not a pornographer, this was an absolutely essential part of the film,' Mitchell says – and *The Entertainers* was left on the shelf. Nine months later, Mitchell and Swallow were surprised to find themselves invited to lunch at the ITA, where Lord Hill, the Authority's Chairman, apologised for having banned the film: he and his colleagues had looked at it again and found it perfectly acceptable. As Hill said later, 'This time we found that we did not boggle.'

Sell, sell, sell: an enthusiastic banker in Granada's series For Richer, For Poorer *(1962).*

Mitchell and Swallow went on to supervise Granada's series *This England* for which, again, the intention was to 'reflect the life of ordinary people'. The programmes were transmitted almost entirely without narration or commentary. 'I've always felt this very strongly,' Swallow says, 'that between me, the viewer, and you, the performer on the screen, there should not be a third person or third voice. Whenever we had any commentary it tended to be at the very beginning, to set up the scene. Thereafter people expressed their own opinions about their own lives, how they lived, what was wrong, what was right.'

One of the paradoxes of televised documentaries is that while presenting 'real life' they can nevertheless often make it seem as new and strange as a film about some tribe in Borneo. *A Wedding on Saturday*, for instance, might have been recognisable to people who lived in Yorkshire mining communities, but for many other viewers it was probably the first time they had encountered the people and places shown in the film, even though they all lived on the same small island.

March 1949: *the dramatised documentary* London After Dark, *based on real cases, involved the construction of a casualty ward at Alexandra Palace.*

Documentary has the capacity to make the unknown seem familiar – as when a group of Masai tribespeople debate an issue in much the same way as any local council. But it can also make the familiar seem unknown – as in a recent Scandinavian documentary which was filmed from inside a penis and a fallopian tube. Most people imagine that they know all about the process of human reproduction, but when they see, in close-up, a sperm fertilising an egg, it becomes as bizarre and wonderful as a picture from the surface of the moon. For more than twenty-five years, documentary producers have attempted to reveal the hidden world which is on our doorstep, as well as to bring back pictures from far-flung parts. In the words of a Japanese documentary-maker, Naoya Yoshida, 'the true role of television is to show people what they hardly ever see'.

For producers in Japan, in the early years at least, this meant revealing to the viewers the secret nooks and crannies of Japanese society. In 1957 NHK started a documentary series entitled *The True Face of Japan*, which lasted for seven years (from 1964 it ran for another seven years under the title *Images of Today*). Yoshida made one of the first documentaries in the series, in which he filmed the *yakuza*, a kind of Japanese mafia. 'I felt that the social rules and the psychological make-up of the Japanese were revealed there very clearly,' he says. 'The relationship between *oyabun* and *kobun* [boss and follower]; *giri* and *ninjo* [the traditional Japanese virtues of social duty and concern for the welfare of people with whom one has some specific relationship]; being locked into a small closed social group, a *habatsu* [clique].' Yoshida admits that he was quite scared when he negotiated with Kunai Shimura, the leader of the main *yakuza* family: 'I said, "I shall attack you, I shall criticise you ruthlessly, but I shan't just attack the *yakuza*, I shall say that both the political world and the academic world are structured in the same way." He said, "Fair enough. I like it. Let's do it." Then he said, "Have a look at my tattoos," and stripped to the waist. Suddenly something black hurtled at me from near the entrance. I was knocked to the floor, and if the *oyabun* hadn't shouted at him I would have had my throat torn out. It was a Doberman. When the *oyabun* strips to the waist it means there's going to be a fight, and the Doberman had been trained to know that.' When the documentary was actually transmitted, he adds, the *yakuza* were 'pleased as punch'; the critics and viewers were also impressed.

Yoshida's interest in exploring Japanese culture is shared by his colleagues. Junichi Ushiyama, the father-figure of Japanese documentaries, won a first prize at the Cannes festival in 1961 for *The Old Man and the Hawk*, which was made for the commercial channel NTV. 'I do current affairs projects on things like the Vietnam war,' Ushiyama says, 'but basically what I'm interested in is ethnic culture – the fundamental culture that is unique to a particular people. However much Japan industrialises, there remains a sort of spiritual culture of the Japanese people which is unchanging. *The Old Man and the Hawk* recorded an almost extinct part of that culture, the old mountain-hunters who used trained hawks to catch rabbits and raccoons. Ushiyama was fortunate enough to find the last man in Japan who was able to hunt in this way, 'so he was eager to cooperate so as to leave on film for future generations a record of his skills'. Nevertheless, a certain amount of trickery was used in the film. 'There are three stages,' Ushiyama explains. 'The first is capturing the wild hawk; the second is the training process; the third is hunting with the fully-trained hawk. We used three hawks

Famous wife-and-husband teams: (top) Michaela and Armand Denis, explorers and photographers, who starred in ITV's first wildlife series in 1955; (below) Jen and Des Bartlett, Australian wildlife specialists.

at the same time. You can't tell hawks apart as easily as people, so the viewers no doubt thought that it was the same hawk. But if we'd really followed all three stages it would have taken ten years.'

Other Japanese documentary makers have had more patience, being prepared to follow a subject over a long period. In 1963 NTV's *Non-Fiction Theatre* ran the first of eleven programmes about Thalidomide, which had affected about 1,000 children in Japan. The series concentrated on one child, Takashi Arai. In June 1975 NTV made a one-hour special about him, *Reach for Tomorrow*, by which time he was a thirteen-year-old attending a normal school. The programme won Japan's first Emmy award in America.

Not all NTV's documentaries have been restricted to Japanese topics. As one might expect of a country which devised *The Ultra Quiz*, some programmes have been both international and sensational. In 1978, the cameraman Susumi Nakasuma filmed an expedition to the North Pole, using a specially adapted 16-millimetre camera. Two years later, Nakasuma obtained even more extraordinary pictures when he 'hiked' to within 300 feet of the summit of Mount Everest with Electronic News Gathering (ENG) equipment – an ultra-lightweight battery-operated camera and quarter-inch video tape recording gear, with a combined weight of just thirteen pounds.

Johnny Go Home, *a Yorkshire television documentary in 1975, looked at the fate of youngsters who run away to London – and in particular a young Scot called Tommy Wylie.*

Necessity is the mother of invention, and the development of new recording equipment for television has often been brought about because of the demands of documentary-makers. Nakasuma's gear had to be light since he was obliged to carry it himself on a long trek in conditions where he would be short of oxygen. In other cases, producers have required lightweight equipment in order to make the cameras more flexible and less intrusive, thereby giving a better *cinema verité* effect – enabling the documentary-maker to become a 'fly on the wall'. The 35-mm film cameras used in the early days of television were frustratingly immobile, and even the first video cameras – as used in *A Wedding on Saturday* – were no less cumbersome.

One man who was particularly exercised by this problem in the United States in the mid-1950s was Robert Drew, an editor at *Life* magazine. 'All documentaries were set up and posed,' he says, 'and you had big crews and cables and cameras on tripods and clap-sticks – and all of this stuff erased the reality that you could possibly get.' *Life* magazine was specialising in picture essays, in which tiny still-cameras were used to capture 'moments of real emotion and feeling in people's lives'. Drew had 'a very simple idea – which was to use the *Life* candid technique in motion pictures'. He took a year's sabbatical, during which he considered whether the story-telling methods of the movies or modern novels could be transferred to television documentaries. 'After that year I was pretty straight on the fact that we had to stop lecturing – that is, we had to stop the narration, and let people talk.' Drew spent the next five years creating more portable cameras, as well as tape-recorders which could work in synch with the cameras without having to be connected to them by an umbilical cord of cable.

The Family made the everyday life of an ordinary family in Reading as addictive as any soap opera, but filming in such cramped conditions was quite a challenge.

By 1960 Drew was ready to shoot 'a real story'. He noticed a young Senator named John Kennedy who was running for the Democratic nomination for the Presidency. 'I went to Washington and proposed to Kennedy that we were going to start a new kind of film-making: the camera would have to live with him from dawn to dusk, day after day . . . We weren't interested in him talking to us. We were interested in seeing what he did as candidate,' Drew says. 'I knew we had to be able to shoot in hotel rooms at night when people were quiet and thinking and worrying, and we had to be able to move through mobs with cameras running, and we had to be able to walk where it would take dollies ordinarily to go.' (Dollies are trolleys on which cameras are mounted to film while moving; Drew's hand-held cameras made them unnecessary.)

Kennedy agreed. Drew then managed to persuade Kennedy's rival, Hubert Humphrey, to cooperate as well. The resulting film, *Primary*, was a remarkable *verité* picture of political campaigning. But hardly anyone saw it: the three networks rejected the film because they wanted to build their own in-house documentary units, and it was broadcast on only a handful of stations owned by Time Inc., which had sponsored Drew.

Kennedy himself did not see *Primary* until after his election, but he loved it. Emboldened by this praise, Drew proposed to the President 'that we do some real recording in the White House of the work that a President does, candidly as it happens'. Kennedy approved, but Drew added that he would have to wait until there was a crisis: 'A man at his desk – whether it is the Oval Office or any other desk – is a man in a closet. A film resulting from that will be a dull film no matter who is behind that desk.'

The crisis which Drew needed finally arrived in June 1963, when George Wallace, Governor of Alabama, announced his intention of defying a court order that the University of Alabama should be racially integrated. Wallace promised that he would personally stand at the schoolhouse door 'to bar the entrance of any Negro who attempts to enrol'. Drew and his colleagues from *Primary* – including Donn Pennebaker and Richard Leacock – went into action, gaining unrestricted access to the White House and the Governor's mansion in Alabama: both Kennedy and Wallace apparently thought that a 'fly-on-the-wall' approach would work to their advantage, showing them to be honest and determined politicians.

By then, Drew and Time Inc. had also reached an agreement with ABC that it would broadcast their films, but transmission of the documentary about Alabama – *Crisis: Behind a Presidential Commitment* – was delayed for four months until October 1963, supposedly because ABC could not find a sponsor. Although it was undoubtedly an exciting drama, not everyone approved of Drew's methods: one critic described *Crisis* as a 'managed newsfilm'. But such objections were inevitable, given Drew's conviction that viewers should be able to watch events unfold without guidance from an on-screen reporter or narrator. As he says, 'What can be done is to develop a form of journalism for TV that works uniquely and best according to TV's own laws, and for me that would be a TV that records real life as it happens without infringing on it . . . and lets these stories tell themselves according to the medium; that is, in a dramatic way instead of fortified with narration.'

Drew believes that his technique requires some kind of drama – 'You enter a subject at the point at which it begins to reveal itself in a dramatic way' – and a beginning, middle and end. Other documentary-makers disagree, arguing that all life is full of drama if one looks closely enough; a camera-crew can enter or leave that life at any point and still produce

Tense phone conversations between Washington and Alabama were a notable feature of Crisis: Behind a Presidential Commitment.

Boldly going . . . An all-woman crew suitably attired for Granada's documentary Some Women of Marrakech *in the* Disappearing World *series.*

Royal Family *(1969): the Queen and Prince Philip had a right of veto but did not exercise it.*

a film as dramatic as *Primary* or *Crisis*. 'That's the fascination of this stuff,' says Roger Graef, one of Britain's most distinguished exponents of the *cinema verité* style. 'It's the drama of everyday life. Soap operas were originally called true-life dramas in America, and these films are true-life dramas . . . I think it is almost universally interesting to watch other people live their lives, and the closer you get to their real lives, the more interesting it becomes.' Norman Swallow uses the term 'kitchen-sink documentary' by analogy with the kitchen-sink dramas which became popular after John Osborne's *Look Back in Anger* in the 1950s.

However, the documentary that attracted a bigger audience than any other involved people who were, at first sight, anything but 'ordinary' – Britain's royal family. That, of course, was precisely the point: the function of the film was to 'humanise' royalty, and in that it succeeded splendidly. The initiative came from Buckingham Palace, in 1968, after several television companies had applied for facilities to make films in preparation for the Prince of Wales's investiture the following year. 'Prince Charles and the Palace realised it just wouldn't be possible to grant facilities to everyone,' says Richard Cawston, who directed *Royal Family* on behalf of a joint ITV/BBC consortium, 'so they decided it might be better if one fully authoritative film was made; and furthermore, since Prince Charles was a young man who hadn't a massive life story to tell, it would be better, instead of making a film about him and his life, to make a film about the job he would one day inherit, namely the monarchy. And the best way to demonstrate the job of the monarch would be to film the existing monarch, the Queen, throughout a year.' At first Cawston believed that the project would be impossible, since he doubted whether he would be allowed the editorial freedom to which he was accustomed when filming documentaries. In fact, however, the Queen and Prince Philip did not exercise their right of veto, and 'the film was made exactly as I would have liked to make it'.

Royal Family *was made to coincide with Prince Charles's investiture at Caernarvon Castle.*

The proposal came at an opportune moment in relation to the development of technical equipment. British television had been using 16-millimetre cameras with synchronised sound for about five years and, as Cawston says, 'we knew how to make them do what we wanted them to, so with that film we were able to hear members of the royal family speaking informally to each other and to other people for the first time. Before then, nobody had ever heard the Queen speak except in a prepared statement made into a battery microphone'. He thinks that the sound of the royal family talking naturally was more important than any of the pictures in the film, although there were plenty of memorable pictures too – a picnic lunch, for example, or the Queen going into a shop at Balmoral. The programme was watched by 23 million people when it was first shown on the BBC, and by 15 million (9 million of them seeing it for the first time) when ITV screened it; it was also sold to more than 100 other countries.

Having dealt with the First Family, in 1974 the BBC turned its cameras as never before on 'ordinary people', in the form of the Wilkins family of Reading. The inspiration for the series had come from a twelve-part documentary transmitted by PBS in the United States the previous year, *An American Family*, for which a camera-crew had moved in with a rich Californian family, the Louds, for seven months. The programmes had been packed with incident, culminating in the break-up of Mr and Mrs Loud's marriage in front of the all-seeing electronic eye.

An American Family had not been broadcast until two years after the actual filming. For the British version, *The Family*, director Paul Watson wanted to have the programmes transmitted as soon as possible after they were filmed, so that later episodes were being made after the early episodes had been shown. The series was thus able to record the effect of sudden celebrity on the Wilkins family: in one of the later episodes, when the daughter Marion married her live-in boyfriend, Tom, there was a crowd of Fleet Street photographers outside the church. The series included several dramatic moments, as when Mrs Wilkins revealed that her husband had not been the father of their youngest son. Richard Cawston thinks that the publicity 'meant that it wasn't quite a natural, ordinary family, as Paul Watson had set out to film; it was a family under these pressures'. Nevertheless, throughout the series, the Wilkins family accepted the presence of the cameras as though they had been there forever. 'A modern camera is so quiet that you don't know when it's running and when it isn't,' Cawston explains. 'The cameraman, Philip Bonham-Carter, was in the Wilkins' sitting-room for twelve weeks all day with the camera on his shoulder for most of the time. They didn't know when it was running and when it wasn't, so in that situation you begin to forget the presence of the camera team.'

In the decade since *The Family* there has been a deluge of impressive fly-on-the-wall series on British television, all of which have obeyed what Cawston calls the law of increasing returns: 'This means that the longer you have a camera team in a closed community, the better and more interesting are the results, for two reasons. One is because the people in that community gradually forget the presence of the team – they are used to seeing them around. And the other reason is that if you're there long enough, something interesting will happen.' This was proved time and again. In *Sailor*, a ten-part series filmed on HMS *Ark Royal* and transmitted in 1976, a sailor with acute appendicitis had to be lifted off an American submarine by helicopter and transferred to the *Ark Royal*; as he was half-way between the two vessels, hanging on the end of a rope, a huge wave swept him into the sea together with the winch-man, who clung on to him. He was eventually rescued. Roger Graef's *Police*, a series about the work of the Thames Valley force which was screened in 1982, included a notorious scene in which an alleged rape victim was treated with appalling roughness and insensitivity by the two officers who were interviewing her. There was such an uproar that the sequence was omitted from the series when it was repeated.

Documentary-makers in Britain have tended to use *verité* methods to deal with people in particular institutions: apart from *Sailor* and *Police*, there have been *Strangeways*, about the staff and inmates of a Manchester prison, and *Hospital*, which did the same for a medical institution. But some of the methods – such as allowing subjects to speak for themselves without a mediator or narrator, and filming incidents as they actually happen rather than reconstructing them – have also been put to use in other types of documentary. Probably the most notable example is Brian Moser's series for Granada TV, *Disappearing World*. 'The idea originated in 1969,' Moser says. 'I thought I'd try and change the whole orientation of making documentary films about tribal groups.' Instead of having a commentator – even one who was extremely good, such as David Attenborough – 'I thought to myself: why the hell can't an Indian tell you about his life.' Moser wanted to record the vanishing way of life of tribes, especially in Latin America and Africa, who were being threatened by the arrival of 'civilisation'. *Disappearing World* would hire the services of an anthropologist who knew the particular tribe well and spoke its language. 'We plugged into a society,' Moser says. 'All right, we were there as a film crew, for just five or six weeks maximum, but we plugged in through the very best means possible, through somebody who understood that group of people very well.' In the early programmes, Moser used the traditional technique of superimposing an English voice reading a translation whenever the tribespeople were talking, but he found this unsatisfactory; so he then took to using sub-titles, a device which British television had previously eschewed because it was too difficult and time-consuming. 'It was magic,' Moser says. 'All these nomadic people, these cattle herdsmen, were talking to you and you were hearing exactly how they said it.' Moser also refused to follow the common documentary practice of reconstructing incidents: 'I thought that it was very important just to observe very minutely what was going on, and record it as best we possibly could, in a truthful way.'

Moser's style, especially the use of sub-titles, has since been adopted by a number of other directors of anthropological films. Alongside the 'unintrusive' programmes of Moser and the fly-on-the-wall directors, however, television has evolved a documentary method which is quite the opposite: the 'blockbuster' series, with a script and a single, on-screen narrator who presents a personal account of some aspect of history. The first was *Civilisation*, a thirteen-part series in which Kenneth Clark traced the history of Western art. Much emphasis was placed on the sheer scale of the series ('Two years to make, 80,000 miles covered, 200,000 feet of film shot – the equivalent of six major feature films. Eleven countries and 117 locations visited. Works in 118 museums and 18 libraries shown,' the BBC announced); its globe-trotting omniscience, and the fact that it was sold to PBS in the United States, set the standards for the blockbusters that followed. Many of them were in fact co-productions with American companies, usually Time-Life. Among the most successful have been Alistair Cooke's *America* (1972), a history of the United States which took two-and-a-half years to make; Jacob Bronowski's *The Ascent of Man* (1974), a history of scientific ideas; Bamber Gascoigne's *The Christians* (Granada, 1977), one of the few not to be produced for the BBC; David Attenborough's *Life on Earth*

Jacob Bronowski visits Auschwitz in The Ascent of Man*: 'Into this pond were flushed the ashes of some four million people'.*

David Attenborough shows Prince Charles and Princess Anne his pet cockatoo Cocky in 1958.

(1979), for which 1.25 million feet of film were shot in more than thirty countries; and *The Living Planet* (1984), again written and presented by David Attenborough, which studied the world's main environments – mountains, islands, jungles, deserts – and the creatures that inhabit them. *Life on Earth*, the most popular blockbuster of all, had been an extension of the wildlife programmes which Attenborough had been introducing ever since *Zoo Quest* in 1955. Indeed, wildlife shows had always been a regular feature of British television. Soon after the inception of commercial television, Granada had begun its series *Zoo Time*, with Desmond Morris, which ran for 331 programmes. During the 1960s, films of considerable distinction had come from both

Desmond Morris, who later achieved international fame as author of The Naked Ape, *presented Granada's* Zoo Time *in the 1950s.*

the BBC, whose Natural History Unit in Bristol was responsible for series such as *The World About Us*, and ITV, for which Anglia Television's long-running *Survival* won many awards.

Not all blockbusters employed such a personal style as *Life on Earth* or *The Living Planet*. Television has sometimes attempted to produce definitive history without the benefit of an on-screen reporter, using instead archive film and interviews. *The Great War*, a twenty-six-part series broadcast in 1964, was produced jointly by the BBC, the Australian Broadcasting Commission and the Canadian Broadcasting Corporation; the scripts were written by a team of historians which included Corelli Barnett and John Terraine, drawing on the reminiscences of more than 50,000 survivors of the First World War. An even more ambitious project was Thames Television's *World at War*, produced by Jeremy Isaacs, a twenty-six-part history of the Second World War which took four years to make and won numerous prizes, including an Emmy for outstanding documentary. More recently, in 1982, Granada Television used the same methods – interviews with survivors, and exhaustive archive research – for its series *The Spanish Civil War*.

Outstanding use of archive film was made by both The World at War *(1973) and* The Spanish Civil War *(1982).*

Programmes such as these are beacons of educational television, surrounded by a mighty ocean of game shows and soap operas. The task of television, it is commonly said, is to inform and entertain. But there is a considerable tension between these two functions and, in the competition for mass audiences, informational programmes are often the first casualty. Nevertheless, some people working in television have consistently tried to use the medium as a teaching aid. ITV and the BBC have both been transmitting day-time programmes for schools since the 1950s, and in their 'children's hour' broadcasts they have also sought to blend fun with education. *Blue Peter*, a 'magazine' show which has been on the air since October 1958, carries many items which are straightforward entertainment but it also seeks to broaden the minds of its young viewers, particularly through filmed reports of the presenters' foreign journeys. A similar show on ITV, *Magpie*, ran from 1968 to 1980.

John Noakes, the go-anywhere do-anything presenter of Blue Peter, *with Shep the dog.*

In Japan, there is an entire channel devoted to educational broadcasting. It was created as a 'second channel' for NHK in 1957, and since then it has transmitted up to fourteen hours a day of programmes for colleges and schools as well as more general cultural programming aimed at the public as a whole. In 1960 NHK decided to study the effects of the channel by installing a television set in a small rural school in the isolated village of Kuriyama: the children's reactions were filmed for a remarkable pair of programmes called *Mountain School Documentary*. In one scene a father returned home from the forest to find his child making a model boat. He was astonished, since no one in the village had ever seen an actual boat, but it turned out that the children had been shown how to construct them by the television. Towards the end of the series, the schoolchildren spoke mournfully about the impending departure of the new teaching aid. 'At the end of the third term we shall have to give the television set back,' one said. 'If the TV set disappears it will be as if the sun had stopped shining.' Another commented: 'When the TV set has gone, I shall pretend that I'm switching it on. I shall probably think, "Those were good times, weren't they? It was something like love."' Finally, NHK gave the school a new set which it could keep.

Muffin the Mule, with Annette Mills, was the star of the Sunday afternoon series For The Children, *which began in 1946.*

In 1983 the children in the programmes – by now all adults, many with their own children – watched the *Mountain School* documentary for the first time since it was transmitted twenty-five years earlier. After seeing it, they discussed their reactions. 'Until that time the village of Kuriyama was completely isolated – there were no buses, and there was no through road past the village,' one woman said. 'So when television came in it really was a surprise to the children. They realised there was a completely different world outside.' A man added that 'compared with the old days you wouldn't recognise our village now. Each house has a couple of TV sets . . . Nowadays the children can watch what they like, when they like, at home as well as at school. When we were small we used to *go* and watch it – it was somebody else's television, and we had no right to say what we wanted to watch.' The attitude of modern children to television was a common cause for complaint. As one woman said, 'I often tell my children, "When Mummy was small she used to watch the NHK Education Channel . . . so you ought to watch the Education Channel." But children prefer cartoons, so the channel gets switched over to that. I sometimes switch it off, saying: "You're not to watch any more!"'

When the Japanese government created NHK's second channel in 1957, it also approved the setting up of commercial 'educational' stations. Unlike NHK, however, these seldom took their responsibilities seriously. One of them, National Educational Television (NET) soon earned the nickname 'National Erotic Television'. Although its licence obliged it to fill half its output with 'education', 30 per cent with 'culture' and only 20 per cent with 'entertainment', it adopted a rather generous interpretation of the word 'education', screening innumerable Westerns, *samurai* dramas or wrestling matches. When challenged, NET would explain that wrestling bouts, for example, were educational because they 'helped people understand wrestling'; similarly, Westerns could be said to teach viewers about American history and animal husbandry. The true reason for the commercial channels' choice of programmes was much less high-minded: educational broadcasts do not attract advertisers.

It is a universal problem. Peggy Charen, who founded the American pressure group Action for Children's Television, says that 'when ACT began there were about sixteen minutes of commercials per hour for children . . . Saturday mornings were wall-to-wall monster cartoons filled with a lot of messages to eat sugary foods and buy expensive toys'. The average American child today watches television for about twenty-five hours a week – a lower figure than in the 1970s, but still enough to make advertisers spend more than $800 million a year on commercials aimed at children.

With such sums of money at stake, it is hardly surprising that networks should screen 'wall-to-wall monster cartoons' which are known to appeal to children. Teachers and other educationalists who are concerned about the effect of this programming on the young viewers have therefore had to put their energy into non-commercial television. As long ago as 1952 the Federal Communications Commission reserved 242 stations for educational broadcasting. Most have existed on shoe-string budgets, and the fact that they have survived at all is largely due to the largesse of institutions such as the Ford Foundation, which in the 1950s financed the creation of National Educational Television (NET) as a centre which would produce programmes for the local stations. In 1961

Andy Pandy with Looby Loo and Teddy; first transmitted in 1950, the series was continually repeated until 1970.

BBC test card girl Carol Hersee was photographed in 1967, aged eight; four years later she won an award as the Most Seen Girl on Television.

NET was boosted when it acquired the licence to Channel 13 in New York.

Six years later, non-commercial television won more support: the Carnegie Commission on Educational Television reported that 'a well-financed, well-directed educational television system, substantially larger and far more persuasive and effective than that which now exists in the United States, must be brought into being if the full needs of the American public are to be served'. Accepting the recommendation, President Johnson set up a Corporation for Public Broadcasting which would provide funds for programmes on non-commercial television. At the same time the Ford Foundation spent $10 million on a Public Broadcast Laboratory to produce the programmes.

Many of the shows were for an adult audience, but children's television also benefited from the new interest in public broadcasting. Joan Ganz Cooney, a producer of documentaries for Channel 13, was commissioned by the Carnegie Foundation to study the potential uses of television for pre-school education. When she completed her report, in 1968, she proposed that a Children's Television Workshop should be set up, and she produced a skeletal outline of a programme which would help pre-school children to understand reading and counting. Under the title *Sesame Street*, the show was first transmitted in November 1969 on almost 200 local non-commercial stations, watched by 7 million small children.

Sesame Street had been offered to all three commercial networks, but they had turned it down. 'We were calling for 130 new hours of television for pre-school children, that would cost between seven and eight million dollars,' Joan Ganz Cooney explains. 'That was an unheard-of amount to spend on a slice of minority audience – children are a minority audience already, and then you are talking about pre-schoolers, it's almost unthinkable from a commercial network's point of view.'

The series was aimed particularly at poor children, and to this end it was set in a street in East Harlem. There was an 'integrated' cast – black and white, old and young. *Sesame Street* also borrowed some of the styles of the commercials with which children were bombarded on the networks. As Joan Ganz Cooney says, 'If television can sell goods to the degree that it does in this country, it can surely do something else. I remember when we first started, people said: how do you know it can teach? And I said, well, I hear every child in America singing beer commercials. If television can do that why can't it do something more constructive?' Hence the series used thirty-second cartoons and, above all, Jim Henson's Muppets – Big Bird, a seven-foot canary who, according to Joan Ganz Cooney, is 'really a clumsy child trying to learn'; Oscar the Grouch, a morose character living in a dustbin; the Cookie Monster; and Kermit the Frog. Kermit had actually begun life as far back as 1954, when Jim Henson first worked in television. 'I made Kermit from an old spring coat of my mother's,' Henson recalls. 'At that time he was an abstract, lizardy-looking character, I didn't call him a frog. He was just made with an old coat and a ping-pong ball and a cardboard mouth. It was a very simple character; he grew over the years.' After *Sesame Street* Henson developed his characters further for *The Muppet Show*, which, like *Sesame Street*, was rejected by the American networks (Henson thinks that 'network thinking in the

Kukla, Fran and Ollie, *an early American children's show, began in 1947.*

The Lone Ranger (Clayton Moore) first appeared on ABC in 1949, aided and abetted by Tonto (Jay Silverheels).

States seldom takes chances – they're not looking for innovations'); in this case it was ATV in Britain which came to the rescue, and *The Muppet Show* was subsequently sold to more than 100 countries.

Sesame Street was also an international success, being exported to fifty countries and dubbed into many languages: in Germany it was *Sesamstrasse*, while the French version was *Bonjour Sesame*. The BBC turned it down ('too American, too middle-class and too authoritarian', according to Monica Sims, head of children's programmes) but ITV bought it.

In the 1960s Batman (Adam West), helped by Robin (Burt Ward), fought off such ne'er-do-wells as The Joker, Catwoman and The Penguin.

One country which did resist the lure of Big Bird and the rest of the crew was Peru, which banned *Plaza Sesamo* for a while 'because the reality with which the child is put in contact through the programme is a reality adjusted to elitism, consumerism, fantasy, unreflexive obedience, a participation conditioned to instruction via formal motivations, very modern and attractive, but conceptually traditional and excluding'. The Peruvian reaction was perhaps predictable, since Latin American governments have always had high ideals in relation to educational television; the trouble is that those ideals have seldom been realised. When television began in Chile in 1952 the government made many self-congratulatory noises to the effect that it would be utterly different from other countries' television: it would be replete with cultural and educational programming, and TV stations would be based in universities. But even academe found itself unable to withstand the attractions of advertising and mass audiences. By 1968, one critic wrote that 'anyone who, after watching Chile's university channels, is able to establish major differences with worldwide commercial television, would deserve the top prize of the biggest game show in town'.

The Colombian government, having had largely unregulated commercial television since the mid-1950s, created a network called Inravision in 1963, which was given control of all studios and transmitters and was made responsible for leasing air-time to production companies in a way that would encourage diversity. During the day, the network was to be used for educational programming designed to counter illiteracy and disease. As in much of Latin America, however, the worthy objectives were sabotaged by the fact that very little money was made available for these programmes.

Big Bird, Sesame Street's seven-foot canary, 'is really a clumsy child trying to learn'.

In Brazil, after the 1964 coup, General Geisel told broadcasters that the era of endless song-and-dance had to end. They took no notice. By 1967, Geisel was introducing new laws which greatly increased the government's power, limited ownership and emphasised 'an educational-cultural orientation and a new awareness of problems of national integration'. Once again, however, the principle was contradicted by the practice: TV Globo, which was on friendly terms with the generals, was able to do largely as it pleased. In 1970, the Brazilian President felt obliged to admonish broadcasters again: 'This is not the first time I have had to speak to you like this. I have reminded you before that it is not enough just to have five hours weekly of educational programmes; it is essential to raise the whole level of programming – poor quality programmes must be forbidden. The creative talent of Brazilians must not be destroyed by television.' Globo's main reaction to this warning was merely to increase its output of *telenovelas*. Nevertheless, some concessions were made to the government. The educational novela *Joao da*

The Muppet Show *was initially rejected by the American networks but was then taken up by the British company ATV.*

Silva was intended to teach viewers basic literacy in 100 episodes. Most impressive was Globo's High School *Telecourse*, a series of 450 episodes accompanied by weekly periodicals, which aimed to enable students to qualify for admission to college. It is still running today, with considerable success.

In a Latin American country, the government's problem is not the lack of an audience – even the poorest slum-dweller will often have access to a television set – but, rather, the difficulty of persuading broadcasters that television should be used for educational purposes. A country such as India has exactly the opposite problem: broadcasting is a ministry of state, so the government can transmit whatever it wants. What is less easy is to ensure that the programmes are seen. India has a population of 600 million, most of whom live in remote villages and do not possess a radio, let alone a television.

Dr Vikram Sarabhai addressed himself to this difficulty soon after founding the Indian Space Research Organisation (ISRO) in 1967. His solution was to have a single synchronous satellite transmitting directly to television sets equipped with small but effective 'earth stations' – antennae which would pick up the satellite signal. This would be the first 'direct broadcasting by satellite' anywhere in the world. The signals would also be received by relay stations for more normal terrestrial transmission.

'Not only television but satellite television appears to be rather incongruous in a country such as India,' says Professor Yash Pal, who worked with Sarabhai and succeeded him as head of ISRO. 'On the other hand, you might say that if TV can do anything in communicating things to people – if it can be used at all for educational purposes – then countries such as India need it more than even the developed countries do . . . We felt that this way we could bridge the gap, we could get to places which we wouldn't get to otherwise for a very long time. Because the signal from a satellite rains down as democratically as sunlight, you don't have to be close to metropolitan areas; so the distant rural areas will not be discriminated against as they have always been in normal development, which proceeds like ink dots on blotting paper, from metropolitan centres.'

Prague: one book per class is all that is needed in this Czech school, where the teacher uses closed circuit television to transmit pages on the screen.

By 1969 Sarabhai had made a deal with NASA for the loan of the American satellite ATS-6. He then spent several years pushing his way through the innumerable layers of the Indian bureaucracy, winning approval from all the relevant government departments. Finally, in August 1975, ISRO started its one-year Satellite Instructional Television Experiment (SITE), transmitting programmes in four languages to 2,330 sets in six backward states. One-and-a-half hours were broadcast for children in the mornings, with two-and-a-half hours for a general audience in the evenings. Each village's set would be placed on the window ledge of the meeting-house, where a large audience would gather. There were twenty-four maintenance centres to deal with technical faults. When the experiment started, many sets did not work, but by the end 95 per cent were functioning properly and were watched each day by 250,000 viewers – an average of 106 people per set. The broadcasts included science programmes for children as well as numerous instructional programmes for adults on subjects such as agriculture, family planning and health.

SITE was an astonishing technical achievement, but many

of those who worked on it believe that it also had a powerful influence on the villagers' lives. 'SITE was an experiment and not an on-going project – one would not expect miracles to happen in a one-year experiment. However, the results were very positive,' says Dr Binod Agrowal, senior researcher at ISRO. 'In Rajasthan I distinctly remember people changing their style of ploughing in the field. Villagers of Bihar adopted new seed variations. These are the perceptible changes. I remember in the villages of Bihar they used a new technique for killing insects.'

It seemed a pity that SITE ended after only a year, having achieved so much in such a short time. But it did not disappear entirely without trace. ISRO quietly set up a tiny station called Kheda TV, based in Ahmedabad. Although Kheda TV is officially run by Doordarshan, the state broadcasting service, it is actually in the hands of ISRO. Villages in the Kheda area usually have sets donated to them, which are then installed in public places such as meeting-houses. Kheda TV's target is 'the underprivileged majority which normally benefits least from the mass media'; it therefore transmits not only 'hardcore' instructional programmes about agricultural problems but also dramas about social issues – superstition, exploitation, the caste system – which are often written and acted by villagers. Kheda TV now has a team of more than 250 'village writers' producing plays about such topical subjects as 'bride burning' – husbands incinerating their wives because their dowry is not big enough. The only restriction on Kheda TV's campaigning dramas is the fact that the knobs on the village sets are usually controlled by someone from a higher caste, who will turn it off during a play about Harijans (Untouchables) or other low-caste people.

Not very educational but full of frenetic fun: South Korea's early morning show Ding Dong, Ding Dong.

A 'developing country' such as India, with a high level of illiteracy, is bound to consider that 'educational television' is as important for adults as for children; but even in the 'developed' world television has been used to reach those people who have, officially at least, finished their education. In the past twenty years several Western nations have had television series designed to promote adult literacy. In one or two cases, television has attempted something more ambitious by offering a complete course of further education. The first venture of this kind took place in Chicago in 1956, when station WTTW started its 'TV College', broadcasting degree courses in twenty-seven different subjects; at the end of the first three years, 200 students had been awarded an Associate in Arts degree.

By far the largest project of this type is Britain's Open University, which was inaugurated in 1971. Ten years later, having already produced 30,000 graduates, it had 65,000 registered students who were enrolled for more than 100 different courses. The proposal for a 'university of the air' had first been made by a Labour Party study group in 1963 and had been adopted enthusiastically by Labour's new leader, Harold Wilson. 'At that time there were very large numbers of people in the country, men in particular, who had missed the chance of a university education because of the war,' Wilson explains. 'During the war they married, they had children, they had to get a job. It was them I was thinking about first, but the ideas germinated.' When Wilson became Prime Minister in 1964, he encouraged discussions between officials at the Department of Education and Science and senior staff at the BBC. In September 1967, after

many battles with the Conservative opposition and within the Labour Party, the government finally announced its support for an Open University which would use broadcasting facilities provided by the BBC as well as correspondence tuition and occasional meetings with tutors. Sadly for Wilson, the Open University's first transmission did not take place until six months after he had been voted out of office in the 1970 election.

It takes considerable determination to be an Open University student. The programmes are usually broadcast late at night or early in the morning, and it is only in the 1980s that students have been able to afford video machines which will record a programme while they sleep. But the thirst for education is such that thousands of people have been prepared to sit up until the small hours of the morning, often after putting in a full day's work elsewhere. Malcolm Watson is typical of the breed. Now in his fifties, he left school when he was fourteen and became apprenticed to his father as a lighterman on the River Thames, where he has worked ever since. When a local teacher suggested that he should join the Open University he assumed it would be impossible because of his lack of qualifications. 'It did surprise me,' he says, 'because with most universities you need a series of A-levels to gain entry. The Open University doesn't require you to have any formal education or qualifications at all.' He devotes between twelve and fifteen hours a week to his degree course, which will take six years to complete. He admits that he often feels like giving up: 'When you finish work and you come home physically tired, it's not easy to come up here and study.' He adds: 'But then nothing that's worthwhile is easy.'

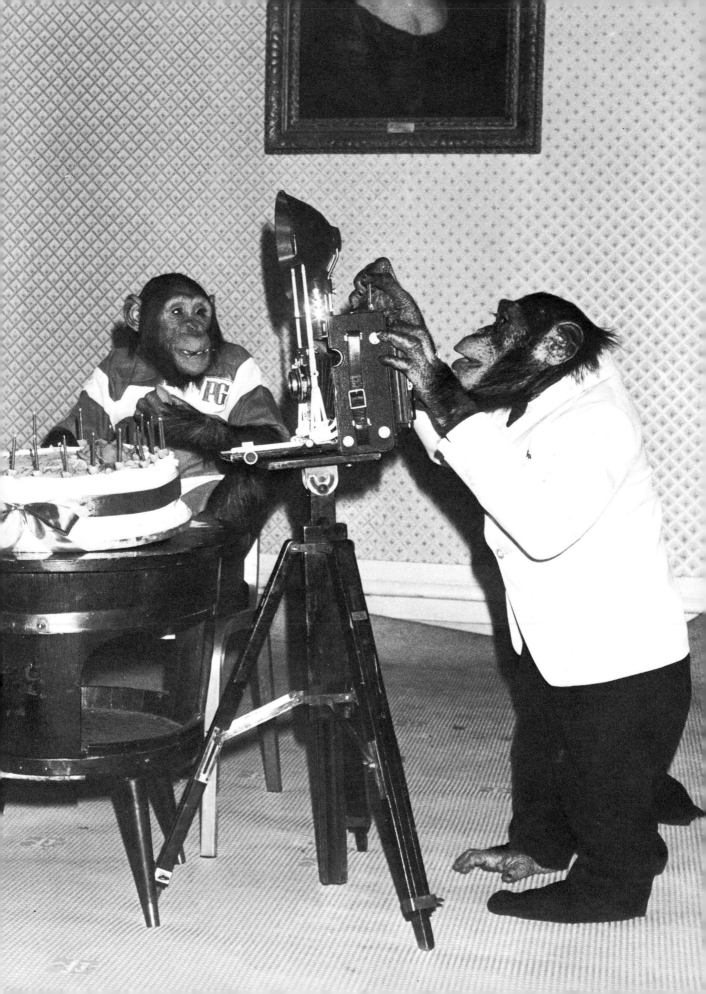

Washing Even Whiter.

Television programmes are the breaks between the commercials: it may be an old joke but it is also, in some parts of the world, dangerously close to the truth. In May 1974 the American Association of University Women (AAUW), having monitored half-hour news broadcasts at 262 local television stations across the United States, found that 43 per cent of them exceeded the National Association of Broadcasters' Code, which restricted advertisements to a maximum of sixteen minutes per hour outside prime time. The AAUW discovered that one station had no fewer than 15 minutes and 45 seconds of commercials in its half-hour newscast; on average, over the 262 stations, there were five-and-a-half interruptions for commercials every half an hour.

In the same year, a survey of Venezuelan television showed that one channel devoted 38.4 per cent of its programming time to advertisements; the figure for the other channel was 35.7 per cent. In Indonesia, at the same time, 10 per cent of transmissions were taken up with commercials – a lower proportion than in some countries, but still enough to worry the government, which reduced it to 8 per cent in 1975. However, the Indonesian authorities were not only concerned by the amount of advertising but also by its effect. Commercials for health products gave the impression that Indonesia was a land of illness; viewers were led to believe that the 'best' make-up – in a country with plenty of traditional make-ups – was Revlon, and that if they wore it they too could drive about in black Mercedes. Advertising revenue had reached the equivalent of US $16 million a year when the Indonesian government took the extraordinary step of banning commercials altogether from 1 April 1981, to 'encourage development without presenting the picture of goods and services that were out of reach of the majority of viewers'.

Indonesia thus became one of the handful of nations whose television contains no advertisements whatsoever. In some countries, such as the Soviet Union, television is financed by the government, and advertising consists only of occasional 'public information' announcements. Elsewhere – in most of Latin America, for instance – television is paid for entirely by the income from commercials and sponsorship. In other places – such as Britain, Japan or West Germany – there is a mixture of commercial channels and 'public' stations. America, too, has a mixture of sorts, but 'public television' has never been able to woo more than a tiny part of the mass audience from the three all-powerful commercial networks.

From the earliest days of television, advertisers have been eager to take advantage of the medium. In November 1930 the hairdressers Eugène Ltd ('perfectors of the permanent wave'), who had branches in London, Paris, New York,

Rex Marshall presenting a rather amateurish early advertisement for Reynolds Aluminium on American television.

Lucky Strike's dancing cigarettes in 1949 were one of the most famous and sophisticated of early American campaigns.

(Opposite) The most popular and enduring characters in British television advertising are the PG Tips chimps; for their first commercial in 1956, Peter Sellers provided the voices.

Berlin and Sydney, used a closed-circuit Baird system to demonstrate their methods at the Hairdressing Fair of Fashion in Olympia, London. Eugène took an advertisement in *Television* magazine to announce that they had been the first 'to discover a real commercial use for Baird Television – that intriguing development of wireless science'. The report of the Selsdon Committee in 1935 argued that advertisements on television would not be acceptable but sponsored programmes, 'for which the broadcasting authority neither makes nor receives payment', could be allowed; the BBC opposed the idea, and when it started its regular broadcasts in November 1936 it paid for them from its licence fee – as it has done ever since. Nevertheless, in those days of 'live' programmes, there was always a danger that someone might slip in a plug for a particular product, as Ian Orr-Ewing learned when he supervised the BBC's first transmission of the Derby at Epsom: 'When we were doing our rehearsal the day before, a man came up – and of course anyone who took an interest in television was immediately a friend, you almost stopped when you saw a television aerial to ask them how they enjoyed the programmes. And this chap said, "Do tell me what you are going to do tomorrow, are you going to be able to see right across the course from the start of the Derby?" We said, "Of course we are . . . on the left will be that tree about fifty yards down the course and on the right will be the starting gate." And he said, "That's very interesting, I shall watch it at home." We went away and the next day when we arrived for an early rehearsal at about 9 a.m. there was a huge sign with "Seager's Gin" written on it, on the tree on the left; and there was nothing I could do to take it down, so it was the first inadvertent bit of advertising that we ever did on the BBC.'

Horror star Vincent Price advertises Haywards, 'the first pickles to bite back'.

When Lord Cadman became Chairman of the government's Television Advisory Committee in 1939 he proposed the use of sponsored programmes as a way of offsetting the costs of the new service, but again the BBC dismissed the suggestion. The BBC had already established its radio service on non-commercial lines and it believed that the same principles should be applied to television, which was regarded as an extension of radio. Exactly the same logic worked in the opposite direction in the United States, where radio was paid for by advertisers: when television arrived, the same arrangements were adopted for that, with little or no public debate. At first, advertisers' interest was limited by the small number of Americans who actually owned sets, but in 1941 NBC's New York station WNBT became the first commercial television channel in the United States (and the world). Its first advertisement was for Bulova watches, who paid $9 for a ten-second plug. WNBT also transmitted the first 'sponsored' programme, a game called *Truth or Consequences* which was paid for by Procter and Gamble.

As the American audience grew in the late 1940s and early 1950s, so did the power and influence of the sponsors. Camel cigarettes issued detailed instructions to the writers of its sponsored drama series *Man Against Crime*, which was first shown by CBS in 1949: 'Do not have the heavy or any disreputable person smoking a cigarette. Do not associate the smoking of cigarettes with undesirable scenes or situations plot-wise.' No character was ever allowed to cough in the series, nor was there to be any mention of arson (because it might make people think of fires started by cigarettes). Camel executives were equally strict with the news programme they sponsored for NBC from 1947 onwards, *Camel News Caravan*: 'No Smoking' signs were not to be shown in any pictures, and no one in the news was to be seen smoking a cigar – apart from Winston Churchill, who was apparently considered a senior enough statesman to be exempt from the rule.

Stories of interference by sponsors were legion. John Mantley, who worked as 'story consultant' on *Gunsmoke*, said many years later that 'to my knowledge, the only people who read my scripts were the sponsor's advertising agencies. They read the scripts and they came to the rough cut, to make sure you didn't "ford" a river if you were sponsored by Chevrolet – honest! As a result, on *Gunsmoke* we always "forded" rivers; on *Bonanza* they only crossed them.' When the De Soto car company sponsored a Groucho Marx show, it insisted that one of the assistant producers – whose surname happened to be Ford – should be removed from the credits. In 1953 Kipling's *The Light That Failed* was transmitted under the title *The Gathering Night* because one of the sponsors was Westinghouse, who made light bulbs.

Hazel Bishop cosmetics sponsored Beat The Clock, *and in return had their name prominently displayed on the clock.*

Probably the most notorious case of censorship occurred with the production of *Judgment at Nuremberg*, a dramatisation of the Nazi war-crime trials, for which one of the sponsors was the American Gas Association. The AGA's advertising agent, Nicholas Edward Keeseley, later described what happened: 'The script came through – and this is why we get paid, going through the script. In going through the script we noticed gas referred to in half a dozen places that had to do with the death chambers. This was just an oversight on somebody's part. We deal with a lot of artistic people in the creative end, and sometimes they do not have the commercial judgment to see things we are paid to see, and we raised the point with CBS and they said they would remove the word "gas", and we thought they would . . . At the last minute we found that there were still some left in. As a result – and this was just, I think, stupidity – the show went on the air where the word "gas" was deleted by the engineer.' The live production of *Judgment at Nuremberg* must have baffled many viewers. As the screen showed pictures of gas chambers, a narrator said: 'They were made to think they were taking baths, the doors were locked . . . [abrupt deletion] . . . chambers.' At the end of the drama, the judge (played by Claude Rains) said: 'The extermination of millions of men, women and children by . . .' Once again the engineers ensured that the dread word was not heard, even though any lip readers in the audience could have seen what Rains was mouthing. To add to the bizarre grotesqueness of the occasion, the performance was punctuated with commercials extolling gas, 'faster, cleaner and cooler than ever before. Today, more people than ever are cooking with gas.'

The American What's My Line, *sponsored by Remington shavers, in 1956 included in its panel the presenter of the British version, Eamonn Andrews.*

Sponsors were not only concerned to protect their own products from bad publicity: broadcasts should create the right *atmosphere*, the most attractive *surroundings* in which to sell a corporate image. Reginald Rose's original script for *Thunder on Sycamore Street* depicted a group of white residents who harassed a black family that moved into the neighbourhood. The sponsors and the network accepted the play on one condition: the black family would have to be removed from the script. It was inconceivable to have black heroes. When the play was transmitted, viewers therefore saw the vigilante activities of the white residents but were not told *why* they had taken against the newly-arrived neigh-

Ted Mack's Original Amateur Hour *ensured that the name of the sponsors, Geritol, was always at the forefront of viewers' attention.*

bour. Some years later, the scriptwriter David Rintels proposed an episode of *The FBI* which would be based on a real incident in which four black girls had been killed by a bomb at a church in Birmingham, Alabama. The network, ABC, and the sponsor, the Ford Motor Company, 'reported back that they would be delighted to have me write about a church bombing, subject only to these stipulations: the church must be in the North, there could be no Negroes involved, and the bombing could have nothing to do with civil rights'.

Sponsors' desire to project 'the right image' was exemplified by the guidelines issued by Procter and Gamble for the shows which it was sponsoring: 'There will be no material on any of our programmes which could in any way further the concept of business as cold, ruthless and lacking all sentiment or spiritual motivation.' There was certainly no coldness in Milton Berle's variety show *Texaco Star Theatre*, which started in 1948 and was introduced by garage attendants with the words, 'Tonight we may be showmen but tomorrow we'll be servicing your car!'

Some TV critics have argued that the era of individually-sponsored shows produced television of a much higher quality than that which followed when the networks took control of programme content and restricted advertisers to commercial 'spots'. A sponsor, so the theory goes, might be more interested in prestige than in winning high ratings; but when a network had to sell a show to dozens of different advertisers it was bound to devote all its energies to acquiring a mass audience.

In support of this argument one can point to the fact that many sponsored programmes were indeed serious and impressive: most of the best productions of the Golden Age of television drama appeared in sponsored 'anthology series', such as *Philco Television Playhouse*, *Kraft Television Theatre*, *US Steel Hour*, *Revlon Theatre*, *Goodyear Television Playhouse* and so on. However, it is also true that the Golden Age came to an end partly because of the sponsors' unease about the glaring discrepancy between the realism of the dramas and the fantasy of the advertising. As the historian Erik Barnouw noted, 'Most advertisers were selling magic. Their commercials posed the same problems that Chayefsky drama dealt with: people who feared failure in love and in business. But in the commercials there was always a solution as clear-cut as the snap of a finger: the problem could be solved by a new pill, deodorant, toothpaste, shampoo, shaving lotion, hair tonic, car, girdle, coffee, muffin recipe or floor wax. The solution always had finality. Chayefsky and other anthology writers took these same problems and made them complicated.'

The FBI: when a scriptwriter proposed an episode about four black girls killed by racists, the sponsors replied that 'there could be no negroes involved' in the cast.

From 1953 onwards, the President of NBC television, Pat Weaver, argued that programmes should have a 'magazine concept': as in printed magazines, sponsors would buy 'spots' in programmes which would be controlled by the networks. Advertisers would have no say in scripts or scheduling. Not surprisingly, sponsors did not care for the idea. A Vice-President of the Association of National Advertisers said that if his members could not be 'identified with the particular programme of their choice, they could not justify, for simple economic reasons, their present investment in television and would feel impelled to withdraw'.

Hovis's nostalgic, lovingly-shot commercials for brown bread were made by Ridley Scott, director of Alien.

It was not until 1959 that sponsors were forced to relinquish their hold over the networks, when the whole television industry was rocked by the 'quiz show scandal'. It was revealed

that some contestants on programmes such as *The $64,000 Question* had been given the answers to their questions in advance, and sponsors themselves had played an active part in this deception. Charles Revson, the head of Revlon Cosmetics, sponsor of *The $64,000 Question*, had often instructed his producers that particular contestants should be allowed to win.

Following these revelations, the networks took away control of programmes from the sponsors. CBS President Frank Stanton promised that 'we will be masters in our own house'. But the advertising industry had to be mollified, so it was given implicit assurances by the networks that the influence of the advertiser would not disappear altogether; in future it would be more subtle, indirect rather than direct. As Stanton put it in 1960: 'Since we are advertiser-supported we must take into account the general objectives and desires of advertisers as a whole . . . it seems perfectly obvious that advertisers cannot and should not be forced into programmes incompatible with their objectives.' The policy has continued, essentially unchanged, ever since. It was inevitable: networks are in the business of maximising their profits, and they can only achieve this by producing programmes that are 'desirable' from an advertiser's point of view.

What this means, first and foremost, is attracting viewers. There is no such thing as a 'rate card' in American television. The price of an advertisement varies according to the popularity of the programme in which it is to be inserted, and the demographic structure of the audience. The networks' obsession with ratings may be criticised frequently, but it is at least understandable. Television advertising was worth $15 billion a year in 1983 and a rise of one percentage point in the rating for a programme produces an extra $70 million in advertising revenue. With sums like that at stake, the networks cannot afford to take chances, and they have equipped themselves with preview theatres, audience research and all the other supposed guarantors of 'fail safe' programming. In 1966 CBS replaced its coverage of the Senate hearings on Vietnam with old episodes of *I Love Lucy* and *The Real McCoys* because advertisers were pressurising the network to put on something that would attract a large audience; the head of CBS News, Fred Friendly, resigned in protest.

The Real McCoys (top) replaced CBS's coverage of Vietnam hearings in 1966; the head of CBS news, Fred Friendly (below), resigned in protest.

Advertising agencies measure the price of commercials in Cost Per Thousand Homes, but this crude yardstick is backed up by much more detailed research into the composition of the audience, which is differentiated by age, sex and social class. One of the most expensive advertising spaces on television is the annual Superbowl match, where a thirty-second spot costs more than $200,000 on the grounds that it is a rare opportunity to reach a massive audience which is almost exclusively composed of men in their prime. Some programmes have been dropped by the networks even though they were achieving high ratings, including *Gunsmoke, The Virginian, The Beverley Hillbillies* and *Green Acres*. The reason was simple: they were being watched by the wrong kind of audience – old, rural and without much spending power.

Although sponsors, in theory, no longer controlled the content of programmes, they were still permitted to 'participate in the creative process' (as CBS put it) by being given advance copies of synopses and scripts. Advertisers may not be able to insist that the word 'gas' should not occur in dramas about the death camps, but it would be a brave net-

The Beverley Hillbillies *was dropped despite its high ratings because the audience was too old to appeal to advertisers.*

work that dared offend them. In 1972 the seafood firm Bumble Bee withdrew all its advertising from CBS after a CBS News report about the pollution caused by seafood canning. Bumble Bee's advertising agency said that 'advertisers select television stations as hospitable vehicles for their messages. Our client, quite reasonably, feels that CBS has destroyed the hospitality of its affiliates for advertising from Bumble Bee, as well as all seafoods.'

One of the most recent examples of advertisers' sensitivity to programme content was ABC's film *The Day After*, a $7 million drama dealing with the after-effects of nuclear war. At the end of October 1983, a month before transmission, *Time* magazine reported that the network was having difficulty filling the commercial spots in the programme: 'The problem, according to Madison Avenue, is not monetary. "It may be one of the most devastating pieces of film I've ever seen, TV or otherwise, but it is artistically unsuitable to most of our clients," says Joel Segal, senior Vice-President of Broadcasting for Ted Bates Advertising.' Since ABC regarded it as a 'prestige project', *The Day After* went ahead anyway, with commercials sold at reduced rates, but many other programmes have been killed at birth by lack of enthusiasm from advertisers.

Elsewhere in the world, advertisers use similar methods to influence what viewers may or may not see. In Japan, particular sponsors can still be associated with individual programmes. 'According to the Broadcasting Law, the sponsor isn't supposed to have any say in the programme's content,' says Junichi Ushiyama, the eminent Japanese producer. 'But in fact, behind the scenes – how should I put it? – it's an inevitable part of the business that they should make their own wishes and opinions known and that these should be acquiesced in. Now most firms in the country don't want to touch political questions, or questions over which public opinion in the country is split, or questions of political ideology. There is a tendency for them to favour television programmes dealing with questions in the cultural sphere or problems in the field of science – that sort of area.'

Sponsored television has been common in Latin America for thirty years. Large firms – usually North American began by putting their money into news programmes or song-and-dance shows. In Colombia, *Telerevista Musical Esso* appeared in 1957 and *El Reporter Esso* the following year. In Venezuela, Shell had sponsored a show as early as 1955, and in 1961 *Noticias Pan Am* started. Latin American soap operas, *telenovelas*, were especially attractive to cosmetics companies: Brazilian television broadcast *Romances Kolynos* and *Teatros de Novelas Coty* in 1958, while Colgate-Palmolive sponsored *Tension* in Venezuela.

No country could resist the advertisers' chequebooks for long. The Chilean government initially refused to allow advertising on the educational television service of the Catholic University of Chile, but the university circumvented the ban by insinuating tins of coffee and bottles of Martini on to the sets of programmes such as *Chatting Among Friends*. The government then relented. As a Vice-President of Time-Life observed in 1966, 'The various underdeveloped countries are having to permit commercials because they can't afford a television system otherwise.'

In the 1960s and 1970s, the dominant form of television throughout Latin America came to be the *novelas* produced by stations such as TV Globo in Brazil, which were increas-

Early uses of animation in commercials: (top) the Gillette parrot asks 'How are ya fixed for blades?'; (below) Ajax Cleanser uses singing elves.

*Sixteen years of Oxo's
'Katie' commercials (above)
attracted a soap opera style
following, the family
changing with the social
climate of the times. In
1983 a new Oxo family was
introduced (right) but the
same theme continues.*

ingly adjusted to suit advertisers. Globo's Director-General said in 1975 that 'a television network's job is to reach those potential segments of the market and reveal, in all its ramifications, the arrival of modernity' – and modernity turned out to mean consumer goods. Globo itself defends the practice of 'merchandising' by arguing that 'it seems unjust not to profit' from the realistic nature of modern *novelas*. One *novela*, called *First Love*, had numerous scenes in which the characters rode bicycles: it was developed by the Caloi bicycle company in collaboration with Globo. Honda worked with Globo to produce *The Steel Horse*, in which Honda motorcycles could be seen in almost every episode.

More recently, in 1984, Globo produced a serial called *The Promise* in which Brazil's best-known actor, Francisco Coco, plays the part of a wealthy banker who goes into politics. He is shot while on a campaign visit to a prison, and from his hospital bed he deals with a procession of visitors including his wife, his mistress, his political adviser and journalists. He expresses his commitment to do something about the plight of prisoners. 'I have made a promise to these men – a moral promise that I insist on keeping,' he tells a journalist. 'To attend to their just claims, to try to set in motion all the bureaucracy of an inflexible penal system, to fight for better living conditions inside the prisons – this is a pledge I have made.' It is emotional stuff, but what viewers are not told is that the *novela* is largely funded by a bank, anxious to improve the image of banking and bankers. Jorge Adib, a 'consultant' to Globo, explains how he 'merchandised' the programme: 'We went to the Association of Bankers in Brazil. We knew that they were trying to make the image of the banker better, and we said, "Look, would you like to sell your merchandise here using our actor? You have to give us a big help to say what exactly is the life of a banker. Our banker in the *novela*, he has a wife, he has three children, he has all the kinds of problems that all husbands have. You have to understand that he is a human guy . . . He is not the guy who is getting your money and charging you interest. He has a real life, a normal life. He is human. He suffers. He laughs. It is what merchandising does."' What it undoubtedly does is to sell things. Adib is particularly proud of two examples. In one *novela* he 'sold the concept of plastic' on behalf of the Melissa plastics firm: 'The important thing is to keep the plastic up-to-date – rich people in our *novela* use the product, and they give an example for all the people.' In another case, a leading *novela* character went to a doctor to ask for treatment for his sclerosis. The doctor replied that he should use a particular product, which was not named. However, an extra-large 'S' was displayed prominently on the doctor's desk. The show just happened to be made by the Sandoz pharmaceutical laboratory, which was part-sponsoring it.

Not everyone approves of this kind of sponsorship. Lauro Cesar Muniz, a Brazilian author, has complained that 'the *telenovela* today makes a dangerous compromise with merchandising and is becoming just a long advertisement. Merchandising took control of the narrative, and now it commands the plot. Today authors think about a theme in terms of the merchandising that it will be related to, rather than the reality it will deal with.'

It is a complaint that has been heard many times around the world in the past thirty years. Whenever a country has considered introducing commercial television, there has

Another chimp: this time in a 1962 commercial for Xerox photocopiers.

always been a powerful lobby to argue that the demands of advertisers will somehow 'infect' the programmes and reduce their quality. This lobby has seldom been successful in preventing the arrival of commercial television, but its predictions have often come true. To take a particularly notorious example: in February 1983 Britain's first commercial breakfast-time channel, TV-am, went on the air. Its franchise had been won by a consortium led by Peter Jay, the former Ambassador to Washington, who was famous for his belief that television news should have a 'mission to explain' instead of what he called 'bias against understanding'. The channel had poor ratings at first, and was therefore unattractive to advertisers. Within three months Jay had been forced to resign, together with Anna Ford and Angela Rippon, Britain's best-known newsreaders. They were replaced by two 'unknown' presenters, Anne Diamond and Nick Owen. More importantly, the 'mission to explain' was abandoned in favour of straightforward entertainment from two puppets called Roland Rat and Kevin the Gerbil, as well as a 'televised agony column' from Diana Dors. The ratings immediately soared.

Hofmeister Lager's bear is keen on rock'n'roll and is generally a pretty cool guy

Warnings of a similar dilution of standards were expressed before the creation of ITV itself, in 1955. The Labour MP Christopher Mayhew formed a National Television Council to campaign against commercial television, to which he recruited such distinguished figures as Bertrand Russell and E. M. Forster. He also wrote a pamphlet, *Dear Viewer*, which sold 60,000 copies. 'I ask you,' he wrote in it, 'to exercise all the influence you have, as a free citizen of the most democratic country in the world, to prevent this barbarous idea being realised.' The Conservative peer Lord Hailsham said that commercial television would be like Caliban emerging from his 'slimy cavern', while Lord Esher described it as a 'planned and premeditated orgy of vulgarity'.

But the forces arrayed on the other side were even more powerful. The pro-commercial Popular Television Association, backed by the advertising industry and the Conservative Central Office, had raised £20,000 by the time of its first meeting, compared with the National Television Council's budget of £840. The Television Act was passed in 1954 despite the doom-laden speeches of its opponents, and on 22 September ITV went on the air for the first time, with a televised dinner from the Guildhall in London.

Dr Charles Hill, the Postmaster-General, said at the opening ceremony that 'we shall not be bothered by a violinist stopping in the middle of his solo to advise us of his favourite brand of cigarettes, nor will Hamlet halt his soliloquy to tell us what toothpaste they are using at Elsinore'. Oddly enough, toothpaste was in fact the subject of the very first commercial seen that night, a sixty-second spot for Gibbs SR. A toothbrush and a tube of SR were shown embedded in a block of ice in the middle of a stream ('It's tingling fresh. It's fresh as ice. It's Gibbs SR toothpaste . . .'). The advertisement also featured a woman named Meg Smith brushing her teeth 'up-and-down-and-round-the-gums'.

The first advertisement shown on ITV: Gibbs SR toothpaste embedded in a block of ice.

Despite Dr Hill's assurances, there were many protests about the intrusiveness of commercials in ITV's first couple of years. Parliament had been assured that advertisements would be shown only in 'natural breaks' or at the beginning or end of a programme, but MPs complained that the 'breaks' often seemed far from natural – in the middle of a boxing match, for instance. On one discussion programme

the editor of the *New Statesman*, Kingsley Martin, was stopped in mid-sentence to make way for a commercial for Tide washing powder. When a live production of *Hamlet* overran its allotted time, the picture was faded out shortly before the end and replaced by an advertisement for Kia-Ora orange drink. Lew Grade, head of ATV, telephoned the producer at Television House in Kingsway to ask angrily: 'What happened? What the devil happened?' 'Oh,' came the reply, 'they all died in the end.'

Critics of commercial television believed that their worst fears had been confirmed, but the advertisements were not universally execrated. The *Daily Mail*'s television columnist, Peter Black, wrote in 1962: 'Some commercials are so well made that although they last only a minute and involve their personages in a single incident, they seem to create a world as detailed as that of any soap operas.' This was particularly true of the advertising magazines (known as 'admags'), fifteen-minute programmes in which a regular cast of characters in a familiar setting would give brief plugs to dozens of products and companies. Many of the admags had sets designed to look like shops, including *Shop in the South*, presented by Sylvia Peters and Macdonald Hobley, and *Watson's Store*, with Vi Stevens and Jack Howarth (who later became better known as Albert Tatlock of *Coronation Street*). Comedians Tommy Trinder, Kenneth Horne and Richard Murdoch starred in the regular admag *In Store*. By far the most celebrated admag, however, was *Jim's Inn*, which was set in a pub presided over by Jimmy Hanley and Maggie Hanley. The programme was so popular that its cast produced an LP called *Singalog at Jim's Inn*. But it was the very familiarity of the admags – their soap-opera quality – that was to bring about their demise. The report of the Pilkington Committee on broadcasting, published in 1962, was highly critical of admags: 'In effect, characters known to viewers as friendly personalities because they appear in regular programmes endorse, as though they were disinterested parties, the claims of the advertisers. They give the impression of having, on the most sensible homely grounds, decided to recommend this article rather than that.' By 1963 the Postmaster-General had announced a complete ban on admags.

Since then, advertisers have used considerable ingenuity in transmitting their message in ways other than conventional 'spot' advertisements. Sponsorship of programmes is not allowed, but there is nothing to stop a company sponsoring a big sporting event which is to be covered by television. This is especially attractive to tobacco companies, which are forbidden to advertise cigarettes on television. In the past twenty years many cigarette firms have either taken over an existing tournament – as Embassy did with the World Snooker Championship – or created a new one. The many one-day cricket contests which have sprung up have often been sponsored by cigarette manufacturers (Benson and Hedges, John Player and Rothmans) though other companies have also been attracted. They include the National Westminster Bank, Gillette, Prudential Insurance, and Texaco. Since 1977, cricket test matches have been sponsored by Cornhill Insurance. Even if a firm does not sponsor an entire sporting event, it can still put its name on the screen. In show-jumping, several firms have 'bought up' riders and re-christened their horses after particular products, so that at the Horse of the Year Show viewers are presented with the curious spectacle

(Opposite) Cadbury's Smash, an imaginative series of commercials for instant mashed potato by director Bob Brooks.

One early 'admag' featured Doris Rogers as a 'store consultant'.

Animals have always been popular in commercials: Dulux paints (top) used an Old English sheepdog called Digby, while Katto-meat (below) found a cat called Arthur which ate with its paw.

In 1968 the original Lone Ranger and Tonto (Clayton Moore and Jay Silverheels) advertised Jeno's Pizza Rolls.

of Harvey Smith jumping the fences on the back of an animal named Sanyo Music Centre. A more common form of 'indirect' advertising is the purchase of billboards around the edges of sports grounds. At the 1970 World Cup in Mexico the British firm Mothercare paid £6,000 for a poster behind one of the goals on the pitch where England's team was playing.

Not all these advertisers and sponsors are interested only in buying cheap advertising time. Texaco, for example, said that it started sponsoring one-day international cricket matches in 1984 because it wanted to shed its purely American image and become associated with something as English as roast beef. In the United States, many large corporations claim to have even more high-minded motives in sponsoring programmes on the supposedly non-commercial Public Broadcasting Service (PBS). Since 1970, Mobil has been underwriting PBS's *Masterpiece Theatre*, which consists mainly of imported British dramas. 'Corporations are like people, they all have distinctive personalities,' says Herbert Schmertz, Mobil's Vice-President. 'One of the facets of our personality is our desire to be associated with excellence, a desire to support what we think are worthwhile cultural and artistic activities.' Other corporations have followed this example: Exxon, for instance, paid for *Theatre in America* and *Dance in America*. With each of these shows the sponsor's name is clearly stated at the beginning and end. The Federal Communications Commission does not permit PBS to broadcast 'commercial announcements of any character' but does allow – indeed, insist on – 'credits' being given. Some enthusiastic sponsors have occasionally overstepped the mark: when PBS transmitted an Almaden Tennis Tournament in 1976, the prizes were presented by an Almaden executive, who remarked that 'these old champions seem to improve with age – like our fine Almaden wines'. For the most part, however, sponsored broadcasts on PBS are decorous and highly praised.

Henry Fonda, one of many film stars to be lured into commercials, advertises GAF cameras.

'I think the networks should be doing this kind of programming,' Schmertz says. 'They obviously don't agree and they have rejected regularly the kind of shows that we want to sponsor. We offered each of the networks *Nicholas Nickleby* and they turned it down.' However, Mobil does sometimes break into commercial television. 'Each year we will have some well above average piece of quality drama to put on what we call our *ad hoc* network, the Mobil Showcase network, which is a loose confederation of about fifty stations which agree to pre-empt the network shows and run our show on a given night at a given time – and that gives us the appearance of being a network.' Each year Mobil spends about $9 million on acquiring programmes for PBS and commercial stations, as well as another $6 million on advertising and promotion for the shows.

Eleanor Roosevelt was paid $43,000 to say 'the new Good Luck margarine really tastes delicious'.

It is significant that this 'trademark publicity' began in the early 1970s, at a time when it was being revealed that several American multinationals had been involved in international politicking. There was a pressing need to restore the corporate images. A Mobil commercial of the period stated: 'Some people want to break up the big oil companies. Is smallness really best? Think hard . . . It's *your* country.' The clear implication was that if the big oil companies *were* broken up, *Masterpiece Theatre* would be the first casualty. The comedian Bob Hope appeared in a series of advertisements for Texaco. 'Who owns America's oil companies?' he asked. 'Fourteen

A 1964 commercial for the Democratic Party picked up a comment of Barry Goldwater's by showing the Eastern seaboard 'sawn off' from the rest of the USA.

million Americans, trusting in companies like Texaco! We're working to keep that trust.'

The company worst affected by the scandals of the early 1970s was ITT, which had helped the CIA to destabilise President Allende's government in Chile. In 1974, ITT spent $4 million producing a children's series called *The Big Blue Marble*, which was given free of charge to any television station that wanted it. The series featured smiling children from many different countries, and was supported by an $8 million advertising campaign which stressed that ITT was devoted to fostering good relations between all the people of the world.

Not surprisingly, all these corporate commercials were attacked for being 'political'. But political advertising has long been established as part of American television, ever since the 1952 Presidential election, when Dwight Eisenhower's advertising agency broke with the tradition of buying large chunks of time for whole speeches and instead prepared a number of thirty-second and sixty-second 'spots' consisting of cartoons, jingles and brief comments from the candidate. The most impressive example of the power of political advertising was in the battle for the Republican nomination in 1964: Henry Cabot Lodge won the New Hampshire primary despite being abroad throughout the campaign (as US Ambassador in Saigon), simply by using an old biographical commercial which had first been seen four years earlier.

Cabot Lodge's campaign soon fizzled out, however, and the Republicans chose Barry Goldwater. Until 1964, political commercials in Presidential elections had concentrated on projecting the candidate – perhaps as a man of action, in full cry on the hustings, or a family man, relaxing with his children. But the hallmark of the contest between Goldwater and Lyndon Johnson was 'adversarial' advertising. Goldwater had once suggested bombing part of Vietnam with 'a low-yield atomic device', so the Democrats produced commercials which showed mushroom clouds. Goldwater had also said, jokingly, that the Eastern seaboard of the United States should be 'sawn off' and floated out to sea; a Democratic advertisement gave a graphic picture of what the USA would look like if the East Coast were indeed removed. Goldwater attacked the Democrats' 'weird television advertising', but he too was capable of punching below the belt. Inspired by reports of Lyndon Johnson driving while drinking beer, the Republicans made a film in which beer cans were thrown from the window of a speeding car.

In a modern Presidential election, about half of a candidate's budget is spent on television spots. Controversy is never far away. When Edward Kennedy challenged Jimmy Carter for the Democratic nomination, Carter's staff made an issue of Kennedy's 'Chappaquiddick problem', so the Kennedy advisers retaliated by including in their commercials a film-clip in which Carter wielded a baseball bat – and missed the ball.

The FCC has tried to minimise controversy with its 'fairness doctrine'. Until the late 1960s this had been applied only to programmes, not commercials, but then a lawyer called John Banzhaf III argued successfully that stations which carried cigarette advertising should also have to broadcast, free of charge, balancing messages which pointed out the health hazards of smoking. These 'counter-commercials' were so persuasive that from January 1971 cigarette advertising was banned altogether. Thus ended the long love

Many well-known British comedians have lent their services to advertisers – for a fee: (from top) John Cleese selling Accurist watches; Penelope Keith advertising Parker pens; Tommy Cooper selling Sodastream ('lovely, really lovely'); Morecambe and Wise with racing driver James Hunt in commercial for Texaco; Alf Garnett (played by Warren Mitchell) extolling Findus foods.

affair between American television and cigarettes, which had begun with *Camel News Caravan* and *Man Against Crime*. In the late 1950s CBS had run a newspaper advertisement in which a television set was made to resemble a vending machine. The slogan was: 'CBS – The World's Greatest Cigarette Vending Machine.' A few years later Leroy Collins was sacked from his job as President of the National Association of Broadcasters after he had argued for some restrictions on cigarette advertising.

In Britain, commercials for cigarettes had been prohibited in August 1965. Political advertising had never been allowed. Some other subjects have also proved too sensitive for the Independent Broadcasting Authority. At the beginning of 1983 London Weekend Television agreed to make a free commercial for the Family Planning Association, in which two teenagers would talk about unwanted pregnancies ('So he's got her up the spout, eh?') and the singer Adam Faith would conclude: 'If you're not man enough to use birth control, you're not old enough to make love.' The IBA refused to let the commercial be transmitted, provoking loud protests. Nevertheless, it did approve a modified version, after long negotiations, which was shown later in the year. The phrase 'got her up the spout' was deleted, and Adam Faith's closing lines had been altered to 'Any idiot can get a girl into trouble – don't let it be you.'

'Public service announcements' of this kind are becoming common in British television as a way of giving admirable but impoverished groups the same access to a mass audience as the richest advertiser. One of the most remarkable experiments, which also began in 1983, was the introduction of a child with Down's Syndrome into the script of the soap opera *Crossroads*. The idea was suggested by the Mencap charity, as a way of demonstrating that mental disability need not prevent someone from leading a fulfilling life.

The introduction of advertising – albeit for a worthy cause – into a show such as *Crossroads* again raises questions about the relation between television programmes and the miniature dramas or comedies which interrupt them in the form of commercials. Some televised advertising campaigns have achieved a popularity and endurance which any soap opera or situation comedy would envy. The actress Mary Holland first appeared as 'Katie' in commercials for Oxo beef cubes in the autumn of 1958. For the next sixteen years Katie and her husband Philip were familiar figures on British screens. At first they were studiously classless, but in the early 1960s they seemed to be upwardly mobile: Katie sometimes put candles on the dinner table, and by 1963 she and Philip were attending the ballet. The advertising agency then feared that this might restrict the appeal of Oxo to middle-class people, so it hurriedly introduced Katie's dad, an unmistakeably working-class character. Kate and Philip were moved to the United States for a while, before returning to British settings in 1972. The series was stopped in 1974, but its memory lives on: it had such an effect on Mary Holland that she changed her name to Katie Holland.

One of the few campaigns to survive for longer than Katie is the PG Tips series of advertisements for tea, in which chimpanzees are seen behaving like humans. The movements of the chimps' mouths are cleverly synchronised with the voices of actors – the first of whom, back in 1956, was Peter Sellers. One of their advertisements, in which two chimps play the parts of removal men trying to carry a piano down-

Joan Collins and Leonard Rossiter in one of their witty half-minute comedies for Cinzano, which were discontinued in 1983.

stairs, has been shown more than 1,000 times – a record for a British commercial. Animals, though notoriously difficult to direct, have always been popular in television advertising. Dulux has been using Old English sheepdogs to sell its paints since 1964. Arthur the white cat, who picked up his food with his paw, appeared in Kattomeat commercials from 1967 until shortly before his death ten years later.

The most successful comic advertisements of recent times have been the Cinzano series, in which Leonard Rossiter invariably managed to tip his drink over Joan Collins. But although these have been immensely popular with viewers, they were terminated in 1983 by Cinzano's directors in Italy, who could not see anything humorous about a man spilling this precious drink over someone: it seemed quite the wrong image.

They may have been right. Witty commercials such as the Cinzano series or the PG Tips chimps may win awards for their elegance and humour, but they may not necessarily be the most effective way of increasing sales, as W.D. and H.O. Wills discovered in 1959 when they launched a new cigarette called Strand. The commercials featured a solitary, handsome figure in a trilby and a trenchcoat, alone in a dark London street. As he moodily lit up a cigarette, the voice-over said: 'You're never alone with a Strand.' The advertisements won great acclaim: Terence Brook, the actor who played the mysterious man, became a celebrity, and the theme music entered the hit parade. It was a perfect commercial – but it did not sell cigarettes. By the end of 1960 it had been discontinued, and shortly afterwards the same treatment was meted out to Strand cigarettes themselves. The problem, according to one theory, was that the audience believed that if they smoked Strand they would appear as friendless and lonely as the Terence Brook character.

Two poultry salesmen who became unlikely celebrities by appearing in their own commercials: (top) Frank Perdue, the American chicken king; (below) Colonel Sanders, begetter of Kentucky Fried Chicken.

Lord Leverhulme, according to legend, once said that he knew half the money he spent on advertising was wasted, but he could never find out which half. What is unquestionable is that television advertising *can* work. For every failure such as Strand, there are several spectacular successes. When the Hazel Bishop cosmetics firm started advertising on American television in 1950, it had an annual turnover of $50,000. Within two years its sales rose to $4,500,000 solely because of its commercials and its sponsorship of shows such as *This Is Your Life* and *Beat the Clock*. An equally dramatic success was achieved by the Northwestern Mutual Life Insurance Company when it spent $1 million on commercials during the Munich Olympics in 1972. A poll taken just before the Olympics put Northwestern thirty-fourth in the 'familiarity' rankings for insurance companies. Two weeks later, in a similar poll, Northwestern came third.

Television commercials have the power to create their own stars. Lorraine Chase, a Cockney who appeared in ads for Campari in the 1970s, became a regular guest on game shows and went on to star in a situation comedy. Even businessmen can be transformed into celebrities. Frank Perdue, the mournful-looking owner of Perdue's Chickens, was invited on to American chat shows because of the public response to the commercials in which he appeared. In Britain, similar status was achieved by Bernard Matthews, the Norfolk turkey farmer whose endlessly repeated catchphrase was 'it's bootiful', and Victor Kiam, the owner of Remington, who appeared in his firm's advertisements to announce that he had been so impressed by the electric razor his wife gave him that he had bought the company.

A British poultry breeder who achieved national fame through advertising: Bernard Matthews, producer of 'bootiful' turkeys.

The importance of commercials can also be gauged by the number of existing stars who have been lured into them. In the 1950s Eleanor Roosevelt was paid $43,000 to do a margarine commercial. One of the earliest advertisements in Britain used the author Sir Compton Mackenzie to sell Horlicks. In 1977 James Coburn was paid $500,000 simply for saying the words 'Schlitz Light' in a beer commercial. The following year Laurence Olivier received a similar sum for appearing in Polaroid advertisements. 'Sometimes I think I'll not be remembered for *Hamlet* nor *Richard III*,' he said. 'Nor even for *Wuthering Heights*. Sometimes I think a whole generation of youngsters will know me only as "that man who did the Polaroid commercials".' It was a feeling shared by many stars who became associated with a particular product. Bert Lahr, the American actor, once said that he was much better known for his appearances in commercials for Lay's Potato Chips than he was for playing the part of the lion in *The Wizard of Oz*. Yet there has never been a shortage of eminent figures prepared to put themselves at the service of an advertiser. In Britain, the former Metropolitan Police Commissioner Sir Robert Mark plugged Goodyear tyres ('a major contribution to road safety') while the former Foreign Secretary Lord George-Brown sang the praises of cross-Channel ferries. In the United States, Henry Fonda has sold GAF cameras as well as vinyl flooring. Even John Paul Getty, the world's richest man, was once prevailed upon to appear in a commercial for a firm of brokers. In his case, at least, it might seem that he did not do it for the money; but given his miserly reputation it is quite possible that he did.

Homepride Flour's little men in bowler hats are a long-running favourite.

Strangely enough, few American film directors have tried their hands at creating a drama in a minute or less, with the exception of Michael Cimino, who filmed commercials for Pepsi Cola and United Airlines in New York before moving to Hollywood, where he directed *The Deer Hunter*. In Britain, however, there is scarcely one film director of note who has not enjoyed the challenge of commercials. The list includes Ken Russell (Black Magic), Lindsay Anderson (Kellogg's Corn Flakes and Guinness), Joseph Losey (Horlicks and Ryvita), Karel Reisz (Mars Bars and Persil), John Schlesinger (Polo mints and Stork margarine) and Jack Gold (Wrigley's chewing gum and Hamlet cigars). Ridley Scott, who later directed *Alien*, created an evocative series of advertisements for Hovis bread, set in the cobbled streets of North England in the 1930s. One of the most prolific of them all has been Alan Parker, who directed not only the Cinzano advertisements with Joan Collins and Leonard Rossiter but also a touching series of commercials for Birdseye which told of the semi-requited love of a young girl for a boy who, though quite fond of her, really preferred his Beefburgers. Parker became better known as the director of *Bugsy Malone* and *Midnight Express*.

In June 1984, an Italian advertising agent broke the startling news that Federico Fellini and Franco Zeffirelli were to make their first-ever commercials. Yet perhaps the news was not quite so surprising: in the mid-1960s Fellini had watched a whole reel of British advertisements and had been awestruck. 'How can these people produce such little masterpieces lasting one minute?' he asked. When he makes his own 'little masterpiece', it will indeed seem that the commercials have become as significant as the programmes they interrupt.

'Only Heineken can do this, because it refreshes the parts other beers cannot reach'

Fun and Games.

In the final episode of *The Mary Tyler Moore Show*, her long-running situation comedy, Mary Tyler Moore addressed her colleagues: 'I thought about something last night: what is a family? And I think I know. A family is people who make you feel less alone and really loved. Thank you for being my family.' The irony was that *The Mary Tyler Moore Show* had been a rarity among situation comedies (or 'sitcoms', as they are usually known) by having a single woman as the heroine. For most of their history, sitcoms have been governed by one rule: the central element is the family. It can have quirks or complications, but it must be a family. A glance at the titles of some British and American sitcoms is enough to make the point – *My Wife Next Door, I Married a Bachelor, Bachelor Father, Father Dear Father, Not in Front of the Children, Mother Makes Three, My Good Woman, Happy Ever After, Bless This House* . . . it can be extended for ever.

Elizabeth Montgomery, the mischievous and trouble-prone spell-binder of Bewitched.

Until the 1960s, the family depicted in sitcoms tended to be the basic unit of wife and husband, without children. These comedies were so prevalent that they soon acquired a generic title in the television industry, where they were called 'Hi honey, I'm home' shows. In almost every episode of *Bewitched*, for example, the long-suffering husband would return home to discover that his wife (Elizabeth Montgomery) had been using her magical powers in his absence. The most famous and successful of all the many comedies in this genre was *The Dick van Dyke Show*, which co-starred Mary Tyler Moore as Dick's wife. 'In retrospect I suppose people would call it a "Hi honey, I'm home" show but in those days it was a little different in that it showed and examined what the husband did for a living,' Dick van Dyke says today. The marriage portrayed in the series 'seemed very real to me . . . there was more than a hint of sexuality between the husband and wife'. Of course the sexuality had to be implied rather than explicit: 'When we showed bedroom scenes they had to be twin beds in those days, you were not allowed to be in a double bed.' Nevertheless, Dick van Dyke thinks that his show was probably more realistic than most family sitcoms. 'One of the highest compliments I ever got for our show was from my wife. On seeing the first few episodes she said it was eerie to her because it was the same things that happened at home – she couldn't see the difference in my behaviour at home and on the show.'

The Dick van Dyke Show, *with Mary Tyler Moore, was the archetypal 'hi honey, I'm home' show.*

Lucille Ball and Desi Arnaz, indefatigable wife-and-husband stars of I Love Lucy.

An even more popular comedy series featured a genuine wife-and-husband team, Lucille Ball and Desi Arnaz. *I Love Lucy* started on CBS in 1951 and continued, under a number of titles, until 1967. Since then it has had a vigorous afterlife, with old re-runs continually being shown around the world. 'It was funny, she was funny, the writing was funny – the

The queen of television entertainment, Lucille Ball appearing in a TV special called Lucy in London.

Harry H. Corbett and Wilfred Brambell playing the frustrated son and the miserly father in Steptoe and Son.

characters and situation still hold up to this day,' says Carol Burnett, another American comedienne. What was especially remarkable about the show's success was that it required the audience to alter their perceptions of Lucille Ball's character. In the movies, she had usually played sophisticated and glamorous women, but when she transferred to television she adopted an utterly different *persona*, scatter-brained and accident-prone.

Throughout her many series, however, the important point about Lucy was that she was lovable. Her family might be driven to despair by her capacity for getting into scrapes, but they could never be angry with her. It was not until the 1960s that a bleaker view of family life smuggled its way into situation comedies.

The trend started in Britain, where some writers and performers had already tried to escape the restrictions of the classic formula. In *Hancock's Half-Hour*, which ran from 1956 to 1961, Tony Hancock played the part of a gloomy dreamer (not unlike his character in real life), partnered by the mischievous Sid James. When Hancock tried to go it alone after 1961 ('Sid makes films without me, why can't I make one without him?') he was a failure; in 1968, after years of alcoholism and depression, he committed suicide.

In 1962, a year after the end of *Hancock's Half-Hour*, the show's scriptwriters, Alan Galton and Ray Simpson, developed their theme of comic pessimism for a new series, *Steptoe and Son*. This reverted to the tradition of having a family at the centre of a sitcom – a father and son running a rag-and-bone business – but broke the rules by keeping the family permanently miserable. The son (Harry H. Corbett) had aspirations of 'bettering himself' and hated the dirt and the penny-pinching economy of their ramshackle home. Whenever he rebuked his father (Wilfred Brambell) for being a 'dirty old man' he was usually rewarded with a scowl and a snarl. The show was a great popular hit in Britain, and its success was repeated when it was produced in the United States in 1972 under the name *Sanford and Son*, with two black actors – Redd Foxx and Desmond Wilson – in the title roles.

Despite their ceaseless battles, however, the father and son never quite managed to conceal their affection for each other. A more radical departure from traditional sitcoms occurred in 1966 with *Till Death Us Do Part*, which might equally well have been called *A Family at War*. From start to finish of each episode, the four main characters argued with each other constantly: Alf Garnett, the working-class bigot who worshipped the Queen, the Conservative Party and West Ham football club but hated just about everything else (brilliantly played by Warren Mitchell); his 'silly old moo' of a wife (Dandy Nichols); their daughter (Una Stubbs), always caught in the cross-fire; and her husband (Tony Booth), a Liverpudlian Marxist – or 'Scouse git' as Alf preferred to call him.

'It took off,' says Dennis Main Wilson, who produced *Till Death Us Do Part*. 'In all my years I've not seen anything like it. The press were ecstatic in that we had broken the conventions . . . there were no feed-line tags, it wasn't format comedy, it was truthful comedy.' Within weeks it was the most popular programme in Britain, attracting an audience of 18 million. 'The BBC left us alone, more or less,' Johnny Speight, the scriptwriter, recalls, 'and it wasn't until the third one had gone out that they realised what was going on because

The American version of Steptoe and Son *was christened* Sanford and Son, *with Redd Foxx and Desmond Wilson in the title roles.*

Three long-serving stalwarts of British television comedy: (from top) Benny Hill, a lecherous Englishman; Dave Allen, a chain-smoking Irishman; and Stanley Baxter, a Scottish impersonator.

the press had suddenly gone mad about it and so had the public – in fact everyone was glued to the set because this character had taken off, and by that time I suppose if they had wanted to stop us it was too late, because it would have to be a brave man or a lunatic to go against all the national press of the day.' But the show came in for heavy criticism in some quarters. Mary Whitehouse's 'Clean Up TV Campaign' kept a tally of the number of times the word 'bloody' was uttered. Mrs Whitehouse now admits that much of the series was 'very clever and very funny – there was many a night when I sat there with my family and had a good laugh. But once again the thing went too far.' The programme reacted to her criticism by showing a copy of her book, *Cleaning Up TV*, being burnt in the Garnetts' fireplace. As Johnny Speight says, 'We were treading on a knife edge, because we were getting to the stage where I was really writing completely uninhibitedly.' What brought about the show's demise – according to Speight – was the arrival as Chairman of the BBC Governors in September 1967 of Lord Hill, a man whose views about 'permissiveness' on television were none too liberal. When the second season of *Till Death Us Do Part* finished in February 1968, Johnny Speight announced that it would not reappear. 'We have been irritated by a number of idiotic and unreasonable cuts,' he said. 'The trouble has been since Lord Hill's arrival at the BBC and I could be the victim of new policies. I would write another series for the BBC but only if this censorship was stopped.' The show did eventually return, four years later, but it no longer seemed as daring as at first.

West German television produced its own version of *Till Death Us Do Part*, called *One Heart and One Soul*. 'I had a letter from the people who made the German version,' Johnny Speight recalls, 'and they said it was very popular over there although they had one difficulty – and that was, they said, that they had no history of racialism in Germany!'

Speight, a socialist, had conceived Alf Garnett as a satire on racists and reactionaries. 'I personally despised, hated, loathed him for a long, long time,' he says. 'The funny thing was, though, that as I wrote him and Warren performed him, we grew to love him ... Even today I still have a soft spot for Alf and so does Warren.' It seems that the viewers felt a similar affection for this repulsive character, thus wrecking the original intention of the show. This was even more noticeable when the series was adapted for American television under the title *All in the Family*. The Garnett figure of Archie Bunker (played by Carroll O'Connor) was as provocatively loud-mouthed as his British prototype; yet he was also, in his own way, as lovable as Lucille Ball. And although the show was praised for 'breaking new ground' in situation comedy, it was in some respects reaffirming the conventions of the genre: the Bunkers may have bickered all the time, but they were indubitably a closely-knit family.

'All successful comedies really have some trap in which people must exist – like marriage,' says Barry Took, the veteran British scriptwriter and producer. He believes that the 'perfect situation' for a sitcom is 'a little enclosed world where you have to live by rules'. However, although the family is the most popular of these enclosed worlds, it is by no means the only one. A highly successful British comedy series of the 1970s, *Porridge*, was set in a prison: its most potent ingredient was the enforced comradeship between two cell-mates, played by Ronnie Barker and Richard

Carroll O'Connor (right) as Archie Bunker, the American version of Alf Garnett, with son-in-law Mike (Rob Reiner) in All In The Family.

Beckinsale. Another enclosed world, which has produced several of the most popular sitcoms ever, is the army. In Britain, it was the setting for Granada Television's series *The Army Game*, first transmitted in 1957, which starred Alfie Bass and Bill Fraser as an unlikely pair of soldiers and Bill Hartnell as their sergeant-major. A follow-up series, *Bootsie and Snudge*, took Bass and Fraser into civilian life, where they worked 'below stairs' in a gentlemen's club; the humour of the original was maintained partly because of the strength of the two characters but also because they were still in an enclosed world – that of the servants' quarters. Moreover, the emotional bond between the two men was strikingly similar to that between husband and wife, the more conventional sitcom coupling.

In 1968 Jimmy Perry and David Croft used a military setting for the BBC's *Dad's Army*, a richly comic series about the adventures (or, more often, misadventures) of the Walmington-on-Sea platoon of the Home Guard during the Second World War. As with most army sitcoms, the central joke was that the soldiers, however well-intentioned, were hopelessly incompetent. They were led by the local bank manager (played by Arthur Lowe), who in the evenings would assume the rank and uniform of Captain Mainwaring, trying to no avail to turn his motley crew into 'a force of fighting men'. His efforts were usually sabotaged by the soft-hearted nature of his second-in-command, Sergeant Wilson (John Le Mesurier), and by the amateurism of the rest of the platoon. They included the milksop Pike (Ian Lavender), angrily referred to by Captain Mainwaring as a 'stupid boy', whose mum was worried that he might catch cold; the local butcher, Jones (Clive Dunn), whose frequent cries of 'Don't panic' always achieved the opposite result to that intended; the 'spiv', Walker (James Beck), surreptitiously puffing at his black-market cigarettes; the doddery old-age pensioner (Arnold Ridley), whose only contribution to the platoon was to supply 'my sister Dolly's fairy cakes'; and the deranged Scot (John Laurie), whose manic belligerence was felt even by Captain Mainwaring to be slightly over the top. The comedy of these characters was able to flourish largely because the unpleasant reality of war never intruded into the enclosed world of Mainwaring's volunteers.

The same was true of America's first popular army sitcom, *Sergeant Bilko*, also known as *The Phil Silvers Show* and *You'll Never Get Rich*, which ran for 143 episodes on CBS between 1955 and 1959. Although it was supposedly set in the Fort Baxter army camp in Kansas, the men seldom seemed to have to bother with ordinary military duties. The essence of the show was Bilko himself (a part especially created for Phil Silvers), the 'fast-thinking, fast-talking, fast-buck artist' whose ingenious schemes for making pots of money always just foundered. But the comedy also rested on the large and crazy group of characters with whom the scriptwriters (including Neil Simon) surrounded Bilko: Colonel 'Melonhead' Hall (Paul Ford), who occasionally tried to turn the men of Fort Baxter into more professional soldiers but was invariably defeated by the immensity of the task; Mess Sergeant Ritzik (Joe E. Ross), the dim-witted compulsive gambler; Private Doberman (Maurice Gosfield), a cheerful simpleton; Private Fender (Herbie Faye), a gloomy pessimist who muttered 'I knew it, he's sold us into slavery' as another of Bilko's schemes was revealed. The machine-gun pace at which the lines were delivered was

Institutions of very different kinds were the settings for these two sitcoms of the late 1960s and early 1970s: Please, Sir *(top) and* On The Buses *(below).*

(Opposite) One of the original features of Monty Python's Flying Circus *was the use of linking animation created by Terry Gilliam and Katy Hepburn.*

reminiscent of the Marx Brothers at their best, and so was the quality: 'Men, this is it – get your hips fitted for Jaguars,' Bilko would exclaim when he thought that, at last, he was in the money.

The camaraderie of Bilko's platoon was one of the influences on the writers of America's most impressive sitcom of the 1970s, *M*A*S*H*, which lasted for 251 episodes between 1972 and 1983. But the show's creator, Larry Gelbart, took *M*A*S*H* beyond the simple laugh-a-minute routine of most sitcoms. The initials in the title stood for Mobile Army Surgical Hospital, and *M*A*S*H* was not afraid of showing the bloody reality of war-time injuries. In one famous episode a character actually died on the operating table – an extraordinary breach of the rules of sitcom. Although the series was set in the Korean War of the 1950s, it had an obvious contemporary resonance, starting as it did at a time when the United States was still deeply embroiled in Vietnam. As *Newsweek* magazine commented: 'The joke – which wasn't a joke to begin with, anyway, but a manifest irony: doctors sent to war to save lives, subversives in fatigues – has steadily gone deeper. Without ever moralising, *M*A*S*H* is the most moral entertainment on commercial television. It proposes craft against butchery, humour against despair, wit as a defence mechanism against the senseless enormity of the situation.' At times *M*A*S*H* abandoned wit altogether and produced something more closely resembling serious drama. In one episode Hawkeye (the undisputed star of the show, played by Alan Alda) and Trapper (Wayne Rogers) protested at the US Army's shelling of a Korean village – an uncomfortable reminder that similar incidents were occurring in Vietnam even as the series was transmitted.

Yvonne de Carlo and Fred Gwynne in The Munsters, *about a family of well-meaning ghouls.*

'The setting was unique,' Larry Gelbart said, many years later. 'It really let us talk about Hemingway's definition of heroism, "grace under pressure". It let us talk about how you'd like to behave in a terrible situation, that you hoped you could be efficient even if you didn't love your job, that you hoped you could maintain your sanity, that you hoped you wouldn't become the thing you hated. It let us use humour as a weapon and as a defence.' Gelbart himself left the show in 1976; by then, too, the Vietnam war had ended. Alan Alda then acquired the title of 'creative consultant', often writing and directing episodes as well as starring in them. (He won Emmy awards for all three functions.) The series continued to win large audiences and critical acclaim until Alda decided to terminate it in February 1983, believing that *M*A*S*H* would soon run out of things to say. The last episode, 'Goodbye, Farewell and Amen', ran for two-and-a-half hours and was watched by 80 million Americans.

*M*A*S*H may have been set in Korea, but few viewers can have missed its relevance to America's involvement in Vietnam; such was the success of the series that it continued long after the end of the Vietnam war.*

One of the few critics to doubt that *M*A*S*H* had departed from the traditions of sitcom was the American writer Roger L. Hofeldt, who argued that the show had not truly challenged the 'family format' of situation comedy: 'By using the characters to create a replica of American society, the producers of *M*A*S*H* have discovered another format for examining issues which are relevant to a vast and highly differentiated audience.' The abiding rule, whether in *M*A*S*H* or a 'family' sitcom such as *The Dick van Dyke Show*, is that a character must not face the world alone: she or he must experience the joys and tribulations of life as part of some larger social unit. When *Happy Days* began in 1974, the ultra-cool Arthur Fonzarelli – 'The Fonz' – was a loner, unconnected to anyone else in the show; the initial ratings

Henry Winkler as The Fonz in Happy Days *became a teenage hero in the mid-1970s.*

for *Happy Days* were poor to average. Towards the end of 1975, however, he moved in as a lodger with the main family in the programme, the Cunninghams. 'I knew that if I got him over the garage I could get him into the kitchen; he could "become" a member of the family,' said Garry Marshall, the creator of *Happy Days*. Almost immediately, the series went to the top of the ratings and The Fonz (played by Henry Winkler) became a teenage hero.

The need to have characters under the same roof also explains the prevalence of 'flat-share' comedies. Notable British examples have included *The Liver Birds* (1969), in which Nerys Hughes and Polly James played the parts of two young women from Merseyside who cling together for mutual support, innocents in an exciting world; *Man About the House* (1973), with Richard O'Sullivan as the bachelor sharing a flat with two bachelor women (Sally Thomsett and Paula Wilcox) and dealing with the demands of the couple downstairs, George and Mildred (Brian Murphy and Yootha Joyce); and *Rising Damp* (1974), which starred Leonard Rossiter as the miserly landlord Rigsby, abusing most of his tenants while trying to win the favours of Miss Jones (Frances de la Tour). A more recent and decidedly different venture into this field has been *The Young Ones* (1982), in which a group of undergraduate flat-sharers often bring their house literally crashing down around them as they hurl vitriol at one another. The actors in *The Young Ones* all made their names as 'alternative comedians', whose humour was much more anarchic than one would normally expect in a sitcom. But their use of a surrogate family – albeit one composed of freaks and maniacs – made them part of a long television tradition.

Nevertheless, *The Young Ones* is one of the handful of programmes which have extended the boundaries of television comedy. Half-way through each episode there would be a musical interlude in which a rock band would perform on the set of the show itself; within any particular episode there might be parodies of other programmes, or a picture of a happy family actually watching *The Young Ones* only to find their television exploding. All these devices served to remind the audience that it was seeing an artefact; the producers revelled in the limitations of the medium, rather than trying to overcome them by encouraging a suspension of disbelief on the part of the viewers.

Only a few comedy shows have dared to take advantage of television in this way. The first British attempt was probably *That Was The Week That Was* (*TW3*), which was screened live on Saturday nights between November 1962 and December 1963. Ned Sherrin, *TW3*'s director, ordered that camera-shots could include not only the stars but also the audience, boom microphones, other cameras and even other performers who were not actually on stage at the time – all of which had previously been unthinkable. *TW3* also broke with tradition by mixing numerous different forms – satire, songs, cartoons, straightforward comedy sketches, as well as more serious items. One reason for this was that *TW3* was made by the BBC's current affairs department rather than Light Entertainment.

Many of the presenters and actors in *TW3* had made their names in university revues such as *Beyond the Fringe* and for the next twenty years the most original comedies on British television often came from these university humorists, including John Cleese, Bill Oddie, Peter Cook and Eleanor

In The Fall and Rise of Reginald Perrin *(1976), Leonard Rossiter played a middle-aged sales executive at Sunshine Desserts who rebelled against his commuter existence and the convenience food industry.*

'That was the week that was – it's over, let it go . . .' Each edition of TW3 opened with a song by Millicent Martin into which new topical comments were inserted every week.

Robin's Nest *(1977), starring Richard O'Sullivan and Tessa Wyatt, was one of two spin-offs from* Man About The House; *the other was* George and Mildred.

Rowan Atkinson, one of a new generation of British comedians in the 1980s, made his name on Not The Nine O'Clock News.

Bron. Various permutations of the members of this group worked on *TW3*'s successor, *Not So Much a Programme, More a Way of Life* (1964), a blend of sketches and live discussions which, like *TW3* itself, was hosted by David Frost. He went on to present *The Frost Report* in 1966 and 1967. Its scriptwriters included John Cleese, Eric Idle, Terry Jones, Michael Palin and Graham Chapman; in 1969 this team came together again to write and star in *Monty Python's Flying Circus*.

Monty Python has passed into legend, and justifiably so. It was not a situation comedy, and it did not obey the rules of any other television form either. It even defied the convention that jokes had to have punch-lines: a sketch would often be terminated after a couple of minutes by the arrival of Graham Chapman, clad in military uniform, who would announce that 'this sketch is becoming silly – stop it'. The picture might then change to Terry Gilliam's weird animations, which would take up an idea that had been explored in an earlier sketch. Yet what might have seemed at first sight to be an incoherent jumble of bits and pieces actually had a remarkable unity of theme and style; particular catchphrases or characters would reappear in many different guises in the course of a show.

Monty Python also drew attention to the fact that it was itself a television programme by subverting the conventions of the medium: its end-credits would sometimes roll only a minute after the show had started. Viewers would then hear what appeared to be the voice of a BBC announcer trailing the evening's next programme – which would turn out to be another Python sketch parodying some archetypal television form such as a chat show or a quiz game. One of the most frequently repeated phrases in *Monty Python* was 'And now for something completely different'; the promise was always kept. What was most extraordinary was the sheer number of ideas which were crammed into each half-hour edition. As one critic wrote, 'The writers seemed to have so many ideas that items which might have been stretched into a situation comedy were consumed in seconds in order to make room for more.'

It was an exhausting way of working, and by 1974 the Pythons felt unable to continue with the show; since then, they have worked together only on occasional feature films. Individually, they have produced some memorable programmes. With his wife Connie Booth, John Cleese wrote and starred in *Fawlty Towers* (1975), a successful series set in a West Country hotel. It was brilliantly funny, not least because of the acting from Cleese and Booth as well as Prunella Scales as the domineering wife, Sybil, and Andrew Sachs as the Spanish waiter, Manuel; in form, however, it was a reversion to traditional sitcom. *Monty Python's Flying Circus* had been something completely different.

One programme which anticipated the Python team's scatter-shot style was *Rowan and Martin's Laugh-In*, which began in 1967 on NBC. Like Python, it was a montage of sketches, surrealist nonsense and catchphrases ('Sock it to me', or 'Veeerrrry interrrresting – but stupid'). Dick Martin, who co-hosted the show with Dan Rowan, says that it was a reaction against the length of sketches in comedy shows, and was inspired by 'the one-frame cartoons from *Punch*, or the *Saturday Evening Post*, or *Playboy*, where they told a rather marvellous joke in one frame'. Within nine weeks of going on the air, *Rowan and Martin's Laugh-In* was the most

Toyah Willcox with Kenny Everett in The Kenny Everett Television Show *(1982), a series for which the adjective 'zany' might have been specially invented.*

Fawlty Towers *was blessed with an unimprovable cast, including John Cleese.*

A typically kooky, wacky, crazy etc. etc. scene from Rowan and Martin's Laugh-In.

popular show in America.

'It was the first show that I can ever remember where there were no rules, there was no beginning, no middle, no end,' Martin says. Scriptwriters were told to 'just write whatever you want and see what happens'. Martin believes that it was also the first 'electronic comedy', specially created for television. 'Up until then there had been televised radio and televised vaudeville,' he says, 'and it was hilarious, of course, it always will be, but it was never an electronic use of the material. In order to do it electronically you had to do it in many, many cuts – so it was really an editor's delight.' No sketch lasted for more than a few seconds.

Dan Rowan and Dick Martin even managed to persuade Richard Nixon of the benefits of appearing on their scatter-shot comedy series.

Martin says that the audience 'would see the most startling things, because they never knew that all of a sudden John Wayne would walk on the stage and do six or eight lines and then walk off'. Wayne was the first of many guest stars with walk-on parts; his own contribution to the show was to utter the line, 'Well I don't think that is funny'. Other celebrities who appeared included Jack Lemmon, Kirk Douglas and – most surprisingly – Richard Nixon, during the 1968 election. 'Our show was politically oriented,' Martin recalls. 'We tried desperately to keep it balanced, and we had writers who were at opposite ends of the pole so that it was really kept balanced; and Mr Nixon was running for office and agreed to come on and say "Sock it to me". He did this, and we offered the same opportunity to Hubert Humphrey, whose advisers turned it down. If you recall, Mr Nixon only won by 1 million votes – a lot of people have accused us!'

Rowan and Martin's Laugh-In lasted until 1973. Two years later, NBC introduced another unusual comedy show, *Saturday Night Live*. It used the formula which had been invented by *That Was The Week That Was* in Britain thirteen years earlier – political satire, songs, sketches – but to an American audience it was refreshingly new. As *TW3* had done, the show launched the careers of several famous comedians, including John Belushi, Gilda Radner, Dan Aykroyd and Chevy Chase, who was best-known for his impersonations of the accident-prone President Gerald Ford: in one typical Ford sketch, Chase stapled his ear to the desk.

Saturday Night Live launched the careers of many of the best comic film actors of the late 1970s and early 1980s, including Chevy Chase, Dan Aykroyd, Gilda Radner, Eddie Murphy and John Belushi.

Programmes such as *Saturday Night Live* may appear to be thrillingly original, but in some respects they are merely modernised and sophisticated versions of the oldest entertainment tradition of all in American television, that of the 'variety show', based on vaudeville. In 1948 comedian Milton Berle inaugurated his *Texaco Star Theatre*, broadcast by NBC on Tuesday nights to an immense audience (restaurant owners complained that no one went out to dinner on a Tuesday because of Milton Berle). Berle became known as 'Mister Television' or 'The King of Comedy', and his acts – which often involved him in dressing up in women's clothes – would be interspersed with performances from jugglers, dancers or acrobats.

'We had tremendous censorship in those days,' Berle recalls. 'You couldn't say "hell" or "damn". I'll never forget one night . . . I said, "Well, I just flew in from La Guardia airport in a heck-acopter." That's how afraid I was. Then I said, "I'm going now to Nevada, I'm going to stop off at the Hoover Darn."' Such was Berle's value to NBC that the network gave him a contract which guaranteed him $200,000 a year for the next thirty years, regardless of whether he was doing a show or not.

Milton Berle was billed as 'Mister Television' and paid $200,000 a year from 1948 onwards, but his Texaco Star Theatre fizzled out after seven years.

The other networks tried to find someone who could compete with Berle. Worthington Minor of CBS decided that 'we had to have two things: one was a non-performing Master of Ceremonies and the second thing was an MC who had the most superb taste in discovering and choosing talent'. The person he selected was a former gossip writer named Ed Sullivan. 'I realised he had grave handicaps,' Minor admits. 'Physically, he was not the most attractive of men.' But no one at CBS could think of a better suggestion and so *Toast of the Town*, presented by Ed Sullivan, was rushed on to the air in June 1948. 'The critics' reaction was devastating,' Minor recalls. 'They had committed themselves to Berle. Berle's great public were kids and bar-flies and that was not what Ed Sullivan was about. So I made a very small bet of five dollars that the Ed Sullivan show would outlast Milton Berle. Well, Milton Berle lasted seven years, if I'm not mistaken. NBC signed a contract whereby he was on the salary for life – a mistake, as he lasted seven years. Now Ed Sullivan worked and worked hard, and he produced a show for twenty-three years.' In the course of those twenty-three years (during which the programme's title was changed to *The Ed Sullivan Show*) Sullivan introduced many new acts to the American television audience, the most famous of whom were Elvis Presley (who had to be shot only from the waist up while he wiggled his pelvis as he sang 'Hound Dog') and the Beatles. The secret of Sullivan's success was that he knew that he could not sing, dance or tell a joke well. He knew that his function was simply to act as the compère for people who did have talent.

Ed Sullivan, a man of no particularly discernible talents, had his own show for twenty-three years and introduced such performers as the Beatles to the American public.

Despite the example set by Sullivan, the networks also continued to produce variety shows hosted by people who were performers in their own right. Sid Caesar's *Your Show of Shows*, which started in 1950 on NBC, featured the usual assortment of dancers and acrobats, but it was dominated by the comedy of Caesar himself, partnered by Imogen Coca. Caesar assembled a formidable team of scriptwriters who included Neil Simon, Mel Brooks and Woody Allen.

A few years later it became fashionable for singers to be given variety shows, such as Perry Como, Dean Martin and Andy Williams. 'Musical variety television was an American art form for many years,' says Dwight Hemion, who produced many such programmes. But it did not last: 'Right now, there is not a single variety television series on the networks.' Hemion suggests a number of reasons for the decline. 'One is that the real artists, the major artists that you wanted to get on your series on a weekly basis, really start to lay back and not want to be on the weekly show because they are too interested in doing their own "Special". So you couldn't get the Bette Midlers and the Streisands and the Manilows and the McCartneys and all those big names to come on and do a spot on a weekly show because they didn't want to over-expose themselves . . . Secondly, a lot of the talk shows that we have in this country, the Carson show, the Douglas show, the Griffin show . . . use the same people that we use, and they go on and they sit and chat and they sing a song – which is not much different than what you do in weekly variety television. Thirdly and most importantly, the really good people realise that you can't do it good every week. Many of the hosts of those shows were not performers, and they were the best ones because they didn't have to be good every week, they just had to be there every week. So we had a whole history of Gary Moore, Arthur Godfrey, Ed Sullivan – non-performing people who were more successful

From the late 1940s Arthur Godfrey had two weekly shows on American television, Arthur Godfrey and His Friends *and* Arthur Godfrey's Talent Scouts.

(Following page) Cher appeared in several particularly spectacular 'specials' in the 1970s. One reason for the decline of variety shows, according to American producers, is that stars prefer to have their own programmes.

Donny and Marie Osmond, Mormon siblings who were protegés of Andy Williams, had their own show in 1976.

at doing weekly television than Sammy Davis or even Dean Martin.' Today, Hemion argues, those 'non-performers' have switched from variety to chat shows.

The variety show may have disappeared from American television but it is still very much alive elsewhere. In the Philippines, one of the most popular television programmes is *Student Canteen*, a lunchtime variety show which has been broadcast ever since 1957. The presenter, Roberto Ledesma, admits that the shape of *Student Canteen* – song-and-dance, quizzes and talent contests – has altered little in the past twenty-seven years: 'But the girls change, because we have to keep them young and acceptable to people.'

Variety galore: (top) Miss Piggy interviews Johnny Carson; (below) Bob Hope joshes with Fozzie Bear.

The part of the world with the greatest appetite for variety shows is Latin America, where, as television became more widely available in the late 1950s and early 1960s, programmers adopted them for their 'mass appeal'. Most of these shows, both then and now, stick to a predictable formula of *'ilusiones, emociones y sorpresas entre risas y canciones'* (illusions, emotions and surprises among laughter and singing), but what distinguishes them is their astonishing duration. In the early days of Argentine television, Alexandro Romay's shows could last for anything up to ten hours continuously; Nicholas Mansera's were only slightly shorter. In Chile, Mario Kreutzberger began his *Gran Show Dominical* which later evolved into *Sabados Gigantes* and is still running today, more than twenty years later. Each edition of *Sabados Gigantes* runs for six-and-a-half hours; Kreutzberger then takes a break before returning with *Nocha de Gigantes* for a further two hours. Kreutzberger is known simply as 'Mister TV' in Chile; he is also the country's wealthiest television personality. Non-stop song-and-dance can be found in Brazil, too, where *The Silvio Santos Show* has been transmitted for two decades, with each show lasting for eight-and-a-half hours without a break – except for commercials, of course. Santos has made so much money that he now possesses his own channel which has, in less than a year, become the second most popular in Brazil. Another Brazilian variety show which has lasted for twenty years is *Chacrinha*, starring Abelardo Barbosa ('The Pope of Communications') and the beautiful Chacrettes.

As Dwight Hemion suggests, in the United States the functions of the old variety shows have been taken over by chat shows. Indeed it is difficult to draw any clear distinctions between the two, for the 'talk and variety' format has been used by the networks since NBC launched its *Tonight Show* in 1954, under the chairmanship of Steve Allen. The ratings shot up when Allen was replaced by the nervy and argumentative Jack Paar in 1957; five years later the show became even more profitable when it was handed over to Johnny Carson, who has presided ever since. By the 1980s Carson was being paid $2,500,000 a year; the amount of money he has accumulated over the years is indicated by the fact that his wife was awarded more than $20 million in alimony when she divorced him in 1984. Carson is *the* star of the show: he employs a large and expensive team of gag-writers, and it often seems that he uses the guests on his programme as a way of projecting his own personality rather than finding out about theirs. From the opening moments, when Ed McMahon announces 'Heeeeeere's Johnny!' only one person is allowed to hold the floor.

Many of Carson's rivals object to his self-aggrandisement. 'Carson's held up as being the example of what a talk show

Steve Allen, first host of NBC's Tonight Show *in 1954, lasted for only three years.*

(Previous page) After the American Quiz-show scandals of the 1950s, British television avoided big-money quizzes; Hughie Green's Double Your Money *was a notable exception.*

When Jack Paar replaced Steve Allen on the Tonight Show *in 1957 the ratings soared.*

should be, and this is where I disagree,' says Michael Parkinson, who hosted a chat show on the BBC between 1971 and 1982. 'Carson doesn't do a talk show as such, he does this talk and variety show. In other words, the people who Carson has on to talk are not important to Carson, it doesn't matter who they are. He just uses people as props to bounce off. He's brilliant – he's a stand-up comic, a magnificent quick-witted man – but he's not an interviewer. In my view, if Carson's life depended on asking three sensible questions consecutively, he wouldn't manage it.' In Parkinson's view, the most important element in a talk show is the guest and the best person to present it is a journalist – which Parkinson was. 'The problem is that it makes you very famous very quickly and you lose that distance that there should be between the journalist and the person you're interviewing – they start treating you on the same level as they are.' Parkinson recalls that in his first series, in 1971, he called all his guests 'Mr' or 'Ma'am', until he interviewed Orson Welles. 'Half way through the interview Welles looked at me and he said, "Tell me, why do you call me Mr Welles and not Orson?' Thinking quickly, in a sick and frantic manner, I said, "Well, because of your huge talent; in deference to that." And he smiled and said "Bullshit", and he was right of course. Next time round I called him Orson and he called me Mike.'

Michael Parkinson, Barnsley-born former journalist, was Britain's longest-running chat-show host.

Parkinson's belief that the host should not try to outdo the guest has sometimes been severely tested. On one occasion he nearly lost his temper when Rod Hull's puppet Emu grabbed him by the tie and wrestled him to the floor. Another time he had to endure fifteen minutes of abuse from Muhammad Ali, who called him a 'honky' and a 'stupid white man'. After the show Parkinson was sitting in his dressing-room feeling depressed when his father walked in. 'My father was a Yorkshire man and a miner and he was not a man who minced words,' Parkinson says. 'He said, "It was thy fault." I said, "My fault, Dad? What could I have done?" He said, "Why didn't thou thump him?" Now my dad would have thumped him, you see – my dad would probably therefore have been a better talk-show host than I was.'

The one British talk-show host who has fought back is David Frost, whose aggressive style of interviewing became famous in the mid-1960s: he sometimes seemed more like a prosecuting counsel than an interviewer, rising from his chair and waving his clip-board dramatically at the guest, inviting the audience to side with him. When he interviewed the swindler Emil Savundra, he was accused of conducting a 'trial by television'. However, as the 1960s wore on, Frost calmed down, and by the 1970s he was a less demonstrative interviewer, even when dealing with such tainted personalities as Richard Nixon or the Shah of Iran.

When Michael Parkinson left the BBC in 1982 for a £3.5 million job on Australian television, he was replaced by the Irish disc jockey Terry Wogan, who soon became the British star of the early 1980s. Interestingly enough, Wogan had won his television reputation by presiding over *Blankety Blank*, a representative of the other type of television entertainment which has not suffered from diminishing popularity – the game show. But although the game show is perennially successful, it has undergone some significant mutations over the years.

At first, it was more usually known as the quiz show. The questions seemed serious and taxing – unlike the inanities of

As a young man in the early 1960s David Frost was famous for his aggressive interviewing style; in later years he toned it down noticeably.

Janice Isaacs of Wembley hugs Michael Miles on ITV's Take Your Pick *(1955). British prizes were more modest than American ones: Mrs Isaacs had won a rolling pin plus the chance of a flight to the States if she gave correct answers for the next three weeks.*

Lenny Ross, aged eleven, from Tujunga, California, won $164,000 in less than a year on TV quiz shows with his knowledge of the stock market (1957).

Randolph Churchill (left) won a mere $64 on The $64,000 Question *after failing to give correct answers to questions on the English language.*

No big prizes – just intellectual glory: Britain's longest-running television quiz show, University Challenge, *has been presented by Bamber Gascoigne since it started in 1962.*

Ever since the 1960s the BBC's Top of the Pops *has been ridiculed by many fans of rock music for being tame and unimaginative; but the show still appears every Thursday evening oblivious to the criticism.*

most modern game shows – and the prizes were stupendous. The trend-setter was CBS's *The $64,000 Question*, which began in June 1955. The atmosphere of the show was tense and deadly earnest – contestants were put in 'isolation booths', and the questions were supposed to be protected by special 'security officers' – but the rewards were so large that it was compulsive viewing: even the loser was given a Cadillac. Within three months *The $64,000 Question* was being watched by 85 per cent of the television audience. Numerous imitations were created, which proved just as irresistible: by 1957 half the top ten programmes were quizzes, including *The $64,000 Question*, *The $64,000 Challenge* and NBC's *Twenty-One*. The first 'celebrity' to be thrown up by these shows was Charles Van Doren, who won $129,000 on *Twenty-One*. Although his winnings were soon eclipsed by a lady who won $250,000, Van Doren was invited to become a guest presenter on the *Today* show; he was also appointed assistant professor of English at Columbia University.

In 1958, publicity was given to rumours that the quiz shows were 'fixed' – that favoured contestants were being told the answers in advance. The following year, Charles Van Doren confessed to a Congressional sub-committee that his appearances on *Twenty-One* had all been rigged. Before his first show, he had been taken aside by the producer and given the answers, with instructions that he should arrange to 'tie' with the current champion that week, to build up tension. The next week he was allowed to win, and he continued to win for several months. He told the committee that when he learned that he was finally going to be allowed to lose, he was relieved.

Dozens of similar revelations were made after Van Doren testified. President Eisenhower said that the fixing had been 'a terrible thing to do to the American people'. All the high-stakes quiz shows were hastily removed from the schedules.

Jack Barry, who created *Twenty-One*, is surprised that there was so much fuss. 'I was reared in the tradition of early radio, as an announcer and master of ceremonies, and I just knew that in any informational programme the participants were given help in one form or another. It was done purely to make the shows more appetising in a productive sense. For example, to draw the largest analogy, you couldn't have a programme be successful if nobody answered any questions, that goes without saying; and consequently the tradition grew.' When *Twenty-One* started, there was no deception for the first three weeks or so: 'But after the third or fourth week we had a couple of contestants who knew almost every question, and it was painful. The sponsor and the advertising agency called and said, "Don't let that happen again" . . . and it didn't. We gave help to the contestants that we wanted to win – it was a standard practice in the United States on all programmes of that nature.' Barry is sure that the networks were well aware of what was happening: 'They would have to have rocks in their heads if they didn't know.' But the consequences of the scandal were particularly harsh for Barry: 'I became the most publicised master of ceremonies in this industry, and somebody had to take the fall for everybody else. Unfortunately it was me, and I was exiled from the industry for ten or twelve years.'

In Britain there was no equivalent scandal, but the trend there, as in America, was to move away from offering large prizes to people who answered reasonably difficult questions (as on Hughie Green's *Double Your Money*) and to concen-

trate instead on 'playing it for fun'. There has thus been a long line of game shows, many of them based on American originals, from *What's My Line* and *Criss-Cross Quiz* to *Celebrity Squares* and *Password*.

'Americans are by and large game players – we are nuts about football and baseball,' Jack Barry says. 'Not everybody can play . . . but you can get some kind of a minimal feeling by participating in a game show, even if it is from your own home – participating in that competitive nature.'

However, it has also been suggested that the popularity of some game shows derives from the audience's sadistic pleasure in watching other people being humiliated in public. One highly successful show in both Britain and America was *Candid Camera*, in which unsuspecting members of the public were used as stooges for practical jokes. In America, the programme ran, off and on, from the late 1940s to the 1970s; a British version was consistently high in the ratings between 1960 and 1967. A variation on the formula had been used in one of Britain's first game shows, *People Are Funny*, broadcast on ITV in 1955: in one edition, a woman was given a hammer and was asked to smash an object hidden under a cloth; when she had done so, she learned that it had been a piece of her own china. There were so many complaints about the poor taste of *People Are Funny* that it was forced off the air, but the idea was revived by London Weekend Television in 1981 with *Game For a Laugh*.

Behind the scenes with Candid Camera*'s hidden camera, filming some innocent victim being duped.*

In America, a programme of the same kind was presented by Dick Martin, the co-star of *Rowan and Martin's Laugh-In*. It was called, appropriately, *The Cheap Show*. 'The person who was the contestant had to bring someone along who, if he missed the question, would get all sorts of diabolical things including green oatmeal poured over them,' Martin explains. 'We had 500 people waiting one day to come on, but they didn't want to be the contestant, they wanted to be the loved one where they would get all sorts of goo poured over them and terrible things would happen to them and they would get a dollar.' He concludes that people 'will do anything to appear on television'.

The most extreme and bizarre of all these 'humiliation shows' is the Japanese series *The Ultra Quiz*, which attracts 30 million viewers for the commercial channel NTV. The quiz begins with 5,000 contestants gathered in a sports stadium, where they have to answer a yes-or-no general knowledge question. Those who get it wrong are eliminated straight away. The survivors are put on a jet at Tokyo airport, but before take-off they are asked another question; anyone who gives the wrong answer is ordered off the plane. While they are in flight, participants have to complete an 800-question exam paper; those who do not achieve the pass-mark are taken off the plane at Guam. There are further eliminating rounds aboard a cruise ship bound for the West Coast of America. By the time the quiz has reached the East Coast, the number of competitors has been reduced to two, who have to answer a final series of questions on the roof of the Pan Am building. The winner receives a substantial prize – a helicopter, for example – while the loser is given the air fare home.

'In the first year of broadcasting *The Ultra Quiz* we had many telephone calls from the audience, saying how can you be so cruel to the contestants,' says Michiyo Saito, who devised the show. 'But after the second year we had no such telephone calls.' Saito thinks that 'it is not a simple quiz show,

I think it is a documentary for three weeks'. One of the secrets of its success is that the contestants 'are always depressed, and we try to keep them frightened and suspicious – they are not ready for a surprise attack'. 'I think the Japanese audience has a very, very huge appetite,' Saito says, 'they digest everything, and even more, and we have been feeding them.' They want 'extreme situations', but *The Ultra Quiz* may not always be enough. He thinks that in about ten years' time Japanese viewers might demand to see someone killed on a game show. Saito concludes: 'The audience is becoming the monster beyond our control.'

World Cups to Royal Weddings.

'The result astonished us all,' the *Daily Herald* wrote after John Logie Baird's first transmission of the Epsom Derby in 1931. 'We had found the stepping-stone to a new era in which mechanical eyes will see for us great events as they happen and convey them to us in our homes.'

The most exciting moments of television history have almost always been the broadcasting of 'great events as they happen'. 'The healthiest curiosity, we may hazard, is that which will demand to see as much as possible of the real world, not of artificially composed entertainment,' *The Times* suggested in November 1936, when the BBC began its regular television service. 'The Coronation procession will obviously give a great opportunity to satisfy an eager public. How delightful, again, to see as well as hear the Derby and the Boat Race; to watch Hammond bat and Larwood bowl; Perry play tennis and Padgham play golf; to follow the expressions and gestures as well as the words of an orator, and get to look at some event or ceremony at which it was impossible to be present. Thus will all the news, all the doings of the great world take on new life and interest.'

An experimental BBC broadcast of a boxing demonstration by Freddy Baxter and Teddy Lewis, August 1933.

At first, television's ability to show the doings of the great world was restricted by the fact that cameras were usually attached to the studio by an umbilical cord of cable. Most of the BBC's early outside broadcasts were therefore staged in the park beside Alexandra Palace, within a few hundred yards of the Corporation's new studios. Yachts were seen on the park's lake. A corner of the park was turned into a 'television garden', which was used to teach viewers how to improve their horticulture. Demonstrations of golf and horse-riding were given, as well as a quite inordinate number of canine performances. ('The dogs were well behaved and made spectacular leaps over obstacles up to more than seven feet,' the *Daily Telegraph* reported after one such occasion. 'Two of them, carrying a stick between their jaws on which perched a parrot, jumped together over a number of low hurdles without disturbing their passengers.')

Baird's outside broadcast van at Epsom for the first televising of the Derby, 1931.

The coronation of King George VI, on 12 May 1937, was a far more ambitious undertaking for the fledgling service. The BBC described it beforehand as the 'first attempt to transmit a real "outside broadcast"', adding that if it was a success 'not only will it add interest to a great occasion but it will mark an important step forward in the progress of television by extending the scope of the programmes beyond the confines of the studios and their immediate vicinity at Alexandra Palace. It will consolidate the lead already won by Great Britain in the world development of television.'

The BBC's engineers devised two alternative methods of sending pictures of the event back to the studio. One was merely an extension of the existing technology, albeit an

(Opposite) Australian tycoon, Kerry Packer, created his World Series specially for television and insisted that cricketers abandon their traditional whites for something more garish. They were handsomely rewarded for doing so.

*Coronation procession,
1937: the royal coach
passes the television camera
at Apsley Gate on its way
to the Palace.*

impressive one – a cable eight miles long, enough to stretch from Hyde Park to Alexandra Palace. No one had ever managed to transmit a television signal over such a length, but it worked perfectly. The alternative system involved a mobile transmitter, equipped with a 'bedstead' aerial fifteen feet high and ten feet wide. On the day, however, the BBC decided to use the cable rather than the transmitter. The whole operation was supervised from a Mobile Control Room – a huge, specially constructed van whose interior was a replica of a normal studio control room.

Tony Bridgewater from the BBC was the engineer in charge of the broadcast. 'Camera positions had to be arranged, and scaffolding and platforms worked out, and where we were going to put the vans,' he recalls, 'so we were probably down there for three or four days before the final event, as well as doing many surveys beforehand, and agreeing with park officials and others where we could stand the vans and run our cables. Of course everything had to be done very carefully, bearing in mind that the public were going to be swarming all over the place.'

Cameras were not allowed inside Westminster Abbey, where the coronation service itself was to take place, so the BBC positioned its three cameras near Apsley Gate, at Hyde Park Corner, which was on the route to be taken by the royal carriages after the service. 'We arranged for two cameras to be facing northwards,' Bridgewater says, 'because the procession was going to come down that way from Marble Arch. The other one was on the other side of the gate, looking across to Constitution Hill, to see the procession passing through and then going on down towards Buckingham Palace.'

Five minutes before the transmission was due to begin, as the procession approached, Bridgewater experienced a moment of terror in the control van. 'The picture suddenly disappeared from our screens. It's very difficult in that kind of atmosphere at such a time to do any kind of quiet diagnosis and work out just what has gone wrong. We had the advantage of the EMI engineers being there and helping a great deal with that side of things . . . One of them, a very bright person called Bernard Greenhead, had a sort of instinct that it was probably somewhere down there in a corner, on a particular panel which had been known to go wrong before; so he risked giving it a most almighty biff with his fist, and that suddenly restored the picture. Evidently there was a loose joint which had just come good again as a result of his biffing, but of course nobody dared move or breathe after that until we were safely through the programme – which happily we were. It didn't happen again.'

The broadcast was a triumph, and nothing gave the BBC more pleasure than the fact that the chief actor – the King himself – had symbolically recognised the invisible audience of television viewers. In the royal coach the King was sitting on the side nearest the camera, Bridgewater says, 'and somehow through a contact much higher than myself it had got through to him at the Palace that it would be very helpful if he would kindly look towards the cameras as he went past them. And we waited anxiously to see if he did this, and sure enough he did – he turned his head at just the right moment so we had a full-face view of him, which was nice.'

It was estimated that 50,000 people watched the event on television, with pictures being received up to sixty miles outside London. Bridgewater and his colleagues believed that

*The Lord Mayor's Show in
November 1937 was
televised via a mobile
control van in
Northumberland Avenue.*

A ten-ton bomb rumbles past at the post-war Victory Parade in June 1946, televised by the BBC.

the broadcast had proved the great potential of television, 'because seeing some event while it was happening was always thought in our minds at that time, and I think in public minds too, as the real job of television . . . Contriving programmes in the studios we always regarded as second best.' The coronation procession of George VI was also the first of many royal occasions which did much to increase public demand for television. More than 1 million people in Britain bought their first television in order to watch Queen Elizabeth II being crowned in 1953; the wedding of Princess Anne and Captain Mark Phillips in 1973 was accompanied by an equally marked rise in the sales of colour television sets; the wedding of Prince Charles and Lady Diana Spencer coincided with a boom in the sale of video-recorders. In other countries, too, the growth of television has been assisted by regal ceremonies. In Japan, for example, 2 million people owned television sets at the beginning of 1959. By the end of the year that figure had doubled as a result of the televised wedding of the Japanese Crown Prince.

In his book *Adventure in Vision*, published in 1950, John Swift wrote: 'It is an accepted fact that it is the Outside Broadcast that "sells" receivers in the first place.' During the late 1940s and early 1950s the BBC worked hard to expand the horizons of outside broadcasts. It was a risky business, of course, because in 'live' broadcasts there is little room for error. As a writer in the *Radio Times* had commented in 1938, 'in television there is the delicious knowledge that at any moment something may go wrong'.

Richard Dimbleby presented Calais en Fête *in 1950, 'live' from France; the fireworks were so vigorous that one of them set fire to a BBC man in the clock tower.*

S. J. 'Lobby' de Lotbiniere: pioneer of BBC outside broadcasts

The people responsible for post-war outside broadcasts at the BBC, led by Peter Dimmock and S. J. de Lotbinière, had their fair share of tense moments. 'In those days live television was very, very exciting indeed,' Dimmock says. He recalls an outside broadcast from a troop ship: 'Unfortunately a company of soldiers halted immediately in front of the main camera. But the situation was saved because we had a very bright young man as stage manager in those days called Bryan Cowgill and he had been a marine officer during his national service, so he simply shouted out, "Company – atten-*shun*, right turn, quick march."'

In 1950 the BBC produced the first outside broadcast from abroad. The location chosen was the French coastal town of Calais, because it was the point nearest Britain, and the occasion was the centenary of the laying of the first cross-Channel cable. The BBC's engineers found that by using very short wavelengths, transmitting on a microwave dish, they could send pictures of good quality from Calais to London – a distance of ninety-five miles. The programme, presented by Richard Dimbleby, was called *Calais en Fête*, and it was a spectacular show, including fireworks, dancers and carnival bands. 'Fortunately, timing wasn't so important in those days,' Dimmock says. 'I think we'd scheduled it to run for about an hour and twenty minutes; in fact it ran for over two hours. But we did everything – we had a circus, and all the usual civic events took place in front of the town hall, and we brought some mannequins from Paris and had a bit of drama.' However, the pictures were not seen in France itself, as the French and British technical standards were incompatible: the BBC broadcast on 405 lines, while the French had adopted an 819-line system.

These difficulties were overcome in 1952 with the invention of a 'line converter' which enabled programmes from the French system to be made suitable for British screens. The

breakthrough was celebrated with a 'French week' in July 1952, during which the BBC transmitted its programmes from Paris. Sir William Haley, the BBC's Director-General, described the week as 'a single stride which makes history', adding that 'it is the beginning of something which will one day be a commonplace. Pictures are not, perhaps, an international language but they are near to being one. To be able to see instantaneously what is happening in another country is going to have a far greater impact than merely to receive a description of the same events.'

This paved the way for the first truly international outside broadcast in television history, the coronation of Elizabeth II on 2 June 1953. Peter Dimmock, who produced the broadcast, believes that the coronation changed the attitude of the Establishment to television. 'Until then, it looked upon it as a bit of a peep-show.' He and his colleagues had twelve months in which to prepare themselves for the ceremony, but it was hard work. 'Everyone in the Establishment was trying to prevent us from televising the actual coronation at the altar. They said we must keep our cameras the other side of the choir screen. Well, we fought that. Then the Cabinet took the decision that there shouldn't be television coverage of the actual crowning. Fortunately, it was then put to the Queen again. We'd done a lot of lobbying in the meantime with the Archbishop of Canterbury, the Queen's press secretary – anybody we could lay our hands on . . . The Duke of Norfolk, who had been very much against it, then changed his mind and was extremely cooperative, and the Queen gave us permission.' Dimmock believes that the initial hostility of the authorities was caused partly by their view that it was an 'invasion of privilege' to allow live television at the ceremony, but also because 'they were afraid that something might go wrong and therefore be seen by an enormous audience'.

The BBC was instructed that its cameras in Westminster Abbey must be unobtrusive. Probably the most important camera of all, the one which transmitted the crowning itself, was positioned among the orchestra on the choir screen. It was operated by the BBC's smallest cameraman, Anthony 'Bud' Flanagan, but even so a number of floorboards had to be removed to make room for his feet. His job was not an enviable one. As a BBC report at the time noted, his back 'was menaced by a ring of steel-sharp cello pegs'; he was also hit on the head every time the orchestra's conductor, William McKie, brought down his baton.

In addition to the five cameras in the Abbey, the BBC deployed another fifteen cameras along the route of the royal procession. These were linked to five Mobile Control Rooms, which in turn were connected to the central producer, Dimmock, in Broadcasting House. The Post Office laid twenty-nine miles of cable to make these connections possible.

The audience was gigantic. In Britain, the coronation service was watched by more than 20 million people, even though there were only 2 million television owners at the time. The BBC estimated that 7,800,000 people watched it in their own homes, another 10,400,000 watched it in the homes of friends and 1,500,000 watched it in pubs and cinemas.

The coronation broadcast was relayed 'live' to France, Holland and West Germany, an unprecedented and complicated feat of technical coordination. The BBC's pictures were sent from London to Dover by three radio links working in

Some of BBC television's commentators at the 1953 Coronation: (from top) Richard Dimbleby, Mary Hill and Bernard Braden.

Anthony 'Bud' Flanagan, the BBC's smallest cameraman, stationed on the choir screen at Westminster Abbey for Elizabeth II's Coronation in 1953.

Scenes from the 1953 Coronation as seen on British television screens by an audience of more than twenty million.

Until the 1950s, American Football was the poor relation of baseball, but when the networks showed an interest, money poured in.

tandem; another link carried them to the French coast, at a point near Cap Blanc Nez, from where the signals travelled by further radio links to Mont Cassel in northern France and onwards to Paris. There the 405-line pictures were converted into 819-line pictures for French television; but the original 405-line signals were also sent on across Belgium to Breda, in Holland, where they were converted to a 625-line standard, the one used by both Holland and West Germany. The quality of the pictures at the end of all this country-hopping was astonishingly sharp. At 11.25 a.m., less than an hour after the crowning, RTF in Paris cabled the BBC: 'VERY URGENT QUALITY IMAGE PASSABLE DEPARTURE FROM BUCKINGHAM PALACE EXCELLENT FROM 10.30 STOP SOUND PERFECT STOP PUBLIC CROWDING ROUND PUBLIC RECEIVING SETS AND CINEMA HALLS FULL STOP REACTIONS ENTHUSIASTIC STOP BRAVO'.

Since the coronation took place before the era of communications satellites, viewers in the United States were unable to watch it 'live'. But there was sprightly competition between the networks to be the first to screen a recording of the ceremony. With the cooperation of the Royal Air Force, the BBC had arranged for telerecordings to be flown to Canada in three stages during the day, carried by Canberra jet bombers. By 4.15 p.m. local time, television stations in Ottawa, Toronto and Montreal were able to transmit a full recording. Both NBC and ABC also received these pictures, via a cable link with Montreal. CBS showed its own telerecording of the BBC's coverage; after a while NBC, too, switched to its own recording, which had been flown over on a chartered DC-6. It was estimated that 85 million Americans watched the coronation, but there was an outcry in England when reports came back of the way in which the networks had treated the event. NBC's *Today* programme had gone on the air at 5.30 a.m. (New York time) with a sound transmission of the coronation accompanied by still photographs, but the broadcast was broken into on several occasions. At one point an NBC commentator asked, 'Is this show put on by the British for a psychological boost to their somewhat shaky empire?' Half-way through the service of holy communion, *Today*'s resident chimpanzee, J. Fred Muggs, was asked whether the monkey world had queens and coronations. CBS's coverage was constantly interrupted by commercials, some of which sought to take advantage of the occasion: a car in one advertisement was described as a 'queen of the road', while another was said to have a 'royal carriage'.

These examples were exploited in Britain by the people who were lobbying against the introduction of commercial television, and they did have one consequence: the Television Act of 1954, which created ITV, stipulated that no programme about royalty could be interrupted by a commercial break.

The coronation broadcasts in Britain confirmed the BBC's reputation as 'the voice of Britain' but added to it the feeling that, with the advent of television, it was now the eyes of Britain as well. On a personal level, the programme was a success for Richard Dimbleby, the commentator, who had made the transition from radio to television with apparently effortless ease. From then on, the BBC took great pride in televising state events, especially royal ones, and until his death from cancer in 1965 the commentary was always provided by Dimbleby. His last such performance was at the

Reception of live pictures of the Coronation by European countries was astonishingly good; these shots (from top) were photographed from screens in France, Germany and Holland.

funeral of Sir Winston Churchill in January 1965, but before that he had also presented the first State Opening of Parliament to be televised, in 1958; the wedding of Princess Margaret to Lord Snowdon in 1960 (watched by 25 million people in Britain and an estimated 300 million around the world); the wedding of the Duke of Kent and Katherine Worsley in 1961; and the wedding of Princess Alexandra and Angus Ogilvy in 1963. Since then, royal outside broadcasts have continued to attract huge audiences, among them the Investiture of Prince Charles at Caernarvon Castle in 1969, broadcast in colour and watched by about 500 million people across the world; the wedding of Princess Anne and Captain Mark Phillips in 1973, seen by an estimated 530 million viewers (including 28 million in Britain); and, most recently and spectacularly, the marriage of Prince Charles and Lady Diana Spencer on 29 July 1981. This wedding was the biggest outside broadcast in British history; it also broke the record for the largest-ever international audience for a television transmission. It was seen, apparently, by an incredible 750 million people in seventy-four countries; in Britain, the audience was 39 million.

In preparation for the wedding of Lady Diana Spencer and Prince Charles, a ferret pulls a nylon cord through a narrow pipe from Buckingham Palace to the commentary position on the Victoria Memorial; the cord is then used to pull through a TV cable.

No other country has succeeded in turning its state occasions, whether royal or Presidential, into such a marketable international commodity. A Soviet leader's funeral or an American President's inauguration may be watched by millions in the Soviet Union and the United States respectively, but its appeal abroad is trifling compared with that of the Prince and Princess of Wales. Nevertheless, outside broadcasts of this kind can have great domestic significance by increasing both the public demand for television and official acceptance of it. For example, the wedding of Emperor Hirohito's son in April 1959, although it was largely ignored by the rest of the world, probably aroused even greater interest in Japan than Queen Elizabeth's coronation had in Britain. 'Japanese television started in 1953, so we had six years' experience by that time,' says Koyoaki Ishiguro, who worked on the broadcast for NHK. 'You could say that all our previous experience was poured into that one effort. A project of that scale and length – when we look back on it now it seems quite commonplace, but at the time it was an epoch-making achievement.' Television cameras were not actually allowed into the Imperial Sanctuary, but they could go into the Palace grounds. More than 100 cameras from NHK and the commercial networks followed the five-mile procession from the Imperial Palace to the Tōbu Palace. 'The fact that we were able to cover this moving event over a long period of time gave us a great deal of confidence in our technical ability,' Ishiguro says, 'and the fact that a large proportion of the Japanese people clearly enjoyed it as a television programme showed us that this sort of broadcast did have audience-appeal.'

Royal weddings are always a crowd-puller for television: Lady Diana Spencer and Prince Charles, 1981.

There is no doubt that the Crown Prince's wedding was televised partly for political purposes, as an attempt by the Emperor to unite the country behind him. 'After the war there was a great deal of talk about the democratisation of Japan,' Ishiguro explains, 'and I think that the Imperial Family themselves were very keen that they should be democratised . . . It was felt that, as one expression of the new "people's Imperial Family", the people should be given the opportunity of rejoicing with them on such a happy occasion.'

This feeling of shared experience occurs with many tele-

vision programmes, of course, but it is especially pronounced with outside broadcasts, where a vast audience is watching an event simultaneously and as it happens, particularly if people could not otherwise witness the spectacle. In the case of royal weddings or Olympic Games, it is at least possible for some people to attend in person. With space travel, however, the only way in which anyone can follow the drama – from the poorest to the richest person in the world – is by watching television. As Bob Schaeffer of NASA says, televised coverage of space flights is 'important to a lot of people because it's an experience they cannot otherwise share'.

When watching space shots, viewers are probably more conscious than ever of the 'knowledge that at any moment something may go wrong', which lends such excitement to live television. Because of its fear of this danger, the Soviet Union has seldom allowed its space flights to be transmitted live, preferring to show edited highlights when the mission is safely accomplished.

Yuri Gagarin, the Soviet cosmonaut, became the first man in space when he orbited the earth in April 1961.

Yuri Gagarin became the first man in space when he orbited the earth in April 1961. Alexander Tikhomirov, the space correspondent for Soviet television, remembers hearing the news from a radio report: 'I was shaving at the time, and I nearly cut my nose off with the excitement.' But there were no television pictures from Gagarin's spacecraft. After his landing, he rested for a couple of days before returning to Moscow, and it was only then that television viewers were able to see him – already a conquering hero, with the element of risk removed. Coincidentally, this happened just as the BBC established its first link-up with the Soviet Union. Paul Fox of *Panorama* had been sent to Moscow to transmit the May Day parade in Red Square; instead, he assembled an impromptu programme called *Moscow Welcomes Yuri Gagarin*, the first live broadcast ever from the Soviet Union to Britain. Richard Dimbleby, in London, provided the commentary.

Moscow Welcomes Yuri Gagarin – an unexpected scoop for the BBC, which had intended to use the May Day Parade in Moscow for its first live transmission from the Soviet Union, but suddenly found itself presented with a far more interesting story.

When the Russians did install television cameras in their space-craft, Tikhomirov was called in to instruct the cosmonauts in the art of communication. 'I am quite sure that there have been some brilliant reporters among the cosmonauts,' he says, 'in particular Sevastyanov and Klimuk – they thought up reports that were really interesting to a wide section of the public. For example, they gave a demonstration of the effect of weightlessness by riding round the space-station on a vacuum cleaner; they let a fly, a fruit-fly, fly about in weightless conditions, they did an experiment on it. In other words, they understood that the attention of a wide range of viewers could be attracted by some sort of amusing detail.' The flight of Sevastyanov and Klimuk, to which Tikhomirov refers, took place in 1975. They stayed in space for nine weeks and 'did a lot of reports', Sevastyanov says. 'We varied them – we tried somehow to show the whole range of work and rest and scientific research on board the space-station. In addition we often made jokes.' The two cosmonauts won an award from the USSR Union of Journalists, and Sevastyanov went on to become the presenter of a popular programme called *Man, Earth and Space*, which has been broadcast regularly ever since.

Valentina Tereshkova, the first woman in space (1963), marries fellow pilot Andrian Nikolayev soon after her successful flight.

Andrian Nikolayev of Vostok 3 and Papel Popovich of Vostok 4, launched within a day of each other, are welcomed by Khrushchev and his deputy, Mikoyan, after their flight in 1962.

Soviet space flights have had a number of tragic mishaps. There was the death of Vladimir Komarov during tests of the first Soyuz ship: his parachute shrouds became tangled and he fell to the earth from a great height. In 1972 the three cosmonauts aboard the first Salyut space-station died when

Gymnastics has attracted a host of new followers since the 1970s because of television coverage of the performances of such graceful limb-twisters as Olga Korbut and Nadia Comaneci.

their air-lock failed as the module was descending through the upper layers of the earth's atmosphere. None of these events was shown on Soviet television – 'for technical reasons', according to Tikhomirov. But it seems unlikely that the Soviet public would ever be allowed to witness a space accident. 'I think they are just far more cautious about how many people know how much about what they intend to do in the first place, which makes it easier to control public knowledge afterwards should something not go according to plan,' says Bob Schaeffer of NASA. 'On the other hand, our experience with them in *Apollo/Soyuz* suggests that given the right set of circumstances they can be very open and candid about their programme.' Curiously enough, it was during the negotiations over *Apollo/Soyuz* that the Russians persuaded NASA to put in its spacecraft a camera which would show the crew's reactions during lift-off – something which had never been done before. Schaeffer remembers it as 'one of the most gripping moments of the flight', but the experiment was not repeated with later launches. As Schaeffer explains, 'it involved scarring the interior surface of the vehicle and fabricating an instrument that would survive the launch G-forces, and touching the surface of a space vehicle is the last thing engineers are willing to do.'

During the earliest years of the American space programme, NASA's managers and engineers were as unenthusiastic about television as the Russians. 'Their concern was supporting life and the safety of the people aboard the spacecraft,' Schaeffer says. 'Television had nothing to do with that. As a matter of fact, the man who became the biggest advocate of television in later years was the man who resisted it most strenuously in those years, Dr George Long. He finally agreed to fly a television camera on *Mercury 9*, Gordon Cooper's flight. That was the first time.'

From then on, however, television became an essential ingredient of NASA's space explorations. There were political motives for this. In 1961 President Kennedy had announced a large increase in NASA's budget so that the Americans could 'beat the Soviets' by putting a man on the moon before the end of the decade. Like every other aspect of the battle between the superpowers, the space race required good international propaganda; television provided it. Apart from their importance abroad, however, pictures of astronauts and spaceships could be used to quieten domestic opposition to the space programme – described as a 'moon-doggle' by some critics because of the millions of dollars that were being spent on it. When John Glenn went into orbit around the earth in 1962, Americans were gripped by the live coverage of his blast-off. Over the next few years NASA staged a succession of similar stunts with its *Gemini* and *Mercury* programmes, culminating in *Apollo*, the most spectacular series of them all and the one which was to land a man on the surface of the moon.

As the historian Erik Barnouw has noted, 'from the start it was all planned as a series of television shows'. On the first manned *Apollo* flight, astronauts Walter Schirra and Donn Eisele held up a placard for the cameras as they orbited the earth: 'Keep those cards and letters coming in folks.' The *Apollo VIII* flight between 21 and 27 December 1968, which was the first manned flight round the moon, produced some extraordinary pictures of both the moon's surface and the earth as seen from the moon. On Christmas Eve, the astronauts treated earth-bound viewers to a reading from the book

President Kennedy helps John Glenn celebrate his orbit around the earth in 1962, in a parade at Cape Canaveral.

An 'earthrise' filmed by astronauts on Apollo 11 as they prepared to descend to the moon's surface, July 1969.

of Genesis ('In the beginning God created the heaven and the earth . . .'). It was the most spectacular Christmas broadcast ever, and a harbinger of what was to come when *Apollo XI* landed in the Sea of Tranquillity the following year.

Apollo XI's flight was billed in advance as 'the greatest show in the history of television'. On 21 July 1969, Neil Armstrong stepped out of 'Eagle', the lunar module, on to the moon's surface. His legs were all that could be seen, but he then moved the camera away from the vehicle and set it on a tripod so that the audience 239,000 miles away had a full view of Buzz Aldrin descending from the module. 'That's one small step for man, a giant leap for mankind,' were Armstrong's words (meaningless ones, too – presumably he meant to say 'one small step for a man'). Thus began a 'moon walk' of two hours and twenty-three minutes. Appropriately and inevitably, a politician got in on the act. On a split-screen picture, viewers saw President Nixon speaking on the telephone from the Oval Office to the two men standing beside the module. 'For one priceless moment in the whole history of man,' Nixon told them, 'all the people on this earth are truly one – one in their pride in what you have done and one in our prayers that you will return safely to earth.' The transmission was seen by 125 million Americans and an unprecedented 723 million people around the world – a record which stood until Britain's royal wedding in 1981.

Nixon's prayers for the astronauts' safe return emphasised the fact that these space shows were the riskiest of all 'live' outside broadcasts. For all the years of planning and preparation, there was still an ever present danger of catastrophe; if something did go wrong, its consequences would be infinitely more serious than, say, Princess Diana's stumbling over her words during her wedding. In 1970, NASA's recurring nightmare became a reality when there was an explosion in the rear of *Apollo XIII* on the third day of its flight towards the moon. The command module lost most of its oxygen and power supply. The three-man crew began a nerve-racking return journey to earth. 'We knew very little about what was going on up there,' Bob Schaeffer says. 'So there was the opportunity to use television to try to understand the nature of the problem. But at the same time, because of the sudden requirement to reduce the use of power aboard the spacecraft, to conserve energy and do everything possible to continue the life-support system, there were not many opportunities to do that – because television, of course, uses exactly the same energy source that the life-support system does.' Pictures were also restricted because the crew had moved into the lunar module, using it as a kind of lifeboat, 'and it wasn't possible to do television coverage in there'. But viewers could see some footage of the main compartment, and a huge audience watched as *Apollo XIII* finally broke through the earth's atmosphere and splashed down safely.

Live broadcasts of this kind – 'unplanned documentaries', as one Japanese producer describes them – are the greatest challenge for anyone working in television. A royal wedding or Presidential inauguration may impress with its panoply and grandeur, but the camera crews, producers and commentators have all had many months in which to rehearse themselves for the occasion. What is much more taxing is to go on the air at a moment's notice and still create a memorable and epic broadcast.

The American networks had just such a task when President Kennedy was assassinated in November 1963. Within

Man on the moon, 1969: (from top) Buzz Aldrin climbs down the steps of the lunar module; he salutes the Stars and Stripes on the moon's surface; an elated Neil Armstrong, back in the lunar module after his moon-walk.

hours of the shooting, on Friday 22 November, all three networks decided to suspend all commercials and entertainment shows until after Kennedy's funeral the following Monday. For four days almost the entire American population, together with millions in every continent, experienced a collective grief through television. 'It was probably the high point of television,' says J. Leonard Reinsch, media adviser to Kennedy. 'I don't know of anything before or after that reached that peak. I was travelling back from Augusta, Georgia, when I heard the news on the car radio, and I immediately went to Washington as soon as I got to Atlanta and was put to work. I was responsible for the television coverage and still coverage of the entire funeral. It was a difficult task but everybody cooperated; we had cameras from everywhere, we had cable from everywhere, and the coverage and cooperation of television was, I think, just absolutely stupendous.'

Broadcasters had a rough idea of the course that events would take: on the Saturday, world leaders would arrive in Washington; on Sunday, Kennedy's coffin would be transported from the White House to the Capitol, where a procession of people would file past it; on Monday, the cortège would set off for Arlington Cemetery for the burial. Nevertheless, there was no time to prepare a script. 'It was all totally ad lib,' says Walter Cronkite, who provided CBS's commentary. 'It came as the pictures developed – I had nothing in mind.' In any case, one of the most startling moments of the whole four days' agony was an occurrence which nobody could have predicted. At noon on the Sunday, the presumed assassin, Lee Harvey Oswald, was moved from the city jail in Dallas to the county jail. CBS and ABC were still showing pictures of the coffin in Washington, but NBC had chosen to show the scene at Dallas live. As Oswald was led towards the police vehicle, a man with a hat – later identified as Jack Ruby – pushed forward and shot him, in full view of NBC's viewers. The other two networks showed videotapes of the incident a few seconds later.

Walter Cronkite believes that the four days of television which followed Kennedy's assassination had 'a calming effect, in the sense that we were all able to share our grief and vent it simultaneously, but also in showing a smooth transition of power'. Reinsch thinks that the broadcasts gave 'a community of interest' to the audience: 'Everyone – whether they happened to be in Atlanta, Georgia, or New York City, or Keokuk, Iowa – felt as one. They joined in their grief for the slain leader and they felt they were participating in this tragic ceremony . . . Television took them there. The sight of this riderless horse going down Pennsylvania Avenue was bound to tug your heart, and little John-John saluting was just world-wide heart-appeal.'

'Unplanned' outside broadcasts became a regular feature of television over the following twenty years, partly because of the growth of 'international terrorism'. Pictures of hijacked planes or besieged houses, for all their familiarity, lost none of their power over the viewers. In 1972 Japan endured what were described as 'ten days of televised national hysteria' when five members of the Red Army faction guerrilla group, fleeing from the police, sought refuge in the Mount Asama Lodge in the mountains near Karuizawa, taking hostage the young wife of the caretaker. For the next ten days they were surrounded by both police and television crews from NHK and the commercial channels. 'The culprits had rifles with

(Opposite) Steve Davis has become a millionaire through snooker; a few years ago, before television took up the sport, he would have been lucky to earn more than a few thousand pounds.

Jackie Kennedy and her children televised at the funeral.

An extraordinary moment of drama during America's national mourning for Kennedy: (top) Lee Harvey Oswald (right) is led out of Dallas City Jail; seconds later (below) he is shot dead. NBC showed it all live.

them, so it was a very dangerous job,' says Kazuo Ōta, who directed NHK's coverage. 'As rifles have a range of 450 metres, we set up one camera – fitted with telephoto lenses – 500 metres away, just out of range, and took a constant full-shot view of the whole lodge.' NHK also had two cameras closer to the lodge, operated by remote control. A cameraman from one of the commercial stations, who were not so careful, was shot through the knee.

On the final day of the siege, NHK transmitted continuous live coverage from 9.45 in the morning until 8.20 p.m. The police arrested the exhausted Red Army members at 6.45 p.m., just as the sun was setting. Ratings were about three times higher than average. In Ōta's view, it was television at its best. 'At that time we had been transmitting television for twenty years,' he says, 'but neither the providers nor the consumers had quite understood what it was that television was supposed to be doing. The Mount Asama Lodge incident taught both us, the producers, and the viewers what the role of television is. In that sense I feel that it was an epoch-making event in the history of television.'

British viewers had a chance to experience something similar in May 1980, when some armed Shi'a Moslems known as the 'Group of the Martyr' took control of the Iranian Embassy in Prince's Gate, West London, holding twenty-six people hostage. On the sixth day of the siege, a Bank Holiday Monday, shortly after 7.20 p.m., Britain's mysterious Special Air Service stormed the building, killing the captors and releasing most of the hostages unharmed. ITV and the BBC both provided live coverage of the extraordinary scenes – masked men, smoke bombs, the sound of gunfire, a corpse thrown on to the pavement – to a large audience, who were given only the haziest idea of what was actually happening. Independent Television News had achieved something of a scoop by smuggling a camera into a nearby building which had a view of the rear of the Embassy, where the SAS men were abseiling down from the roof; however, for fear of jeopardising the rescue, ITN did not transmit these pictures until after the hostages had been freed.

ITV's live transmission from Prince's Gate had begun immediately after *Coronation Street*, replacing the scheduled film (called, appropriately, *Detour to Terror*). BBC-1 had interrupted a John Wayne movie, *Rio Lobo*. Not everyone approved of the change. 'My seven-year-old son was indignant,' John le Carré wrote afterwards. 'After a couple of minutes of the real thing, he found the reality formless and wanted to go back to Wayne and clearer issues. His feelings, as we now know from the BBC, were shared by a great many adult viewers who phoned in to complain.'

Significantly, however, the greatest number of complaints came from viewers of BBC-2, who protested at the interruption of the final of the World Snooker Championships between Cliff Thorburn and Alex 'Hurricane' Higgins, which had reached a particularly tense stage at 16 frames all. Given a choice between two different forms of 'live' outside broadcast – an unfolding news story and a great sporting encounter – it seems that many viewers would have preferred the latter. The fact that it was the Embassy World Snooker Championships was peculiarly fitting, since snooker has become emblematic of the relationship between sport and television. As recently as 1972, Alex Higgins received just £480 in prize money when he won the world championship. In 1978, however, BBC-2 decided to transmit lengthy coverage of the two-week competition, which immediately acquired a sponsor in the shape of Embassy Cigarettes. The game was transformed. When Steve Davis became world champion in 1981 the prize had risen to £20,000 and sponsors were falling over each other in the scramble to be associated with snooker; in the following year, a brewery announced that it would pay Davis up to £220,00 for forty personal appearances; by 1983 Davis was not only a millionaire but also the highest-paid sportsman in Britain. John Pulman, a veteran professional snooker player, says that the arrival of colour television made snooker's success possible. 'I would say it's an ideal television game. The playing surface is twelve feet by six feet, which makes it quite easy to cover camera-wise. It's colourful, with a nice green cloth and coloured balls, the players are nicely dressed and it's a very clean game.' It is also a cheap way of filling time for the television companies. BBC-2 usually broadcasts about eighty hours of snooker during the fortnight of the world championship, and both ITV and the BBC give saturation coverage to many other snooker tournaments which have been invented in the last five years to cash in on the popularity of the sport. Television exposure has influenced the viewers to take up the game themselves: hardly a month passes in Britain today without some old cinema being converted into a snooker hall.

The Arsenal football side of 1936 inspect a television camera on their ground at Highbury, North London.

Television coverage of horse racing was transformed by the use of cameras attached to the roofs of vans which drove along the side of the course at the same speed as the horses; hitherto, viewers had been able to see only the winners flashing past the finishing post.

Snooker is by no means an atypical example of what can happen to a sport when it attracts the attention of the electronic eye. In the past twenty years, numerous sports which had hitherto been considered as 'minority interests' – show-jumping, golf, gymnastics, ice-skating, darts – have been extensively covered on British television; riding clubs, ice rinks, gyms and so forth have all reported a huge increase in membership applications from people hoping to emulate Olga Korbut, Princess Anne or Torvill and Dean. Television has even created its own sports: rallycross, a type of car race, was invented for ITV's *World of Sport* in 1966.

Television has also brought about changes in the appearance of some sports which have been prepared to adapt to the demands of the medium. Burke Crotty, who was a cameraman for NBC from its first broadcast in 1939, recalls that black-and-white cameras could not distinguish between the shorts worn by boxers: in those days one contestant would wear black trunks with a purple stripe and the other would wear purple trunks with a black stripe, all of which came out as a dark splodge on the screen. 'So we went to the boxing commissioner and got permission to make some tests. We had sixteen different kinds of trunks – we had gold with white stripes, and pink . . . you name it, we had it. And they finally agreed to let us use white with a black stripe and black with a white stripe, provided that we made them available to the boxers for every fight.' From then on, those colours became standard.

December 1938: amateur boxing from Alexandra Palace, with a camera platform on scaffolding above the ring.

Ian Orr-Ewing, who worked on many of the BBC's early outside broadcasts, had similar difficulties when covering football matches. 'We had to group our cameras together roughly in the middle of the field, fairly high up to give a good sense of perspective,' he says, 'and then we discovered we couldn't see the ball very well, particularly in the fading light of winter. So I went along to Stanley Rous, who was then head of the Football Association and very cooperative – he welcomed television more than anyone else – and I said would it matter very much if we had the ball white? He said, "Not a bit, let's try white," and therefore we gave to posterity the white ball which is now universally used . . . And that started because you couldn't see a leather-coloured ball against the grass.' Many years later, in the late 1970s, cricketers who signed up for Kerry Packer's World Series games, specially created for his Australian television channel, had to accustom themselves to wearing yellow shirts and blue pads, which Packer thought looked better on colour television than the traditional white outfits.

From the very beginning of television, sport has been considered to be one of its greatest attractions. As early as 1924, in a piece of propaganda for John Logie Baird's rudimentary equipment, *Kinematograph Weekly* reported that 'it is not too much to expect that in the course of time we shall be able to see on the screen the winner of the Derby actually racing home'. By 1931 Baird had indeed televised the Derby, although the horses were indistinguishable. It is clear that most pioneers in television had the same thought: sport was a cheap way of winning a mass audience. In February 1931, four months before Baird took his cameras to the Derby, a Japanese scientist at Waseda University televised a baseball game by closed circuit on to a three-foot screen in his laboratory; later the same year, the university transmitted forty minutes of baseball for the benefit of the handful of enthusiasts in Tokyo who possessed a receiver. In the United States, a baseball game between Princeton and Columbia universities was the first outside broadcast shown by NBC after the channel's inauguration at the New York World's Fair in 1939. In that first year NBC also screened a six-day bicycle race from Madison Square Garden, athletics from Randall's Island, boxing from the Yankee Stadium and Ridgewood Grove, swimming from Manhattan Beach, the Eastern Grass Court Tennis Championships from Rye, New York, American football between Philadelphia and the Brooklyn Dodgers from Ebbet's Field, professional wrestling from Ridgewood Grove, fencing in the studios, skating from the Rockefeller Center Ice Rink, soccer from Starlight Park, hockey and basketball from Madison Square Garden, and much, much else. As NBC proudly announced, 'sport enthusiasts throughout New York's metropolitan area have had thrills a-plenty'.

The technical limitations of the early cameras made some sports difficult to televise well. Baseball, for example, was a constant headache for American producers because of the vast size of the pitch. In Britain, Ian Orr-Ewing felt that boxing and tennis were the two sports most suitable for television, since they take place within a restricted area. When covering games that needed more space, such as football, cameramen often had to change the lenses on their Emitrons and set up the focus again, which took several minutes. 'In the last Cup Final before the war, in the last minute of extra time, a penalty was given and we hadn't got a camera available,' Orr-Ewing recalls. 'So we just talked and went off the air for a moment. We rushed the telephoto lens into the only serviceable camera and focused it on the goal-mouth and the spot-kicker. We got it perfectly.'

The BBC was determined that the London Olympics of 1948 should be as much of a propaganda triumph for Britain as the Berlin Olympics of 1936 had been for Hitler, but it was still reliant on the old Emitron cameras from the 1930s, fitted with a single lens and a viewfinder which showed the picture upside down. At the last minute, the BBC managed to acquire a new camera with three interchangeable lenses and a viewfinder which gave an image the right way up – the

The first baseball game ever televised: Columbia versus Princeton, May 1939.

New York Yankees' coach sits on the sidelines at a football match with the Brooklyn Dodgers in 1947, watching the game on television to get a clearer view.

Roller derbies were a popular sport on American television in the early days because they were fast-moving.

Just as the 1936 Olympics had been a propaganda triumph for Hitler, so the 1948 Olympics in London were a triumphant re-affirmation of Britain's victory in the Second World War, and of Britain's success in the television race.

Image Orthicon from America, which produced bright pictures even in overcast weather. Live coverage was achieved with just two mobile units, one in Wembley Stadium and the other in the adjacent Empire Pool. Olympic events which took place outside the stadium were recorded by the BBC's newsreel team and shown in the evenings.

Some sports welcomed television from the start; others were distinctly uneasy. 'Most sports were a little frightened,' Orr-Ewing says. 'They thought we would take away from the attendance – which of course perhaps in the long run we did. But Wimbledon was a classic place because there was tremendous over-application for seats on the Centre Court, and they could fill it ten times over. So we went to see the secretary and said, look, you are the ready-made example of a perfect game for television . . . They were terribly cooperative. We had to find an optimum camera position for all our three cameras and I placed them just behind the royal box, fairly high so that they could dominate the whole court – there was no question of panning with the ball. And I'm glad to say that when I went there last year I went to look at the camera positions and they were exactly the same as they were forty-five years ago.'

Another event which was happy to be televised was the Oxford and Cambridge Boat Race, since it had no paying spectators to lose anyway. In 1949, for the first time, the BBC managed to place a camera on a launch and follow the race from behind; two years later it won a scoop when the Oxford boat sank in full view of the camera, while no press photographers recorded the incident.

This picture from the television screen is the only record of the Oxford crew sinking in the 1951 boat race; no press photographer recorded the incident.

Other sports were uncooperative. The Football Association allowed the BBC to cover the FA Cup Final every year, but the Football League did not like the idea of having its Saturday afternoon matches televised: when a game between Charlton and Blackburn was broadcast in 1947 there was uproar from the other clubs. 'Live' Football League matches were not seen on British television again until the 1980s. The British Boxing Board of Control and the Greyhound Racing Association were similarly resistant to the cameras, largely because the BBC refused to pay for the rights to cover the events, merely offering a small 'facility fee'. In 1944 the dog-racing authorities, together with the people who ran the Grand National and the Derby, formed the Association for the Protection of Copyright in Sport to lobby for proper fees. As it argued with the BBC over the following ten years it was joined by several other sports groups, including cricket and rugby controllers. But it was only in 1954, with commercial television due to start the next year, that the BBC was goaded into action: exclusive contracts were signed with numerous sports promoters, and the BBC's leading producers of sports programmes were also put on contracts to prevent them from being poached by the new channels. In the same year, the BBC introduced a weekly show named *Sportsview*, the brainchild of a young producer called Paul Fox who had proposed 'a really fast-paced journalistic sports programme'. It was regularly watched by 8 million people – a huge audience for those days. When ITV went on the air in 1955, it had to do the best it could with the few sports that the BBC had not sewn up – professional wrestling, for instance – as well as the handful of 'important events' such as the FA Cup Final which were not allowed to become the exclusive property of either channel.

Since then, television sport has become big business.

The Grand National, the most famous horse race in Britain, was not televised until 1960.

The BBC programme Sportsview *won an impressive scoop only a few weeks after it began in 1954 when Roger Bannister became the first man to run a mile in under four minutes.*

Michael Angelow, a 'streaker', ran naked across the cricket pitch at Lord's in 1975 in full view of the television cameras.

The World Cup, held every four years, causes large parts of the world to come to a halt for the duration; in 1966 England, the host nation, won the trophy for the first time.

Aware that they could not resist the cameras, the controllers of particular sports concentrated instead on securing the best possible deal from TV companies; and, as we have seen in the case of snooker, 'minority' pastimes have been as eager as the more established sports to take a share of the huge sums of money available. Until the 1950s, American football had always been the poor relation of baseball; but when the networks began to take an interest in it, money poured in. The American Football League signed a five-year contract with NBC, worth $42 million. In the mid-1960s, CBS paid $14 million a year for exclusive rights to National Football League matches. At the same time it broke new ground by actually *buying* a baseball team, the New York Yankees. Four years later a station in Atlanta, Georgia, went one better by purchasing its local basketball *and* baseball teams. But American football has remained the dominant television sport. The annual Superbowl has been watched by audiences of more than 90 million in the US, and in 1982 the three American networks paid a record £1,000 million for the right to televise National Football League matches over the next five years.

The launching of communications satellites has made it possible for viewers around the globe to watch the same sports match or tournament simultaneously, but time-differences have tended to restrict such live coverage to massive international contests, notably the World Cup for soccer and the Olympics. The last World Cup, held in Spain in 1982, caused almost the whole of Latin America to come to a halt for the duration, since Argentina was the cup-holder and Brazil was the favourite. (In the event, surprisingly, the Italians won.) Channel 4 in Peru paid the salary of the country's national coach, while Channel 5 simply 'bought' three of the star players in the Peruvian team. Chilean television spent so much money on covering the World Cup that for months afterwards it had to show nothing but cheap programmes imported from abroad, as it could no longer afford to make its own shows.

Nothing better illustrates the importance of television money than the Olympics – which are, ironically, supposed to be the last bastion of 'amateur' sport. Every four years the American networks engage in a fierce competition to win the right to cover the games. In 1960, CBS paid a trifling $550,000 to broadcast the Rome Olympics. By 1972, at the Munich Olympics, the price had risen to $13.5 million; ABC was the successful bidder, as it was four years later with an offer of $25 million for the Montreal games. After that, ABC was confident that it would also be allowed to cover the Moscow Olympics: it was said that no less a figure than the Soviet Prime Minister himself, Alexei Kosygin, wanted ABC to do the job. However, the head of the Soviet Olympic Committee, Ignati Novikov, defied Kosygin by accepting an astonishing bid of $87 million from NBC. (Kosygin was demoted soon afterwards.)

ABC redoubled its efforts when negotiations started for the rights to the 1984 Olympics, to be held in Los Angeles. It won with an offer of $225 million. 'Without television funding we wouldn't have a Los Angeles Olympic Games,' says David Wolper, who chaired the negotiating committee. 'The Los Angeles games are financed wholly by independent sources, not by the federal, state or city government, so we must get all our funding from television, tickets and the sale of commercial rights to sponsors.' The single largest contribution

Television cricket commentators in 1955: (left to right) Peter West, E. W Swanton, Roy Webber (statistician) and Brian Johnston; Peter West still introduces cricket broadcasts to this day.

ABC sportscaster Howard Cosell has his toupee felt by Mohammad Ali, a sportsman who manifestly loved appearing on television.

was ABC's $225 million; payments by television companies in all the rest of the world added together came to a mere $125 million.

When ABC is paying the piper so handsomely, it expects to call the tune. At the Winter Olympics in February 1984 (which ABC had acquired for $92 million) there were frequent complaints from performers and journalists about the network's heavy-handed behaviour. At one point Princess Anne's private detective asked an ABC man to stop poking his camera in Her Royal Highness's face. 'Listen, buddy,' came the reply, 'we're ABC television. We bought the Olympics. And we do what the hell we like.' ABC has already demonstrated the truth of that by having the 1988 Winter Olympics in Calgary lengthened so that they extend over three weekends of prime viewing time. The organisers of the Winter Olympics objected to this interference at first, until they saw the size of ABC's bid – $309 million. It all seemed a far cry from John Logie Baird's first flickering pictures of the Epsom Derby half a century earlier; but as one ABC executive put it, 'To bring the best athletic competition in the world back to the United States and at the same time receive high ratings – nothing could be greater.'

Winter Olympics, 1964: an ABC cameraman uses a new, 'streamlined' camera fixed to his shoulder, which leaves his hands free.

Live coverage allows little room for editing or censorship: some athletes took advantage of this with 'black power' salutes at the Mexico Olympics in 1968.

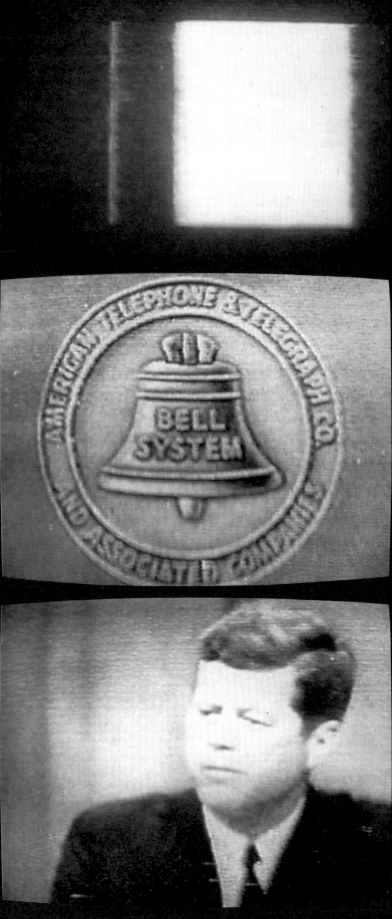

Technology of Tomorrow.

In the mid-1980s hardly a week passes without someone predicting that a new development – cable, satellite, inter-active TV, teletext and dozens of others – will 'revolutionise' television. These announcements are usually countered by an equally confident assertion from someone else that the development will never be more than a passing fad. If there is one thing that can be learnt from the history of television, it is that both types of prediction should be treated with great caution: during the past half-century many eminent figures have been left with egg on their faces after trying to imagine what will happen to the new medium.

In his pamphlet *What To Do With the BBC*, published in 1935 Raymond Postgate listed a number of reasons which could prevent television from supplanting radio. 'The first is that any picture must be shown on a screen. If it is to be a permanent amusement, and not a mere oddity, the screen must be large enough to show action, and detail of facial expression. It need not indeed be quite so large as a cinema screen, but it is difficult to imagine it much less than five feet by four. Now such a clear wall-space is almost impossible to secure in a working-class or middle-class home.' Postgate concluded: 'It seems, therefore, that television will only become a home amusement in homes that have several rooms. Not more than 10 per cent of the population will take it up permanently. But in cinema houses as a rival feature to films, it may become very popular.'

A demonstration of an early prototype Emitron camera; it had no viewfinder.

Postgate's mistake can, perhaps, be excused by the fact that he was writing at a time when television was in its infancy and had not proved itself. No such defence can be offered for Bertrand Russell, who chided Grace Wyndham Goldie when she moved into television from radio in 1948. 'My dear girl,' he told her, 'it will be of no importance in your lifetime or mine.'

Derek Horton's book *Television's Story and Challenge*, published in 1951, suffered from the same misconceptions that Raymond Postgate had had sixteen years earlier. 'Many types of television broadcast in future will demand a large screen,' Horton wrote. 'Big-screen television will open a new era of mass viewing. There will be special theatres showing events as they occur, not days or weeks later as in present newsreels: all the entertainment of television will become available for the viewer who prefers to absorb his enjoyment in the company of fellow-beings.' Horton added, without a hint of doubt: 'I don't believe television will ever make families want to stay at home, night after night, peering at their little screens, but I have been amazed at the number of people in different parts of the world who fear that television may bring all sorts of social changes by keeping everyone indoors.'

Douglas Birkinshaw, the BBC's first research engineer in television, pictured at a control panel in 1932.

First pictures transmitted via Telstar satellite, July 1962.

One should be just as wary of those whose blithe enthusiasm for any new form of television leads them to predict its success. The history of the medium has been littered with exotic ideas, such as three-dimensional television, which have fizzled out because there was no public demand for them. Peter Eckersley, the BBC engineer, made the point well in an article about television which was published by the *Daily Mail* in January 1933: 'Some ingenious technician may invent a means of smelling the flowers of Tahiti while the smeller is in Chipping Norton. The fundamental value of the invention lies not in its technological ingenuity but in the extent to which it meets a real need. And who wants to smell *any* flowers all day and all night?'

Many of the 'new' ideas which are being peddled today are, in fact, revivals of inventions which are as old as television itself. One scheme which has been touted in recent years is the use of television as a sort of telephone with pictures – a two-way videophone, as it is sometimes called – which will enable business executives to hold conferences with colleagues in other cities by arranging a row of screens on their desks. Yet something of the kind had been visualised by George du Maurier in his famous *Punch* cartoon of 1879: the parents were able to hear and talk to their daughter in Ceylon at the same time as watching her on the screen. The idea was first put into practice in 1936, when the German Reichspost set up a 'television telephone' between Berlin and Leipzig; the service was extended to Munich the following year. For twice the price of a normal telephone call, any member of the public could go into a 'television telephone' booth. One problem was that the user had to arrange in advance for the person whom she or he wished to address to be present at the other end. There were other drawbacks: 'This video telephone booth was very small and one had to sit in an armchair, because a very precise distance had to be kept between the Nipkow disc, which was doing the scanning, and the person who was speaking,' says Karl Tetzner, a German who remembers using the service. 'The booth was very dark, and once one had sat down, a very harsh beam of light came towards one from out of an aperture, and it was most unpleasant. It dazzled one, and above this light aperture there was a Braun tube which had the picture of the person at the other end.' His wife, Anne-Marie Tetzner, adds that the picture was 'very faint . . . one could only just recognise the outlines'. However, the quality had improved considerably by the time of the 1939 Berlin Radio Exhibition. 'I think it was on the third or fourth day of the exhibition,' Herr Tetzner says, 'that I received another call requesting me to go to the Postal Directorate in Leipzig where the booth was. We talked for about twenty minutes to each other, and the picture quality was so good that my friend was able to ask me, "What sort of a tie have you got on today? It doesn't match your suit at all." I had thought that it was all right, but I had a look and it was exactly the wrong tie.' The service was suspended when war broke out in September 1939, but it had never been particularly popular anyway – a bit of fun, rather than something of real benefit to the public.

This may also prove to be the case with another development which, according to its proponents, is about to transform our lives – 'shopping by television'. As with the video telephone, the idea has a long ancestry, having been predicted by the French artist Albert Robida in 1882. On 25 July 1934, the London *Sunday Express* printed a rather over-excited

The 'television telephone' between Berlin and Leipzig in use in the 1930s; it was suspended with the outbreak of war in 1939.

The BBC's three-tube colour camera, used experimentally at Alexandra Palace from 1955.

John Logie Baird with his 'Telechrome', developed during the Second World War in an attempt to provide good colour transmission.

News and weather from Ceefax teletext service, BBC's electronic newspaper which started in 1974, available on suitably equipped televisions on both BBC TV channels.

article headed 'FIRST MAN TO SHOP BY TELEVISION: A Foretaste of the Wonders That Are Coming'. The 'first man' turned out to be the *Sunday Express*'s Special Correspondent, who began his report thus: 'I saw wonders yesterday that will transform life within a few years. I was the first man in the world to buy goods by television. I saw the goods displayed in front of me although they were lying miles away. I made my choice as easily as I would have done in a West-end store . . . I was the first person to have these experiences, but within a year or so you will be able to do these things, too. It was just television.' In fact, shopping by television did not become a reality until 1979, when British Telecom launched Prestel, the first 'viewdata' service in the world. (The international generic title for such systems is 'videotex'.) The Prestel signal is sent along telephone lines by a central computer, and viewers can use the keyboards of their home computers to 'talk back' to the service and order goods. Videotex should not be confused with 'teletext' services such as the IBA's Oracle (which began in 1973) and the BBC's Ceefax (which was inaugurated the following year). These are 'one-way' systems, broadcast over the air like any other television channel. They are normally used for transmitting news, weather forecasts, recipes, 'What's On' listings, jokes and sports results; they also give sub-titles to some television programmes, since teletext can be called up on to the screen without losing the picture transmission. Teletext services are sometimes described as 'electronic newspapers', and the claim has some justice: viewers can buy video printers which will turn the text on the screen into a printed page.

A trend discernible in many recent developments, of which Prestel is but one manifestation, is to enable viewers to 'answer back' rather than being passive consumers of whatever is placed on the screen. Since 1972, all new cable systems in the United States have been obliged by law to have a 'two-way capability', which means that houses have to be linked directly to the cable station instead of being connected to the house next door, which is connected to another house, which is then connected to the cable station. The common phrase for this service is 'inter-active television', and the first station to put it into practice was Qube in Columbus, Ohio, which started in 1977. All subscribers were given a hand-held gadget containing five 'response buttons': the audience could thus give an instant opinion on the programmes which were being shown – choosing, for instance, between several possible endings for a drama. Should the hero be killed or should he survive? By pushing the appropriate buttons, the viewers could decide. They could also react to political speeches or new products, allowing advertisers to use the station for market research. In its principle, it was no different from the Preview Theatre in Hollywood, where for many years audiences have given the thumbs-up or thumbs-down to pilot shows for the networks. In practice it was little more than a gimmick; Qube was closed in 1984.

The Japanese, inevitably, have gone one better. Since the 1970s they have been experimenting with HI-OVIS (Highly Inter-active Visual Information System). Like Qube subscribers, HI-OVIS viewers are given a key-pad with which they can reply to questions asked by the station. Unlike Qube subscribers, however, they can actually take part in the television programmes themselves. This extraordinary facility is achieved by having a camera and microphone in every home, linked to the studio by two-way fibre optic cable. Up to two viewers can appear at a time, so three-way conversations can take place – between one viewer, another viewer and the studio. The HI-OVIS experimental station near Osaka delights in taking advantage of this technology. In one programme, for example, a viewer learned what was wrong with her tennis stroke: she was at home, demonstrating her technique in front of the living-room camera, while the expert was in the studio, taking part in a chat show. HI-OVIS executives seem to be confident. In the words of their evaluation report: 'Visitors to the system said that it would be ten years before the system becomes practical. It won't be that long.'

More disinterested observers are more doubtful. Until every home really does have its own camera and microphone, there is every reason for scepticism about ventures such as HI-OVIS; it may well turn out to be just another expensive gimmick, with all the public appeal of Peter Eckersley's imaginary system transmitting the smells of Tahitian flowers.

Baird's Phonovision: a recording is about to begin as J. D. Percy puts a wax record on the turntable/scanner.

The only forms of new technology about which one can afford to be less tentative are those which have begun to establish themselves. The video cassette recorder (VCR), for example, has already changed the way in which many people see television, liberating them from the tyranny of scheduling, so that they can go out for the evening and yet not miss the episode of *Dallas* which is being broadcast at the same time. The idea that viewers might wish to record television programmes was anticipated by John Logie Baird as long ago as 1927, when he patented his 'Phonovision' system. As Baird explained, 'the sound of the living face can be recorded on the phonograph record and on playing this record again the moving face is reproduced on the televisor screen so that we have here a method of storing living scenes on phonograph records.' But Baird's Phonovision was not commercially viable, and it was only in the 1970s that video-recorders for home use came on to the market. It was not until the 1980s that the true successor to Baird's apparatus, the videodisc, became available. As its name suggests, the videodisc looks like a gramophone record; each side contains 54,000 numbered frames (lasting about an hour), and the most advanced systems use a laser rather than a stylus for scanning the disc. However, whether using laser or stylus, the machines can only play back; they cannot record. This makes it unlikely that they will offer serious competition to video-cassettes in the next few years.

October 1969, London: unveiling of the Vidicord, a machine which enables people to show normal 8mm films on their television set.

During the 1970s, some hopes were expressed that the advent of cheap cassettes would enable ordinary people to become television producers. A community group, for example, could use a video camera to make a film about its neighbourhood, which could then be watched by local people on their VCRs. Although there have been a few moves in this direction, on the whole the hopes have not been realised. Instead, video cassette recorders have been used largely for watching movies. In Britain, which has a higher concentration of VCRs than any other country in the world, every town now has a shop which hires out tapes of feature films – including many of a particularly gory or pornographic nature, known as 'video nasties'.

Similarly idealistic hopes have been voiced in connection with cable television. As with video, little has come of them: the audience seems to prefer sports and movies to 'narrowcasts' by community groups. Cable television started as a way of bringing television signals to areas which could not

Duplicating pre-recorded videocassettes: the rise in sales of video recorders in the early 1980s also led to 'video piracy' on a huge scale.

receive them from normal transmitters – perhaps because of their remoteness, or because they were surrounded by mountains. In the past ten years it has become big business, as entrepreneurs have taken advantage of the fact that cables can carry many more channels than conventional 'over the air' broadcasting; the potential of cable has increased still further since the 1970s with the invention of 'optical fibre' cables made out of very thin glass, down which signals can be sent as pulses of light. Attached to an optical fibre cable, a television set can receive an almost unlimited number of channels.

Cable News Network (CNN), a 24-hour service run by the ebullient Ted Turner from Georgia.

In Manhattan, cable subscribers already have a choice of more than thirty-five channels – including Spanish-language channels, financial news channels, local educational channels, live programming from the United Nations and the House of Representatives, a 24-hours-a-day health channel, a 24-hour sports channel, a channel called MTV which shows nothing but rock videos all day and all night, a 24-hour news channel called CNN which is run by Ted Turner from Atlanta, Georgia, as well as Home Box Office, a 24-hour entertainment channel owned by Time Inc. and beamed to cable stations across the country by satellite. 'People are looking for new programming choices,' says Susan Green, of Manhattan Cable's experiences in the early 1980s. 'Americans have had three national broadcast networks plus a variety of independent stations, and they have not found that those have satisfied their needs.' She is proud of Manhattan's 'public access'

The first ever pop video: the Beatles' Strawberry Fields Forever. *In America today, there is an entire channel devoted to pop videos.*

Subscribers to Manhattan Cable have a choice of more than thirty-five channels – everything from sport to Spanish drama.

policy: 'We do 12,000 hours a year of locally-produced programming by people who live in New York City. That's 1,000 hours a month, and we do it on three different channels, and essentially the policy is wide open: anybody who lives in New York City can come to us with a tape, or a schedule time when he wants to do a live programme out of a particular studio. We have no control over the content of the programming . . . our only responsibilities are for the scheduling, the administrative aspects of getting that programme on the air and making sure it meets minimum technical standards.' This facility is used not only by pressure groups but also by an extraordinary assortment of individuals who fancy themselves as television stars, such as the group of schoolchildren who regularly present their own news programme. The lack of regulation in cable TV has also enabled it to screen such bizarre shows as *Ugly George's Hour of Truth, Sex and Violence*, in which the self-styled Ugly George takes a video camera down to 42nd Street and propositions young women, usually out-of-town visitors; a surprisingly high percentage are prepared to accept his invitation to go back to his apartment and disrobe in front of the camera.

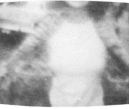

A typical sequence from Ugly George's Hour of Truth, Sex and Violence: *a woman is approached in the street and chatted up by George; within minutes she has agreed to go into Central Park and strip; she later became a regular on the show, under the name 'Melinda the Rescinder'.*

However, the public access programmes and the freaks like Ugly George are mere sticklebacks in the huge lake of cable. For most people in America, cable means Home Box Office, showing movies and sports games, which has 13 million subscribers. HBO does not disclose its profits, but a reliable estimate in 1982 put them at $100 million, pre-tax. Frank Biondi of HBO thinks that his channel's success has influenced the three old networks – forcing them to produce more 'made-for-TV' movies, for instance. He also believes that cable channels have changed viewers' habits. 'People are now planning their viewing, and probably using television a bit more intelligently because they use it for what they want. If there is nothing on the networks at 9 o'clock then maybe there is something on HBO; or maybe they have already seen

Cable television has unleashed all sorts of unusual programmes, including 'Kids' News' for Sun Prairies cable viewers.

what's on HBO because of our repeat cycle, so they may go to Cable News Network, or maybe they will go to the sports network or the health network and try something new. That's the way it should be – it's a much more intelligent use of that box than what it's been in the past, which has been Paul Klein's theory of Least Objectionable Programming.' That theory, in Klein's own words, is that 'you come home at night and you say you're going to watch a little television, but in effect what you do is you turn on the television and, irrespective of the content, you watch and you turn the dials to watch the least objectionable programme'.

Playboy's cable channel: 'When somebody hears the word Playboy, *they think of sex. So they're going to plonk down their money and make that initial payment for sex'.*

This idea was highly influential in discouraging adventure or experiment at the networks, but Frank Biondi is unduly optimistic in his belief that cable has somehow destroyed it: Klein himself, only begetter of the concept, has moved into cable television, running the channel which is owned by Hugh Hefner's Playboy Organisation. Klein is candid about his intentions for the Playboy channel: 'When somebody hears the word Playboy, they think of sex. So they're going to plonk down their money and make that initial payment for sex, and that's what's called a "targeted pay service" and if I don't deliver that, they're not going to buy it any more. They're going to be disappointed, and so I have to deliver sex – sophisticated, funny, raunchy, all the variations of sex – that one target, all day long.'

March 1966: the world's first battery-powered transistor television tape camera is displayed in California; it weighs just seven pounds and takes half-an-hour of broadcast-quality pictures without recharging.

Klein believes that the proliferation of cable channels will bring about the death of the traditional networks. 'The advertisers have consistently paid more and more money for a dwindling audience because they had no other place to go, and they still don't have any place to go. So the networks will get smaller, the advertisers will pay more and eventually there has to be a revolution. The advertisers have to say, "To hell with you, I ain't paying this much, I can put together a lot of different ways to get the same amount of audience more cheaply." And that will be the end of the network system.' The three big commercial networks' domination of the market has already been eroded. In the 1970s, they used to capture well over 90 per cent of the television audience in the United States. In November 1983, when HBO presented the first television screening of the film *An Officer and a Gentleman*, the networks' share of the national audience was just 66 per cent.

September 1950: a Marconi 'Image Orthicon' camera is used by the BBC from an aircraft to take aerial pictures of London.

What is questionable is whether the cable companies have the financial strength to survive. HBO is the only American cable channel to have made money so far, and several large cities – including Chicago and the whole of New York except Manhattan – have not yet been 'wired up' because of the huge cost. By 1984, American firms had spent $4 billion on laying cables; to have even half of the United States wired up would cost another $5 billion. It will take many years before the large corporations involved – including Westinghouse, Warner Communications and American Express – see a return on their investment.

Doubts about financial viability have also been heard in Britain, whose first cable franchises were awarded in 1984. One million homes were due to be within reach of cable by 1985, but there was no guarantee that they would want to subscribe. One City accountant estimated that it would take twenty years for cable companies to become commercially self-supporting, because of the initial capital investment required: to cable a single London borough would cost about £25 million, and the price of wiring up the whole country would be £3.5 billion. Although the Conservative government has been enthusiastic in its support of cable, the Minister responsible for broadcasting, Douglas Hurd, admitted at the end of 1983 that 'it won't be a bonanza for everybody . . . There will be some red faces and some red bank balances.'

In America, Mobil's Vice-President in charge of broadcasting, Herbert Schmertz, thinks that the potential audience has been over-rated: 'There is just so much that the public out there is going to pay for. They will pay for better reception as a result of cable, they will pay for movies, they will probably pay for a little bit of sports, maybe some pornography, and that is about it. The so-called "narrowcasting" of the cable operations is just not going to generate enough subscribers to be economically viable, and I am not surprised that the Entertainment Channel has gone out of business, and that one of the two news channels is now going out of business. I would be very surprised if there was any actual increase in the cabling of large cities, because with the technology that is coming along, cable itself is going to be in a fight with direct satellite broadcasting, which is potentially less expensive. What was hailed as the new technology a few years ago may well become obsolete at a rapid rate.'

Certainly the other possible threat to conventional television corporations does seem to be direct broadcasting by satellite (DBS), a system in which viewers connect their television set to a miniature satellite dish (the size and shape of an upturned umbrella) on the roof of their house. In many ways DBS is no more than a logical extension of the existing use of satellites for broadcasting – a use which was first suggested by the science fiction writer Arthur C. Clarke in *Wireless World* magazine in 1945. In a famous article, headed 'Extra-Terrestrial Relays: Can Rocket Stations Give World-Wide Radio Coverage?' Clarke pointed out that if a satellite could be sent into orbit at a height of 22,000 miles it would revolve at the same speed as the earth, and would therefore remain stationary above the same point of the globe's surface. Three strategically positioned satellites would be enough to cover the whole world, bouncing radio messages to and fro.

The first satellite used for international television transmissions was *Telstar 1*, launched by the United States in 1962, but it orbited at a much lower height than that proposed by Clarke and was consequently 'out of synch' with the earth's rotation; in each of its two-and-a-half hour orbits, there were only eighteen minutes in which it was able to transmit signals between the United States and Western Europe. However, in April 1965 the USA launched *Early Bird*, the first commercial communications satellite to use Clarke's 'stationary orbit' (they are known as synchronous satellites). This made possible such historic transmissions as the fight between Cassius Clay and Sonny Liston, shown 'live' in Western Europe in May 1965, and the international live coverage of the Mexico Olympics in 1968.

Since then, satellites have also been used for domestic purposes, enabling huge countries such as Canada, Indonesia and the Soviet Union to have truly national television services. Cable companies have taken advantage of the technology to create their own 'networks', starting with HBO in the United States, which bought a lease on part of RCA's domestic communications satellite in 1975. This meant that an HBO programme could be sent by satellite to an HBO station in some other region, whence it would be passed on to the local subscribers on cable.

A huge parabolic antenna 50 miles north-east of Tokyo, 30 metres in diameter, used for relaying television pictures of the Tokyo Olympics in 1964 to North America and Europe via the Syncom 3 communications satellite.

Richard Dimbleby, the voice of the BBC, explains the mysteries of space satellites to British viewers in preparation for the first transatlantic transmissions.

The fight between Cassius Clay and Sonny Liston for the heavyweight boxing championship of the world was shown live via satellite in Western Europe in May 1965.

The next step, inevitably, was to 'cut out the middleman' with direct broadcasting by satellite. By the 1980s America, Japan and most European countries had decided to introduce DBS. But the economics of DBS may turn out to be an impossible obstacle: when the BBC mooted a seven-year lease with Unisat in 1983, for instance, it was set to pay £24.4 million a year for just two channels. This money can be recouped only through the subscriptions paid by individual viewers, and there is no evidence that all that many people will want to subscribe. The original plan for DBS in Britain was for two channels run by the BBC. In 1983 another two were allotted to the IBA. They would start in 1986. But a technical wrangle followed. By the beginning of 1984, both the BBC and the ITV companies were becoming jittery about the cost. A third group, of outside commercial producers, were allotted a share, and a new authority created. But this only added to the complications of agreeing on programme ideas – and the expensive contract for the satellite was still not settled. The new system seemed unlikely to begin transmissions before 1988. The early euphoria had been replaced by gloom. As the *Guardian* asked in March 1984, 'Who wants satellite broadcasting anyway? As the crisis over the space-age telly scheme deepens, the fundamental question does not go away. On the contrary, it forces itself nearer the front of the debate.' Ironically enough, by 1984 the only successful use of DBS anywhere in the world had been in a country where people did indeed want it – India, where the one-year SITE experiment in 1975 had brought television programmes to remote villages for the first time.

Melanie Garland, aged twelve, holds up a rather bulky 'portable' television in London, 1964.

The Beatles, singing 'All You Need Is Love', were the British participants in an international television link-up called Our World *in 1967; but the experiment was not popular with viewers.*

Even if DBS does fail, the pace of technological advance is unlikely to slacken. Despite all the wonders of modern science, there is still no common technical standard for television around the world. European countries broadcast on 625 lines while American stations use 525. There are no fewer than three different systems of colour television, all of which are widely used. The American colour standards, based on the work of the National Television System Committee (NTSC), have been adopted in Canada, South America, Japan and the Philippines. The French SECAM system (Sequential Colour with Memory) is used in the Soviet Union and in parts of Africa and Asia, while the Anglo-German PAL (Phase Alternation Line) is the standard in all of Western Europe except France.

In recent years, some television sets have reverted to the screen-size of the very earliest receivers: in 1983 the British inventor Sir Clive Sinclair created the first 'pocket television', the size of a paperback book.

The strongest demand for a world agreement on standards has come from Japan, where NHK's engineers have been working on HDTV (High Definition Television) for more than ten years. HDTV is a 1125-line system which achieves even better resolution than that of 35-millimetre film; the 'lines' are invisible even on large screens, and the detail is remarkable. HDTV has won powerful support in America from CBS, but there are still many hurdles to be cleared. The new system would make all existing television sets obsolete: at the moment, the ratio between the width and depth of a screen is 4:3, but the ratio on an HDTV receiver is 5:3, like a cinema screen. After lengthy research, the Japanese scientists have discovered that the human eye prefers to look at pictures in this shape. Dr Takashi Fujio, the inventor of HDTV, is convinced that 'it will come'. It is, however, unlikely to come soon: every camera, television set and video-tape recorder in the world will have to be replaced first. Nevertheless, one should be wary of dismissing completely the chances of HDTV; in the 1930s, television itself was

(Opposite) In May 1983: Seiko announces that it is to sell 'television wrist-watches' in the United States. The suggested retail price is $495.

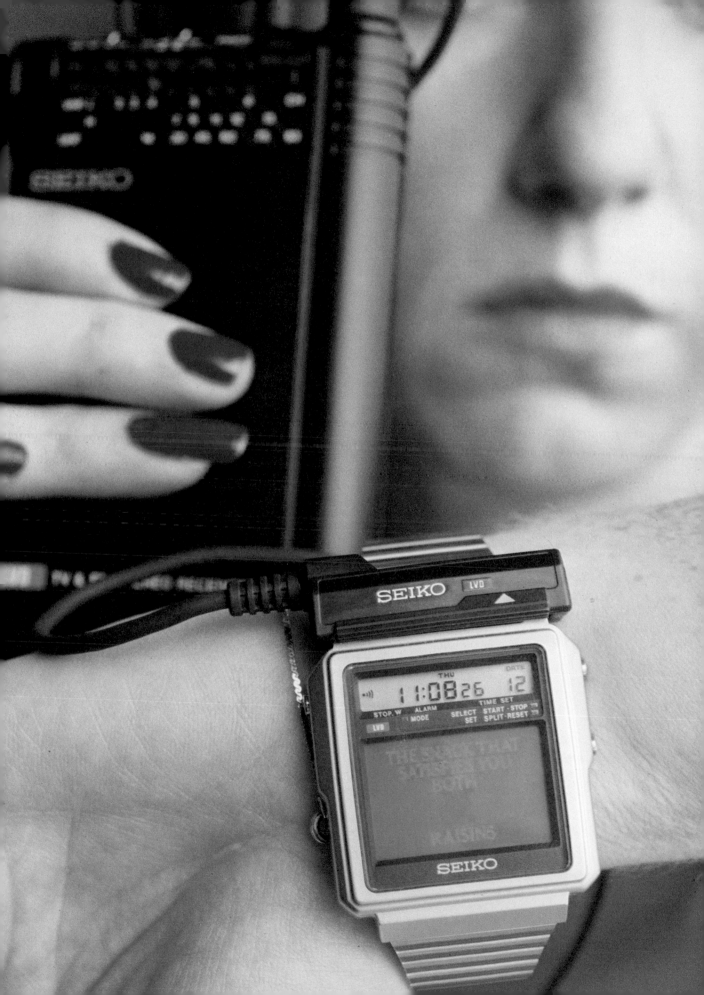

derided by many intelligent people as a crackpot scheme dreamed up by wild eccentrics, yet within a few years it had found a place in people's homes around the world.

All one can say for certain about the television set of the future is that it will be a very different beast from the one to which we have grown accustomed. It will still fulfil its normal function of providing programmes from broadcasting companies, but these may be supplemented by video, cable and satellite. It will be a Visual Display Unit for one's home computer and a play-park for computer games. It may be an electronic shopping arcade or a business conference centre. With a print-out machine attached, it could even put newspapers out of business.

Les Brown, the former television correspondent of the *New York Times*, believes that this Third Age of Broadcasting – following the radio age and the television age – will create new inequalities. 'Already we see a division in this society,' he says, 'the formation of a new caste system of information "haves" and information "have-nots". The people at the poverty line clearly cannot afford these things, the wealthier families can . . . and since information is power, the power is flowing more to the people with money and away from the people without the money.' He adds: 'Silly as it sounds, the only solution that anyone has come up with is cable stamps, information stamps. Just as we give food stamps to the poor, we might very well have to give cable stamps.'

Doom-laden prophecies about television are, of course, as old as the medium itself. Some of them have turned out to be justified, but none has managed to stop the onward march of broadcasting. As an article in the *Daily Mirror* put it, in 1950, 'If you let a TV set through your front door, life can never be the same again.' George Bernard Shaw feared that television would kill the theatre; head teachers said that it would prevent children from doing their homework. In a changing world, some things remain constant: in 1957, a Japanese politician described television as a 'complete national fatuity'; in 1961, Newton Minow, Chairman of the Federal Communications Commission in the United States, compared television to 'a vast wasteland'; in 1966, the Ceylonese politician Dudley Senanayake said that television was 'the deadliest instrument to create a non-thinking generation of people'; in 1983, the British director Jonathan Miller spoke of the 'continuous, incontinent, unremitting triviality of television'. These trumpets have been sounded outside Jericho for some time now, but the walls have still not come tumbling down. Will they ever?